FRANK LLOYD WRIGHT

TO 1910

Fig. 1. Frank Lloyd Wright as he looked at 35 in the heyday of The Studio.

FRANK LLOYD WRIGHT

TO 1910

The First Golden Age

GRANT CARPENTER MANSON

VNR VAN NOSTRAND REINHOLD COMPANY
New York Cincinnati Toronto London Melbourne

Copyright © 1958 by Litton Educational Publishing, Inc.
Library of Congress Catalog Card Number 58-7195
ISBN 0-442-26130-6

Printed in the United States of America.
Designed by William Wilson Atkin

Published by Van Nostrand Reinhold Company
A division of Litton Educational Publishing, Inc.
135 West 50th Street, New York, NY 10020, U.S.A.

Van Nostrand Reinhold Limited
1410 Birchmount Road
Scarborough, Ontario M1P 2E7, Canada

Van Nostrand Reinhold Australia Pty. Ltd.
17 Queen Street
Mitcham, Victoria 3132, Australia

Van Nostrand Reinhold Company Limited
Molly Millars Lane
Wokingham, Berkshire, England

16 15 14 13 12 11 10 9 8 7 6 5 4 3 2

Contents

Acknowledgments

This book is the result of two campaigns of concentrated work: the first in 1938-40, the second in 1953-57. During these periods I have received, in the form of discussion, interview, correspondence, and hard fact, invaluable assistance from many people. To all of them I owe a debt of gratitude. But my first gratitude is to Mr. Wright himself for making everything possible in a sense that goes all the way from the obvious to the intangible. Particularly, I am grateful to him for the wonders of the Husser house which made me his fan at the age of six (when I voted it the most captivating object in my neighborhood) — and for his unfailing kindness to me ever since I became old enough to try to put my admiration into publishable words. It would have been impossible to do so without personal consultations with Mr. Wright and the opportunity to study the records in his possession.

In the early days of my research, my most valuable co-worker was Miss Marion Rawls (now Mrs. William Herzog), then associated with The Burnham Library of The Art Institute of Chicago. There was nothing about my subject, it seemed to me, which Miss Rawls didn't know or couldn't find. Latterly, I had generous assistance from the late Mrs. T. M. Hofmeester, Jr., also of The Burnham Library. Miss Ruth Cook (retired) and Miss Katherine McNamara of the Harvard Library of Design have contributed their skills cheerfully and continually through the years, and have borne my nuisance value with fortitude. Lewis Mumford and Henry-Russell Hitchcock have steadily shared my enthusiasm and curiosity about "the early Wright," and have offered direct, practical help when it was most needed. To Charles P. Graves of Clemson College I am indebted for many hours of expert drafting without which certain illustrations would not have been possible. Finally, special mention must be made of the part played in this work by Mrs. Irene P. LeCompte of the library of Temple University; she assumed the task, which in the last months of the second campaign I found myself unable to continue, of compiling the bibliography for this book, scrupulously edited to cover the same years as the text.

Grant Carpenter Manson
Philadelphia
May, 1957

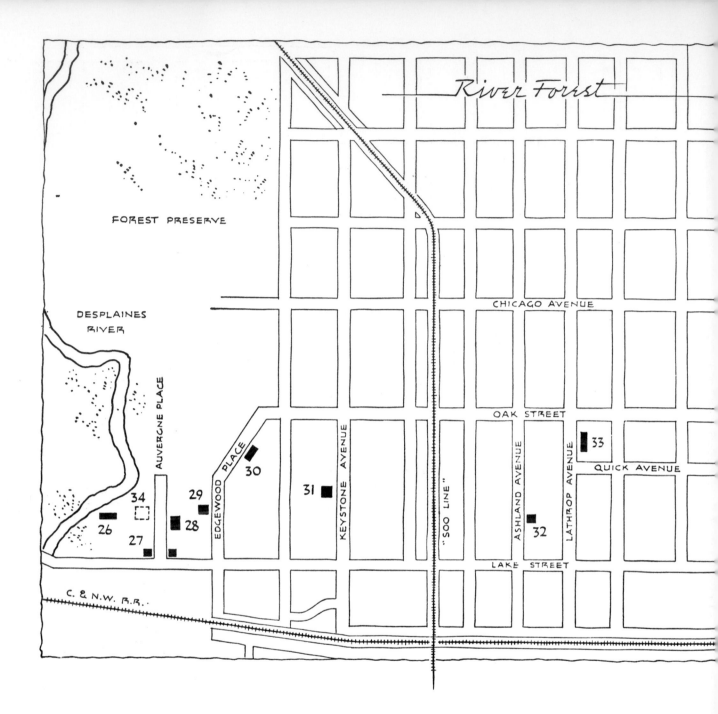

River Forest

FOREST PRESERVE

DESPLAINES RIVER

AUVERGNE PLACE

EDGEWOOD PLACE

KEYSTONE AVENUE

"SOO LINE"

CHICAGO AVENUE

OAK STREET

ASHLAND AVENUE

LATHROP AVENUE

QUICK AVENUE

LAKE STREET

C. & N.W. R.R.

34
26
27
28
29
30
31
32
33

OAK PARK KEY

1 F. L. WRIGHT HOUSE AND STUDIO
2 DR. COPELAND HOUSE
3 HEURTLEY HOUSE
4 MRS. THOMAS GALE HOUSE
5 BEACHEY HOUSE
6 THOMAS HOUSE
7 HILLS HOUSE (MOORE II)
8 MOORE HOUSE
9 WOOLLEY HOUSE
10 WALTER GALE HOUSE
11 THOMAS GALE HOUSE
12 "   "   "
13 O. B. BALCH HOUSE

14 YOUNG HOUSE
15 UNITY CHURCH
16 LAKE STREET FOUNTAIN
17 GEORGE FURBECK HOUSE
18 HARRY ADAMS HOUSE
19 W. E. MARTIN HOUSE
20 FRICKE HOUSE
21 GOODRICH HOUSE
22 CHENEY HOUSE
23 ROLLIN FURBECK HOUSE
24 GEORGE SMITH HOUSE
25 PEBBLES & BALCH SHOP

RIVER FOREST KEY

26 WALLER HOUSE (BARN)
27 WALLER GATEWAY
28 WINSLOW HOUSE
29 WILLIAMS HOUSE
30 ROBERTS HOUSE
31 INGALLS HOUSE
32 DAVENPORT HOUSE
33 RIVER FOREST TENNIS CLUB
34 SITE OF WALLER HOUSE
35 SITE OF RIVER FOREST GOLF CLUB
36 SITE OF CUMMINGS REAL ESTATE CO.

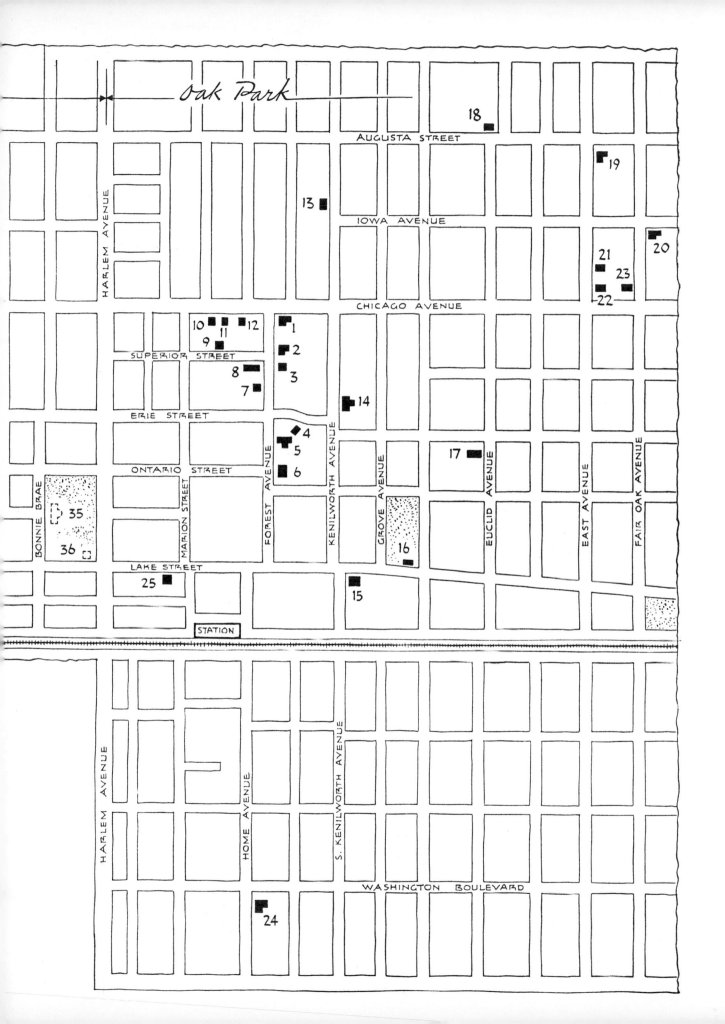

THE FORMATION OF
HIS ARCHITECTURE

1. Inheritance and Environment

The Family

Students of the career of Frank Lloyd Wright inevitably discover that any attempt to account for his accomplishment in customary terms of example and influence does not work. Sooner or later, they are faced with the fact that it is essentially spontaneous. This conclusion does not imply that Wright has lived his life in a vacuum; on the contrary, he has always been, in the broadest sense, a public figure. It may come as a surprise to those who are not acquainted with the Wright of fifty years ago that his present fame, although different in tone, is no novelty in his career. He has, furthermore, as a man of enormous perception, felt and responded to many attitudes other than his own. But the conclusion does imply that the architecture for which he stands and which he brought forth in his first maturity is so radical and so personal that it can only be explained as coming from within. Many competent critics and colleagues have, indeed, gone no further than this. If, however, we are no longer content to rest our case with the supernatural, an inquiry into Wright's inheritance and environment becomes important as a clue to what "within" might mean. We learn that his family was certainly the sort from which an unfettered and rebellious genius could spring.

Let us begin with a statement of the circumstances of Wright's life to his eighteenth year. He was born to William Russel Cary Wright and Anna Lloyd-Jones Wright in Richland Center, Wisconsin, on June 8, 1869.[1] Presently, the family moved to Weymouth, Massachusetts, to remain until 1877; here Wright's formal education began, first in the new kindergarten tech-

Note 1
A conflicting birth year, 1867, has been published (Henry R. Hitchcock, "Wright," Chamber's Encyclopaedia, New ed., New York, Oxford University Press, 1950, XIV, 757-58); it was presumably suggested by personal recollections of some members of Wright's family. Since no birth records exist to be consulted, the author continues to rely upon the date given in Wright's autobiography (Note 3 below) and long established in the public mind. The chronology of this book, therefore, is based upon the birth year of 1869.

nique, later in ordinary grade school. By or before 1880, the family[2] was established once again in Wisconsin, this time at Madison, the capital, where Wright continued his primary education in the old Second Ward School, spending his summer vacations at work on the Lloyd-Jones land at Spring Green, forty miles to the west. In 1885 he entered the University of Wisconsin as a special student to undergo his one brief experience with education at the college level under the tutelage of Allen Conover, then Dean of the Engineering School at the University. Also in the year 1885 William Wright walked out on his family, never to return. In the spring of 1887 young Wright decided to try his luck in Chicago; after a few months, his mother joined him there. This move plunged him into young manhood and a career.[3]

William Cary Wright died in 1904 and lies buried in a little cemetery in Bear Valley, Wisconsin; aside from the indisputable fact that he was the father of Frank, Jane and Maginel Lloyd Wright, this is the most definite thing we know about him. His nebulous place in the chronicle is the result of a calculated effort on the part of his second wife to dismiss him from her awareness (and that of her children) after he had finally failed her. He was of an English non-conformist family which had emigrated to America and settled in New England. There is indeed some reason to believe that William Wright was born in England and brought across the Atlantic in infancy. His father was for many years a Baptist minister in Hartford, Connecticut, where the family took root. Thus, William Wright grew up in a New England environment and regarded himself as a New Englander. At Amherst College he had studied with the law in mind, but he was decidedly not the stuff of which a lawyer is made. Artistic, visionary, moody, and egocentric, his only real enthusiasm was for music. Upon leaving college, he became a wanderer, earning a bare living as a music-master

in the raw communities of the Middle Frontier. It was in this capacity that he eventually reached the hinterland of the Wisconsin River valley. He married Permelia Holcomb, the daughter of substantial valley settlers, by whom he had three children. Left a widower in 1864, he seems to have disavowed altogether the issue of this marriage; certainly, he resumed his footloose existence. One day, while he was conducting a singfest near Spring Green he met Anna Lloyd-Jones; he was then forty-six years of age, she was twenty-nine. Although they were both, by Victorian standards, beyond the customary age for romance, they fell in love and were soon married. There was in this ascetic Easterner something which appealed to and satisfied Anna Lloyd-Jones's desire for life on a more spiritual plane than the black earth of primitive Wisconsin could offer. William Wright not only embodied through his music and his educated speech a traditional culture, tarnished by time and misuse as it may have become, but he revealed to her that he was about to answer a "call" to preach, and religion ran full and strong in the Lloyd-Jones clan.

In a sense, it was natural for William Wright thus, suddenly, to turn to preaching, for there were many ministers among his forebears; but the impulsive way in which he did so, as well as the curious, formless adventure his entire life had been, points to a strain of irresponsibility and unconventionality in his character which must have been at odds with his New England background. He was a solitary — a man upon whom no one could make a permanent claim. The history of his first marriage forecast that of his second, in which he proved to be an erratic husband and father. He supported his family at times by giving music lessons, at times by preaching, but always precariously. It was only in the realm of music that any active interest in the education of his children was aroused. With a certain ferocity, he had taught young Frank, by the age of seven, to play Bach upon the piano. Wherever the Wrights lived, no matter how little of anything else there might have been, there was always music. Listening to the concertos of Beethoven, which would sometimes swell through the house far into the night, young Frank in his bedroom would conjure up "an edifice of sound." But in all other respects than music, the father was remote and unreachable,

Note 2
Two daughters, Jane and Maginel, completed the family and had been born by this time.
Note 3
For such biographical data in this book, the author is indebted to "An Autobiography," by Frank Lloyd Wright (Longmans, Green, New York, 1932).

inexplicably concerned with the preservation of an ego which, while it offered him no comfort, he valued above all else. His desertion of his wife and children in 1885 was perhaps inevitable; in any case, it was a prophetic act which his son was to repeat twenty-four years later. His departure was actually a disappearance; his family in Madison neither saw nor heard from him again, and his going seems to have meant little more to them than a welcome release from domestic conflict. William Wright was one of life's vagrants who wandered from one impasse to another, who sought nothing from life but privacy, yet who was destined to be recorded as the father of a genius.

Anna Lloyd-Jones Wright was, on the other hand, a very integrated and resolute person whose character is intimately bound up with the development of her son. As William Wright had an uncontrolled passion for music, Anna Wright had an impassioned respect for education. Much as she had originally admired her husband's musical talent and religious fervor, it was his college degree that really overwhelmed her. The motto of the Lloyd-Jones clan is "Truth against the world," represented by an old druidical symbol[4] which the family seems to have adopted as a device. They are proud, gifted and energetic people of direct Welsh descent. They brought with them from Wales an ancient, druidical animism which in no way impaired the strength of inspiration which they drew each day from the Bible, but which did facilitate the process of transferring their love of land from the old soil to the new. They identified themselves so quickly and thriftily with Iowa County, Wisconsin, that they convey the impression of having lived there for centuries. Actually, Frank Lloyd Wright and his cousins are the third generation to own the land which the Lloyd-Joneses settled some hundred and ten years ago. It consists of small, level valleys opening southward from the Wisconsin River and bounded by low, round hills from the summits of which outcroppings of yellow ledgestone jut forth in curiously weathered shapes. In these outcroppings the Lloyd-Joneses saw all around them fanciful forms and profiles which captured their Celtic imaginations and suggested the words of Welsh folklore; it is not surprising,

Note 4
The symbol is: **/|**

therefore, that, when it came his time to build in the valley, it occurred to Frank Lloyd Wright to call his famous house "Taliesin" — "Shining Brow" — the name of a mythical bard to whom much that is memorable in ancient Welsh literature is freely ascribed.

Grandfather Richard Lloyd-Jones, the pioneer, had the typical immigrant's stalwart individualism. Born plain Jones, he was a hatter by trade, and an outspoken Unitarian in a country where Unitarianism was unpopular. He attracted to himself a girl of the superior Lloyd family, who defied all the conventions of class-conscious Welsh society to marry him. Together, now calling themselves Lloyd-Jones, these two hopeful rebels with a family already consisting of seven children made their way in the 1840's from Wales to Wisconsin. One child died en route, but four more were eventually born. Fraternizing with Indians as he plowed his virgin land, Richard Jones must have felt the pride and exhilaration of a man who makes a momentous decision and executes it within his own resources, asking favors of no one. Upon his grandson, Frank Lloyd Wright, has fallen a large share of his pioneer strength and self-confidence, his contempt for outmoded human patterns of behavior. Such sturdy independence as he and his family had was tempered, however, by equally strong concerns with self-improvement and a profound respect for the advantages of education. It was this which lifted them above the level of the average emigré homesteaders and gave them a sense of high purpose. One must learn, and one must, in turn, disseminate truth by teaching or preaching.

Next to his nephew, Frank, Jenkin Lloyd-Jones became the most celebrated member of the clan. Turning to account with Celtic persuasiveness the deep religious strain which he inherited, he organized, and was the lifelong pastor of, All Souls' Church on Chicago's then suburban South Side, whose congregation was at one time the largest in the city. In so doing, he was the first of the clan to prove that Richard Jones's descendants had goals in life that were not to be bounded by the simple satisfactions of farming. Nor were these goals to be conventional. Jenkin Lloyd-Jones was fired by an ambition to strip Christianity of its old burdens of sect and ceremony, to approximate in congregational worship the uncomplex religion he had absorbed at home. Nature and the "natural man" played an important role in the resultant faith; it was not without significance that the Rev. Mr. Lloyd-Jones chose the name Lincoln Center for the congregation's enormous final home— a building with whose curious history Frank Lloyd Wright was to become unhappily involved. The Rev. Mr. Lloyd-Jones was an immense, magnificent person with a compelling eye. Like his father and brothers, he wore long hair and a full beard, and when these turned white he unquestionably brought to mind the picture of the inspired patriarch. As is customary with men who owe their success to themselves, he could be opinionated, contradictory and difficult, as he was in the protracted affair of designing Lincoln Center; but he also had the ability to withstand and triumph over any hostility or ridicule. During the First World War he remained an avowed pacifist, although it was obvious to him that, as a result, he was being deserted by many of his congregation. Politically mistaken as the pacifist attitude proved to be in those last moments of the Edwardian Age, it had in it much of that optimism which, on all fronts, gives the Age in retrospect such a buoyant quality. Chicago in particular, with regard to the United States, adhered to the belief that a fresh start, unclouded vision and hard work could not fail to bring about the utopia for which the inventions of the nineteenth century had roughly prepared the way. Jane Addams and Jenkin Lloyd-Jones, who were friends and colleagues, labored in the sociological aspects of the common purpose; it does not diminish their accomplishment, nor the degree of their courage, to point out that they, and all those others who made the region of Chicago such a wonderful place in the first decade of our century, drew their strength from the general buoyancy around them.

A courage of a more quiet sort characterized the maiden daughters of Richard Lloyd-Jones, the Misses Jane and Nell, who in the 1880's undertook the organization and operation of a boarding-school for adolescents on the family land at Spring Green, an immensely remote place in those days. This was the Hillside Home School, for which Frank Lloyd Wright designed several buildings culminating with the large group erected in 1902. The militant Lloyd-Jones motto, "Truth against the world," was adopted for the enterprise, implying a belief in education as a weapon with which to combat superstition and ignorance. Accordingly, the Misses Lloyd-Jones explored and put to practice new methods of instruction, such as coeducation and direct application of knowledge through work-programs, that were remarkably advanced. The celebrated educator, Mary Ellen Chase, had her first post at Hillside, and devotes part of her autobiography, "A Goodly Fellowship," to a lively description of the maiden aunts and their highly unconventional school.[5]

While Miss Jane and Miss Nell dedicated their skill to the education of the children of others, Mrs. Wright addressed hers to the rearing of her own family, and of Frank in particular. She was determined that her son should be a great builder, and she was convinced that she could predestine him to that end. Secure in her faith that her firstborn would be male, she hung engravings of English cathedrals on the walls of the room which his crib was to occupy. From the day of his birth, she never ceased to concentrate her willpower and her ingenuity upon fortifying that architectural ambience which had been established prenatally. She, unlike her husband, also taught her son much by simple precept. Against obstacles of remoteness and undependable income, she created an atmosphere of sensitivity and good taste in the very nadir of Victorian ugliness, so that young Frank never suffered any intimacy at home with the ill-formed or the banal. She had an innate appreciation of the natural quality of things, whether food or clothing or household furnishings, and refused to torture or overload them in the current mode. Whatever the crudeness of the dwelling in which the Wrights lived, there was a fine simplicity inside: plain, good things, and not too much of them, relieved here and there by a print in a maple frame or some sprays of seasonal foliage in a glass vase (so you could see the shape of the stems).

Strangely, it is Anna Wright who seems in retrospect, much more than her moody husband, akin to the best of the Concord spirit, physically distant and unconnected from that center of New England Brahminism as she was. But she

Note 5
The School was disbanded many years ago, and the buildings are now used for the various activities of the Taliesin Fellows.

was never effete. She always had the self-reliance and sense of purpose of her pioneer parents. When, in 1885, matters between her and William Wright had reached a stalemate to the detriment of her children, she did not hesitate to advise him to leave, although she clearly realized how difficult her lot would be as an abandoned wife and mother.

Weymouth

Weymouth, Massachusetts, is now engulfed by Boston's sprawling suburbia, but in 1874, when William Wright took his family there to live, it still retained its identity as a crooked, compact New England village shaded by great elms and threaded by tidal streams. For William Wright, the move to Weymouth was a return to familiar scenes, but for his wife and children it was a revelation in every way. The Weymouth period, therefore, was as significant to the development of the Wright family as it was brief, and embraced the most important single event of Frank Lloyd Wright's childhood. The financial circumstances of the family, during the three years that William Wright managed to hold the parsonage of Weymouth's small Baptist church, were somewhat more secure than usual, permitting exploratory contact with the interests and values of a segment of American society which, in contrast to that of the frontier, knew and utilized every advantage of civilized living. Mrs. Wright, particularly, seized the opportunity offered her to find means of advancing and improving the education of her children; she was determined that her family, and especially Frank, should derive some permanent benefit from the experience of living in the East.

In 1876, Mr. and Mrs. Wright, availing themselves of the special railway excursion rates, traveled from Boston to Philadelphia to "take in" the great Centennial Exposition of that year. In the welter of Victorian things spread out to view in Fairmount Park, Mrs. Wright made, for her, a tremendous discovery: an exhibit setting forth the principles of the new Froebelian kindergarten concept. She was fascinated by the clean toys, the intelligent way in which the games were organized, and the conversation of the young woman in charge, Ruth Burritt, who had been trained by Froebel in Austria. Here,

indeed, was a radical departure in child education which, Mrs. Wright believed, she could put into practice back in the Weymouth parsonage. It seemed to her that her son particularly (whom she had predestined to be a builder) could not fail to derive a sense of structure and a feeling for simple materials from playing with the wonderful Froebelian toys. She made up her mind— and, in so doing, contributed one source of influence upon her son's career which seems certain and undeniable. Frank Lloyd Wright is fully aware of the enduring effect of his kindergarten experience[1], and he used to speak of it to George Elmslie.[2] No doubt, he also discussed it with Robert Spencer, who so wisely stressed it in his valuable early article on Wright,[3] pointing out that Wright was probably the only American architect of his generation to have received kindergarten training.

In any case, Mrs. Wright, upon her return to Massachusetts, went at once to Boston to make further inquiries about the kindergarten principle and to see what was available in the way of equipment. She found that another of Froebel's disciples, Mme. Kraus-Boelte, had established a small kindergarten there in 1872, and that others were currently in operation under Mme. Kriege and Mrs. Shaw. A Boston bookseller carried textbooks in English published a

Note 1
Wright has acknowledged the influence upon him of his kindergarten experience, specifically in "An Autobiography."
Note 2
Wright and George Elmslie first became acquainted as fellow draftsmen in the office of Lyman Silsbee in Chicago. Elmslie's eventual association with Sullivan was of long standing (see Morrison's biography of Louis Sullivan); later, he practiced independently and became a member in his own right of the so-called "Chicago School" of progressive architecture. Further references to Elmslie, with whom the author corresponded, are made in this book.
Note 3
Robert C. Spencer, Jr.: "The Work of Frank Lloyd Wright," Architectural Review (Boston), Vol. 7, June 1900, pp. 61-72.

year or two before by Steiger of New York[4] and Milton Bradley's store stocked a line of Froebelian kindergarten chests.[5] There had been nothing like this in Wisconsin! It was out of the question to send her children into Boston to the kindergartens, but Mrs. Wright was more than ever convinced that she could apply the new method at home. She bought the necessary equipment.

The fact that Frank was then going on seven, well beyond the accepted kindergarten age, did not in the least deter her. She knew that her son was, both by predestination and suggestion, highly susceptible to the Froebelian objective, and, since she realized that its lesson had the broadest implications, he could well derive more profit from it at six than at four. She proceeded — and to inspect the old Steiger textbooks, crammed with diagrams and minutely practical, is to get an explicit insight into how she proceeded.

Today it is difficult, perhaps, to understand that the idea of directing children's play into organized, constructive patterns could ever have been revolutionary. But, under the happy name of "kindergarten," revolution is exactly what Froebel and his colleagues had brought about. The name reveals Froebel's basic theme: that direction of play must be so sympathetic as not to be obtrusive nor to diminish its joy. It was only that, without the child's awareness, play was transformed from a random energy-outlet into an appreciation for natural objects and laws upon which mature human life depends. To this end, the first and most obvious change was in the character of the toys with which the games were played. Froebel provided nothing amorphous or merely pretty. Instead, the child was given objects simple and crystalline in shape, primary in color, truthful in material. The toys, known in the early days of the kindergarten experiment as "gifts," were presented in a series beginning with the three fundamental shapes — the cube, the cylinder, and the sphere — followed at intervals with other "gifts" increasing in complexity. With each "gift," there were dozens of games to be played, gradually progressing in difficulty. Granting that only a Victorian child would have submitted to even such velvet-gloved regimentation, he allowed himself to be shown the mastery he had gained over these materials, giving him the necessary confidence to take another step up the Froebelian ladder. While such pedagogy is possibly debatable by modern standards, it is indisputable that, by contrast with the gingerbread toys of the Victorian Age, Froebel's "gifts" were admirable, and any child familiar with them had the advantage of developing an early feeling for simple, uncluttered shapes and plain surfaces, and the additive relation of form to form in structure.

In "An Autobiography," Frank Lloyd Wright devotes several passages to this stimulating experience in his childhood. "The strips of coloured paper, glazed and 'matt,' remarkably soft brilliant colours. Now came the geometric by-play of these charming checkered colour combinations! The structural figures to be made with peas and small straight sticks; slender constructions, the joinings accented by the little green pea-globes. The smooth shapely maple blocks with which to build, the sense of which never afterward leaves the fingers: so *form* became *feeling*. And the box with a mast to set upon it, on which to hang with string the maple cubes and spheres and triangles, revolving them to discover subordinate forms.... And the exciting cardboard shapes with pure scarlet face — such scarlet! Smooth, triangular shapes, white-back, and edges, cut in rhomboids, with which to make designs on the flat table top. What shapes they made naturally if only you would let them!" And again: "That early kindergarten experience with the straight line; the flat plane; the square; the triangle; the circle! If I wanted more, the square modified by the triangle gave the hexagon — the circle modified by the straight line would give the octagon. Adding thickness, getting 'sculpture' thereby, the square became the cube, the triangle the tetrahedron, the circle the sphere. These primary forms and figures were the secret of all effects . . . which were ever got into the architecture of the world."

Note 4
Heinrich Hoffmann: "Kindergarten Toys and How to Use Them," E. Steiger, New York, 1874.
Note 5
For further details of the early kindergarten developments in this country, see Anon.: "Pioneers of the Kindergarten in America," The Century Co., New York, 1924.

Such passages, highly illustrative of Wright's literary style, give the impression, as they are meant to do, of a tremendously receptive child responding to the fascination of pure forms and patterns at the precise moment when his thought-habits were acquiring definition. The phraseology underscores the very genuine experience that lies behind it and the fact that it endured and became basic. The two- and three-dimensional schemes of the Froebelian exercises bear a distinct resemblance (Figs. 2 and 3) to designs incorporated in the work of what is referred to subsequently in this book as "The First Golden Age" — the completed buildings and projects carried out from 1900 to 1910. The determining factor in these resemblances is always the avowed attempt to give expression to the nature of materials[6] and the forms they naturally suggest.

Froebel insisted that his miniature structures be built carefully, with a plan marked out first upon the floor. The child's imagination was called upon to give the resultant structure a name: "barn," "barge," "pipe-organ," "newsstand," "farmyard," etc. The child thus felt that he had the power to build anything he could

Note 6
This fact was signalized by Henry-Russell Hitchcock in the title for his book on Wright: "In the Nature of Materials," Duell, Sloane & Pearce, New York, 1942.

Fig. 2. The Froebel games, beginning with the first "gift": a cube, a sphere, a cylinder.

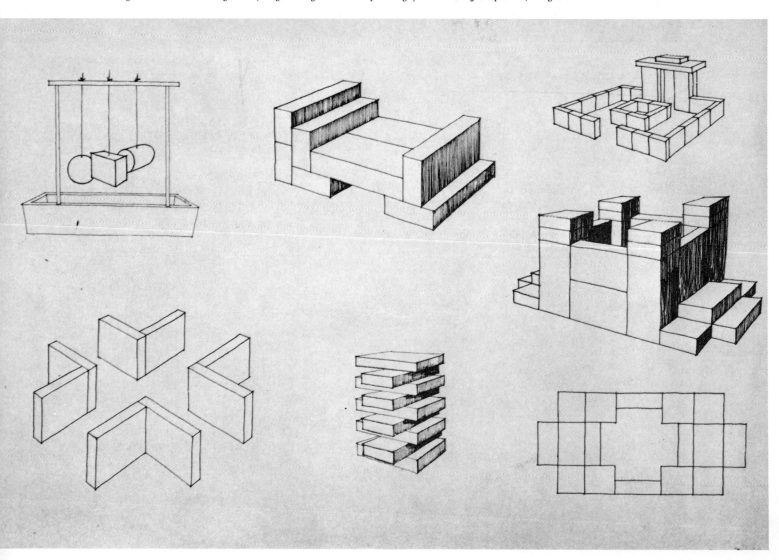

Fig. 3. Here and on the facing page are examples of the Froebelian "gifts"—wood blocks, paper-plaiting, paper folding, beads and string, etc.—compared with actual designs by Wright.

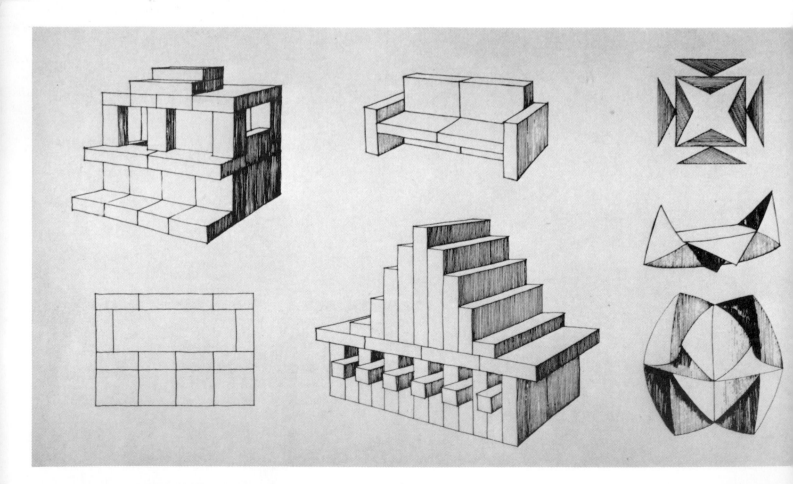

ideate, a sort of self-confidence which Wright has subsequently shown to a marked degree.

The curve, lying within the sphere, was limited in application, and the kindergarten builder knew that he could only use it as ornamental relief for his prevalent straight lines. The chief decoration for his block houses was vigorous effects of light and shadow, with which he could produce satisfactory rhythms that gave his buildings interesting richness without applied ornament. There was an emphasis on good balance and an acceptance of unbroken surface for structural strength. Sometimes partial enclosure of space was the aim, as in walled "farmyards," and here the imaginative child could take pleasure in fusing structure and environment; even the problems of town-planning were touched upon in such exercises as "street scene" and "street crossings." Furniture, too, was built, likewise abstract, and looking very modern.

It is significant that Froebel did not recommend drawing or painting until the last stages of the kindergarten experience. Thus there was little direct imitation of nature; natural objects

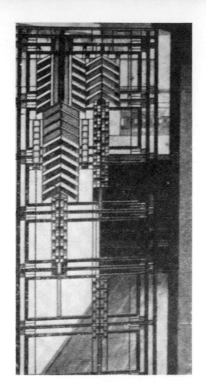

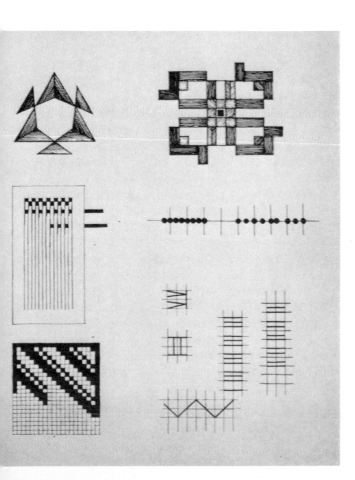

were translated into the crispness of geometry. At the same time, the child was encouraged to see that geometric forms underlie all natural manifestations and are readily arranged into satisfactory approximations of them. Letting his mind run free in the pleasantly ordered world of the abstract, Froebel's child could produce unlimited designs that were independent of "nature" in the banal Victorian sense. It was an enormous advantage.

How many hours Wright devoted in the Weymouth parsonage to the Froebel "gifts" is an incalculable sum, but the effect is not. It was a fateful moment when Mrs. Wright, that day at the Philadelphia Centennial, stopped to study Miss Burritt's exhibit, for, as a result, she certainly opened to her builder-son, in the heyday of Welsbach and "Eastlake," a vista of better things to come. Wright's immediate and powerful declaration of faith in direct expression of function, simple form and tailored surface when he made his first independent design as an architect bespeaks a long-established taste; and, since he was only twenty-two at the time, it stands to reason that we must look for its inception in childhood, and probably at Weymouth.

Madison

William Wright's tenure of the Weymouth Baptist pastorate lasted a little more than three years, from August, 1874, to November, 1877. Concerning his service in the neo-Romanesque frame church on the hill above the main street, the chronicles of the congregation are both revealing and non-committal. The booklet published on the occasion of the church's semi-centennial[1] informs us that the Rev. Mr. Wright "baptized eleven and received ten others, twenty-one in all; he left a membership of one hundred and twenty-six. It was during Mr. Wright's stay in Weymouth that the Church put in the valuable pipe organ which is still such a great help in our worship; this enterprise evidently owing not a little to his large attainments as a musician." This is the organ which, according to the anec-

Note 1
Frank B. Cressey: "Semi-Centennial, Baptist Church, Weymouth, Mass.," Gazette Publishing Co., 1904.

dote in "An Autobiography," young Frank once pumped for his imperious father until he lay exhausted upon the floor. The Rev. Mr. Wright and his wife were made members of the congregation immediately upon their arrival, having been "baptized by letter," but their names were removed from the church register in 1878, and it is a curious fact that their children were never registered. Apparently, the Wrights remained Unitarian at heart, or foresaw that the connection in Weymouth was to be, like everything Mr. Wright inaugurated, short-lived.

When the connection was severed, the family returned to Wisconsin and occupied a wooden cottage in Gorham Street, Madison, for the following seven or eight years. William Wright now resumed his old profession of music-master. There is uncertainty as to the exact year of the Wrights' return to Madison; "William Wright, music teacher" is first listed in the Madison Directory in 1880, which suggests that he had hung out his shingle sometime during the previous year and that there are some two years in the family history unaccounted for.

Despite the dignity of being state capital, Madison in the times of which we speak was a scattered, slovenly Midwestern settlement with a few retail streets of false-fronts, blocks of humble balloon-frame dwellings, a pretentious "Period" Capitol, some nondescript university buildings, and a score of jigsaw mansions in which the wealthy lived. Although hardly, as yet, graced by man, the capital enjoyed a superb natural setting on an isthmus between two round blue lakes enframed with low hills. The Wrights' Gorham Street cottage had the edge of Lake Mendota at the bottom of its yard. Second Ward School, in which young Frank Wright and his elder sister were now enrolled, a short distance to the west, was a forbidding brick structure in the folk-style derived from the Renaissance Revival with the exaggerated floor-heights and narrow, beetle-browed arched windows which the style called for. From this oppressive institution the Wright children escaped every summer to live and work on the Lloyd-Jones farm at Spring Green; Uncle James Lloyd-Jones came for them on the appointed day in a creaking wagon drawn by a massive team.

These farm interludes familiarized young Wright with hard physical labor and gave him rugged strength. They also served to renew his ties with his mother's people and their remarkable attachment to the land which they cultivated and loved. These acres of rolling black earth were the ultimate reality against which every achievement of man must be measured.[2] Nature so powerful, normally benevolent, could be rough and uncouth, too. Notwithstanding the animistic tone of the traditional Lloyd-Jones attitude toward nature and the natural life, young Wright's was realistic enough. He hated the back-breaking toil, the incredibly long hours of the workday, the often overpowering sights and smells of the barnyard, the relentless struggle against weeds and pests. But because the total effect of life on the Lloyd-Jones farm was one of kindliness and abundance the lasting impression which summertimes made upon Wright was that of the goodness of nature. In common with his uncles and aunts, he came to understand and to respect the timeless appeal of their beloved homestead and the rolling landscape in which they could feel strong, secure and free.

Back in Madison, Mrs. Wright bravely maintained the Brahmin atmosphere which she had at first instinctively created and then had actually perceived in New England. Undistinguished as the Gorham Street house may have been outside, its interior was an oasis of simple good taste. "The modern refinement of the home grew from the yearning, ambitious mother's hands: the new-laid, white, waxed maple floors, the cream-colored net curtains hanging straight beside the windows. The centers of the room-floors covered with India rugs — cream-colored ground with bright-colored patterns and border. Maple and rattan furniture. And everywhere, books. Simple vases gracefully filled with dried leaves. A simplicity, yes — but not of the soul." With only a few modifications, this could be a description of one of Wright's own early essays in in-terior decoration. Unhappily, these tranquil rooms were increasingly filled with discord as the breach between the parents widened. There were evenings of real contentment, however, when everyone indulged in a musical family party — then, and only then, could William Wright break down the barrier of self-concern which isolated him from his wife and children, and be one with them. The "conservatory of music" which he had hoped to establish, while unsuccessful financially, at least attracted to the Gorham Street house most of the livelier young folk in town who organized themselves into an informal civic band. Naturally, each of the Wright children had been taught to play one or more instruments. Young Wright's specialty, although he had commenced his instruction on the piano, was the viola. He also developed an insatiable appetite for reading, and, in a household which was bookish, there was a good deal of material to satisfy it, albeit haphazardly. On one occasion, his aunts Nell and Jane presented him with a copy of Ruskin's "Seven Lamps of Architecture," no doubt at his mother's suggestion, indicating that the word had already been passed in the family circle that Frank was to be an architect; yet, oddly enough, no other book with an architectural subject seems to have come his way until his formal training (such as it was) began.

The first step in this direction was probably taken prematurely due to sudden pressure of family circumstances. Some clue may be had from the Madison Directory of 1885: it is the last edition in which the name of William Wright appears and the first of two in which there is listed the entry "Frank L. Wright, draughtsman." William Wright's abandonment of his family and his son's debut into the world of architecture apparently coincided. Young Wright, at fifteen or sixteen years of age,[3] found himself the man of the family, faced with the necessity of contributing something toward its upkeep. It is characteristic of his mother that she made a virtue of necessity, and launched her son forth-

Note 2
Frank Lloyd Wright: "Recollections—United States, 1893-1920," Architects Journal (London), Vol. 84, July 1936, pp. 76-78: "When I was eleven years old I was sent to a Wisconsin farm to learn how really to work. So all this I saw around me [i.e., upon beginning to practice architecture in Chicago] seemed affectation, nonsense, or profanity. The first feeling was hunger for reality and sincerity. A desire for simplicity. . . ."

Note 3
This reckoning depends upon whether he started to work sometime during the year prior to the publication of the 1885 Directory; it is the usual assumption, but there is no proof.

with upon his career by placing him in the office of a local builder named Allen D. Conover.

This is unquestionably an exciting moment in any account of Frank Lloyd Wright's career, yet its details are prosaic enough. Young Wright, of course, knew nothing of any practical value to Conover, so the relationship commenced with Wright acting as officeboy and most junior apprentice. Conover was the one professional builder in Madison at the time; one hesitates to use the word "architect" since his bias was strongly toward engineering rather than design, as is attested by the fact that he also served as Dean of Engineering in the University up on the hill — and by the fact that he often supervised the erection of buildings designed by others, as in the case of the University's Science Hall whose architect was a Milwaukee man named Koch. Nevertheless, there fell to Allen Conover the commissions for some of the most prominent buildings in Madison, like the University Armory, which he designed in the popular Richardsonian style, complete with high-pitched roofs, turrets, and massive arches, the standard equipment of this kind of picturesque architecture. Derivative as such buildings are, they have something of the ponderous dignity of Richardson's famous manner, being "built to last."

The lessons which Wright learned in Conover's office were impressive because they were the first, and they were certainly lessons in sound engineering practice rather than pure design. It was an apprenticeship in the school of hard knocks. The sort of job which was meted out to very junior draftsmen in those days was more than paper work. Wright describes as a typical example the task of installing the metal clips on the roof trusses of Science Hall during the winter of its construction. Such precepts in sturdy building as the work at Conover's afforded young Wright were sharply highlighted by the coincidence of his witnessing the disastrous collapse of the new North Wing of the old Capitol. A great scandal ensued upon the discovery that dishonest contractors had fatally weakened the building by filling the supporting piers with loose rubble.

Wright remained in Conover's office for over two years, and although the designs on which he worked were unimaginative in the extreme, he could not have been exposed in Madison to any higher manifestation of the architectural profession. Madison was not a hothouse of architectural ideas. The only building in the town, other than those with which he had some connection as Conover's apprentice, that impressed him sufficiently to be mentioned, years later, in "An Autobiography" was the William Vilas house in Gilman Street. Like the old Second Ward School, the Vilas house would probably have been catalogued as "Renaissance," but its design was of a higher order. It is one of those rare mansions of the Civil War Era which, despite a loading of jigsaw ornament, achieves by sheer proportion a certain air of distinction. Free of the ubiquitous mansard roof (and therefore coming under the subheading "Italian"), it is really a composition of simple cubes, with plenty of bare brick wall to carry, and act as a foil to, the ten-foot sash windows, each with a cast-iron balcony beneath. By some miracle, the house is low upon its site, thus stressing the horizontal in a period when houses thrust themselves upward in direct proportion to their owners' bank-accounts. It is conceivable that the Vilas house (as could not possibly be said for any of Conover's buildings) stands as one source of inspiration for the epochal Charnley house, Wright's first masterpiece of domestic design.

To proceed with the matter of Wright's formal education in Madison, his job with Conover was so arranged as to leave him some part of each day free so that he could take courses in the Department of Civil Engineering at the University under the tutelage of Dean Conover and Professor Bull. Such courses were as close as the curriculum of the University of Wisconsin then came to offering in architectural training, and they are all that Wright ever had. At that, he managed to take only a sampling, as will be seen. The University catalogue for 1885-86 describes the Civil Engineering program as one of four years' duration, comprising technical instruction and daily practice in drafting;[4] it was aimed primarily at proficiency in machinery- and shop-practice. "All drawings [i.e., of machinery] are required to be executed in such a way as to be fit for use as working-drawings in a machine-

Note 4
A complete transcription of the curriculum for the freshman and sophomore years of the School of Civil Engineering is included in the Appendix of this book, p. 215.

shop. For the sake of gaining some practice in tinting, the students are required to tint them . . . ."[5] That her son might enjoy the dubious benefits of such a training, Mrs. Wright contrived, with many sacrifices, to pay the fees, and Frank was registered as a "special student" in civil engineering;[6] the prefix "special" meant that he could not meet the scholastic standards for regular registration — nor give it the hours per week that it required. He was a part-time student, and his University career was brief. His name appears in the catalogue of 1885-86 as "one of the students present during the latter part" of the academic year; in the catalogue of 1886-87, it appears again under the heading of "special students." The only course for which there is any complete record of his attendance is Geometry, in which he received a final grade of 90. This must be the abbreviated title for the course in Descriptive Geometry that was prescribed as part of the curriculum for the third term of the freshman year, which corresponds with his late registration as indicated in the catalogue of 1885-86. As Wright ran off to Chicago in 1887 before the University had adjourned for summer vacation, he received no final grades that year. His entire attendance was considerably less than two academic years.

This, in sum, was his college education. It is hard to imagine what he could have gained from so desultory an experience other than a natural disgust which he takes no pains to conceal and which drove him to leave Madison and seek his destiny elsewhere. Henry-Russell Hitchcock was right, in the light of the information revealed by these Registrar's records, when he said that "never having studied in the American architectural schools of the eighties, there was much he [Wright] never had to unlearn."[7] Up to the day of his arrival in Chicago, Wright could literally be classified as a "native" genius.

Note 5
Quoted from the prospectus of the course in Draughting under Prof. Bull, 1885-86.

Note 6
All data pertaining to Wright's attendance at the University of Wisconsin were taken from records kept by the Registrar.

Note 7
Henry-Russell Hitchcock, Jr.: "Frank Lloyd Wright," Modern Architecture; International Exhibition . . . Feb. 10 to March 23, 1932 (New York, Museum of Modern Art, 1932), pp. 29-55.

2. Apprenticeship

Silsbee, the Conventional

The exact date of Wright's arrival in Chicago is not available. By his own statements and by the records of the University of Wisconsin, it was some time in the spring of 1887 that he left Madison and came to the big city. It was a calculated risk — and a classic move in the biography of all country-bred geniuses. Wright's description of Chicago's first bewildering impact upon him as he emerged into its clamor one rainy evening from the old Wells Street Depot is also in the best tradition. But the purely conventional has no real part in Wright's life, and the critical eye which he turned upon the buildings in The Loop in those first days was the eye of a rebel. With what was he armed, at the age of eighteen, for rebellion?

He had been born to a determined, aggressive mother and a weak, temperamental father, a combination which usually leads to conspicuous disaster; he had absorbed from the former an innate ability to discriminate the good from the tasteless, from the latter (strangely enough, considering the tactless way in which he had imparted it), a love of music; he had been exposed to the "gifts" and lessons of the Froebel method of child training, from which he had distilled with precocious understanding its message of respect for simple forms and crystalline structure; he had experienced farm-life and the peculiar agrarian cult of the Lloyd-Jones clan from which he gained a strong, somewhat confused, and ambivalent belief in the "rightness" of nature; he had known some contentment, but also disillusionment and anxiety; he had been a voracious and catholic reader of everything from Alger and Henty to, by the way, Ruskin; he was practically ignorant of the benefits of "higher" education, but he was aware of himself as a predestined architect, and he had learned directly from Allen Conover many of the secrets of good construction. To quote Hitchcock again,[1] "... the most absurd conventional discipline of imitation could hardly have dimmed a youth so nurtured in a tradition of emotion and rebellion. His education advanced on either side of architecture, below it in the field of construction and above it in the field of aesthetic theory. The middle plane of artistic actuality he had from the first to fill in alone. Indeed, in that mid-Western town [i.e., Madison] ... architecture hardly existed except as it grew new and fresh in Wright's imagination."

The second sentence in this book (and it could

Note 1
Henry-Russell Hitchcock, Jr.: "Frank Lloyd Wright," Modern Architecture; International Exhibition . . . Feb. 10 to March 23, 1932 (New York, Museum of Modern Art, 1932), pp. 29-55.

well be repeated as the last) is to the effect that Wright's art is spontaneous. But it is a form of idolatry which Wright himself does not admire to say that nothing from "outside" helped to give expression to what he felt. One of the chief purposes of this book is to itemize and explore those experiences of Wright's which contributed to the formulation of that feeling. From the moment he set foot in Chicago, his perceptive mind was bombarded with experiences of which a few were to prove significant. Within this limitation, the months he spent in the office of Joseph Lyman Silsbee, his first Chicago master, can probably be evaluated as neutral but salutary. Lyman Silsbee was the best practitioner of conventional Eastern-inspired architecture in Chicago at the time. An Easterner himself by birth and training, Silsbee's work was gentle and well-bred in a way that much of the architecture of Chicago's youth was not. However unexciting, Silsbee's houses were always in good taste, derived from the work of Norman Shaw and his contemporaries in England, but sensibly adapted to the American scene in respect to size, disposition and materials. They had something of the simple, fresh elegance of those wonderful shingle-sides which were beginning to dominate Atlantic coast architecture in the United States, about which Vincent Scully has recently written with such penetration;[2] and indeed it would seem to be Silsbee who introduced the "Shingle Style" to the Chicago area. It was really fortunate for Wright that he should have had his first and inevitable experience with the conventional in architecture under Silsbee's guidance.

By the year 1887, Lyman Silsbee had become sought after and highly successful in the realm of house design and related kinds of architecture such as clubs. Among other things, he was then engaged upon an important venture, the development of "Edgewater," J. L. Cochrane's new lakeside suburb on the northern fringe of the city. He had also been commissioned by the Rev. Mr. Jenkin Lloyd-Jones, Wright's dynamic uncle (who was instrumental in bringing Silsbee to Chicago from Syracuse) to design a new build-

Note 2
Vincent J. Scully, Jr.: "The Shingle Style: Architectural Theory and Design from Richardson to the Origins of Wright," Yale University Press, New Haven, 1955.

ing for All Souls', which had grown from a little band of enthusiasts first gathering in a store in Cottage Grove Avenue to a congregation of impressive size and wealth ready to finance the construction of a new church to its own liking. Jenkin Lloyd-Jones had been attracted to Silsbee by the sensible, "homey" touch of his house architecture, and it was a house for his congregation, rather than a church in the routine sense of the word, that he had in mind. Wright had heard of this commission before he left Madison, and this justifies the use of the phrase "a calculated risk" to explain his sudden departure for Chicago, for, although he did not want to lean upon his uncle in any obvious way, he knew that he had one foot in the door. He was, of course, despite the best intentions, introduced to Silsbee as "Jones's nephew," and, just in the nick of time, he landed a draftsman's job in Silsbee's office; he had already spent the last of the few dollars that he had in his pocket when he arrived.

Wright duly reported for work the next day, and thus it was that All Souls' Church was the first piece of architectural design with which he had anything to do in Chicago. It was a curious design (Fig. 4). Silsbee's style was, for reasons mentioned, strongly domestic. This, coupled with Jenkin Lloyd-Jones's determination to have a

Fig. 4. The single surviving photograph of All Souls' Church.

Fig. 5. The J. L. Cochrane house. Observe the signature of the draftsman.

church that expressed freedom from cant, accounts for the eccentricity of the design. With studied informality, it looked like a suburban clubhouse rather than a church — asymmetrical, picturesque, eschewing all the appurtenances of ecclesiastical architecture. Like the Edgewater houses, it was made of a pleasant mixture of brick and brown shingles, and was graced with an oriel and some pargeting here and there.

In the published drawings for J. L. Cochrane's house in the Edgewater development (Fig. 5), the hand of Silsbee's newest apprentice can actually be seen, for the pen-and-ink perspective is neatly lettered in the corner "Frank L.L. Wright, Del." It is interesting to notice the an-

gular, stylized rendering of shrubbery around the house; this small contribution to the modern viewpoint in the imitation of nature apparently caught on and became the vogue in Silsbee's drafting-room, as it was copied in pen renderings by Henry Fiddelke and other draftsmen after Wright had left. As a matter of fact, Wright's urgent need to find avenues for expressing his own ideas about design began to exert itself as soon as he felt the stimulus of Chicago, and it was not to be satisfied by having his way in a few renderings for Silsbee's commissions. He managed to break into print under his own name.

There are four extant independent projects of

Wright's dating from the Silsbee period. The design for a little "Unitarian Chapel for Sioux City," which was published in the early summer of 1887[3] (Fig. 6), has the honor of heading the chronological list of Wright's authentic works.

Note 3
Inland Architect & News Record, Vol. 9, June, 1887, plate: plan and perspective drawing.

The unconventional form which this chapel takes could be a reflection of the club-like appearance of All Souls' Church. The simple one-room interior can be subdivided by movable screens into parlors for social gatherings; there is a fireplace at one end, a speaker's platform at the other; a small recess serves as the pastor's study, balanced at the other side by that indispensable feature of the Shingle Style, a circular alcove with a cupola above. We may ascribe the fluidity of the plan to a lack of experience in controlling

Fig. 6. Unitarian Chapel for Sioux City, probably Wright's first independent design and to this day his bête noire.

enclosed space, or to the free nature of Unitarianism — or we may read real significance in it and ascribe it to a precocious realization on the designer's part that standardized attitudes toward compartmentation of space were open to attack. The broad sash windows, both in their oblong shape and their leadings, are certainly progenitors of the type of fenestration Wright was later to use in the Winslow house and other designs of the early Oak Park period. As for the rest, the building is unprotestingly picturesque and reminiscent of Silsbee's interpretation of the Shingle Style.

Also sometime in 1887, Wright undertook a youthful job for his maiden aunts, the Misses Jane and Nell Lloyd-Jones: this was the first building for Hillside Home School at Spring Green (Fig. 7). Since this design was not merely paper work but was actually going to be built, Wright sought practical assistance from Silsbee in solving his problem. The vernacular and the general effect of roofs and gables are picturesque in Silsbee's Shingle Style manner.

The whole story of the development by Wright and his aunts of the Hillside Home School complex is difficult to grasp. It was a project that continued sporadically into the opening years of the twentieth century and that will be referred to again in this book. It undoubtedly began under the immediate supervision of Lyman Silsbee, and then gradually became the responsibility of Wright alone, any exact moment of transference being impossible to define more nearly than the date of severance of Wright's employment by Silsbee.

Aside from the Sioux City Chapel, there are two other published designs by Wright from this earliest period: "Country Residences I & II for Hillside Estate" (Figs. 8 and 9). Both designs appeared in the Inland Architect & News Record, the first in August, 1887, the second in February, 1888. Again, these designs have some connection

Fig. 7. First Hillside Home School, where Aunts Nell and Jane began their experiments in teaching the young.

Fig. 8 (above). One of the "Helena Valley" houses, an early project never carried to completion. Fig. 9 (below). This "Helena Valley" house was more than a project, as Fig. 7 indicates.

with schemes for development of the family land at Spring Green; that they may have been seriously intended is indicated by the location lettered on the drawings — "Helena Valley, Wisconsin" — a locale which does not exist today but which can be found on contemporary maps of the state. It is natural to assume that the Lloyd-Joneses wanted to give every encouragement they could to the debut of the architect in their midst, an event so long heralded. As for the "Country Residences," they are the least original and most derivative from Silsbee's Edgewater manner of all these early projects.

Wright remained in Silsbee's office for seven or eight months, up to the late fall of 1887. There was a brief interval of a week or two when he went over to the office of the architect Minard L. Beers, but, finding nothing there to interest him, he managed to recover his position with Silsbee. There were other promising young men serving an apprenticeship with Silsbee at this period, among them George Maher, George Elmslie, Cecil Corwin and Henry Fiddelke. They were all to evolve with considerable success their own versions of progressive architecture within the compass of the Chicago School and the vigorous style which that term has come to imply. Due to various circumstances, which will be explained, Wright later formed close associations with two of them: Elmslie and Corwin. All these beginners had their first brush with the practice of architecture in the late Victorian atmosphere of quiet good taste which Silsbee created; although they diverged sharply from conventionalism in their several ways as time went on, they were to remember and occasionally to copy, Wright no less than the others, certain features of the so-called Shingle Style. This is not in any sense an indictment. Silsbee was a man of good background and judgment in whose conventionality there was usually something fresh. Furthermore, there was much in the picturesqueness of the Queen Anne tradition, from which the American Shingle Style was derived, that, if not carried to excess, was a splendid introduction to the world of informality and invention. No one could ever be too sure of what "Queen Anne" meant; of all the revival styles, it was the least specific. From its very vagueness, its intelligent devotees conjured up some rather significant things: in the guise of the oriel and the bay, the idea of continuous fenestration and

the centrifugal plan; from the English porch grew the spacious American verandah, spreading the house out upon its site and giving it low, informal lines; the translation of the English pantile for siding into the old Colonial gray shingle and the flowing contours it suggested such as the eyebrow dormer and the bell-shaped cupola; bold, fanciful chimneys, moulded brickwork, plastic ornament in terra cotta and carved wood. Despite its puzzlements, the net result in America of the vogue for the Queen Anne was an adaptable, elastic kind of domestic and related achitecture that was perhaps better suited for living on the North American continent than any style which had preceded it. It was essentially conservative in that its aim was still to recreate the flavor of the past, but in the hands of a few architects, as Vincent Scully has shown, it could rise to very real heights of accomplishment and challenge.

We cannot, of course, bracket Lyman Silsbee with such great practitioners of progressive conventional architecture as Stanford White in the 1880's, but, nevertheless, to have worked with him for a while was not wasted time for any of the young architects of Chicago mentioned above. Wright himself acknowledges three benefits from this period of his career: "With Silsbee . . . I had gained considerable light on the practical needs of the American dwelling . . . Silsbee could draw with amazing ease. He drew with soft deep black lead pencil strokes and he would make remarkable free-hand sketches of that type of dwelling peculiarly his own at the time. His superior talent for design had made him respected in Chicago. His work was a picturesque combination of gable, turret and hip with broad porches quietly domestic and gracefully picturesque. A contrast to the awkward stupidities and brutalities of the period, elsewhere." Planning skill, the secrets of drawing, a sense of propriety in design — these were valuable precepts; there was one other hint he took from Silsbee, a clue to a ruling passion in his life and a source of very real influence on his work which will be recalled in a later chapter when the relationship of Japanese art to Wright's style is being discussed.

Despite acknowledged benefits, Wright soon began to feel restive under Silsbee, and he was eager to move on when the opportunity came to join up with Adler & Sullivan. He never quite forgot Silsbee, however. Traces of Silsbee's picturesqueness remained in his work throughout the 1890's, after he had begun to practice independently. Just before 1890, Silsbee introduced to the Chicago area another importation from the East, the new rage for the "Colonial," and the fact that Wright had actually erected two houses in this manner by 1894 — the Blossom and Bagley commissions — shows how closely he watched his former employer's development. It was not until the close of the century that Wright altogether discarded the high, steep roofs which the picturesque demanded. The most stubborn after-effect of his experience with Silsbee was a tendency to incorporate diamond-shaped and polygonal elements in plan, sometimes delightful in themselves, but sharply opposed to the ultimate achievement of the Prairie House. The polygon and the circle as prime units of the modulated plan, after lying dormant for almost three decades of Wright's career, have again risen since 1940 to form the basis of much of his design, and it is logical to trace them back to the turrets and oriels of Silsbee.

It is interesting to note in passing that Wright at last began, while he was with Silsbee, to make a serious study of books on architecture and to learn something of its history. For example, he made one hundred onion-skin tracings from the "Grammar of Ornament" by Owen Jones and the "Dictionnaire Raisonné" of Viollet-le-Duc at this time. Horizons were widening.

Sullivan, the Unconventional

So much has been said, written, and inferred concerning the association of Frank Lloyd Wright and Louis Henry Sullivan that it deserves every scrutiny. Yet it is a relationship that has the qualities of a mirage: it grows less substantial the closer it is approached.

"Der Liebe Meister," as Sullivan was called by his disciples, was elevated by them in the heyday of his creative power to the role of (to carry on the vernacular of the cult) *Uebermensch*. The fact that he must always have had buried within him the seed of that spiritual weakness which was eventually to bring about his tragic retirement from the field was either unknown or unadmitted in the architectural circles of late-nineteenth century Chicago. For some twenty years, he was, indeed, a towering force felt by all those younger architects, including Wright, who may lay claim to membership in that group now known as the Chicago School.[1] It was a matter of pride to wear the disciple's mark, and upon most of them the effect of Sullivan's influence was tangible. In Wright's case, despite the fact that he chooses to wear that mark, Sullivan's influence can neither be specifically isolated nor measured. Wright and Sullivan were, at the very least, of equal stature, and it is open to question whether any influence that may have been exerted in the relationship did not flow more in Sullivan's direction than in Wright's. We begin to look upon Wright's continuing maintenance of the disciple's status as nothing more than an amiable fiction.

An effort to evaluate the relationship was first made by Robert Spencer, Wright's early protagonist, who wrote in his previously cited article of 1900: "No one more than he [i.e., Wright] realizes and is grateful for the significance in this work of the early influence of Sullivan. Working together as master and trusted pupil, . . . there must have been between two such ardent natures an interchange of thought and influence not wholly one-sided. Today both are influencing in the same direction the enthusiastic youths who are taking up the burden of an architectural career in this free western hemisphere." But almost forty years later, with his more mature knowledge of the situation and with the advantage of hindsight, George Elmslie said in a paper read to the Illinois Society of Architects in November, 1939: "A fine sense of camaraderie existed between those two men at that time, giving and taking with fine accord and equanimity of spirit. Wright, even then, bore all the earmarks of what he has become, the outstanding figure of our day. A Brahms in Architecture, if you like. Sullivan did not, of course, need Wright; while the latter has emphasized in glowing terms the benefits he received in communion with his master. Wright, however, would have come into his own if he had never met Sullivan. Sullivan did not make Wright in any sense, each

Note 1
To the author's knowledge, the term "Chicago School" was inaugurated by Thomas Tallmadge in his article of that name in the Architectural Review (Boston), Vol. 15, April 1908, pp. 69-74.

was *sui generis* and both marked men of the ages." This puts a bolder light upon the matter, and probably comes very close to the truth.

However this may be, one thing is certain: Sullivan's personality gave Wright's its first real professional stimulus. It was a day to be reckoned with, therefore, when, in the late fall of 1887, Wright applied at the office of Adler & Sullivan for a position as draftsman. He had heard from a fellow-draftsman at Silsbee's that there was a vacancy there; he had already begun to crave release from the limited world of reminiscent architecture, and he felt sure that he would find something novel on the boards at Sullivan's shop. An interview was arranged, and Wright stayed up late for three nights preparing a sheaf of drawings to take along. "Some of Silsbee's own drawings of mantels and ornament I took, and drew them my own way, directly and simply with clear definition. Not sentimental and 'sketchy.' Silsbee's way was magnificent, his strokes like standing corn in the field waving in the breeze. So I imitated his style in some few drawings just to show I could do that. Then I improvised some ornaments such as I had seen, characteristic of the Adler and Sullivan buildings. I had studied them a little since I had learned of their work . . . Another evening I took the onion-skin tracing of ornamental details I had made from Owen Jones, mostly Gothic, and made them over into 'Sulivanesque.' " Sullivan studied the drawings during the interview and his reactions were caustic; nevertheless, he hired Wright at twenty-five dollars per week.

It is important to understand the precise position in his career which Sullivan had reached when Wright reported for duty with the firm. He was busy with the Auditorium designs, and it is easy to imagine how the sight of them exhilarated Wright and made him think that he was at last taking part in the making of architectural history. But, in actuality, Sullivan was just on the threshold of his significant career; he had only begun to make history a few months before when Adler & Sullivan won the coveted Auditorium commission. Here is a circumstance of considerable weight in evaluating the Sullivan-Wright relationship. The Master, having passed through a period of most painful experimentation with the business of applying cumbersome eclectic detail to routine mercantile buildings, became aware sometime in 1885 of Henry Hobson Richardson — and of the inner meaning of architecture as a creative art. Wright, in his recollections, describes the event wryly: "Richardson at this time had a decided effect upon Sullivan's work, as may be seen in the outside of the Auditorium building itself, the Walker Wholesale, and other buildings. The effect is unmistakable, although he [i.e., Sullivan] seemed to hold Richardson in no very high esteem." Richardson had died in 1886, but he had partly completed three buildings in Chicago — the Marshall Field Wholesale Co. Building, the Glessner and the MacVeagh houses — which were brilliant examples of his final phase, one of hitherto unparalleled penetration and freedom. Local architects of indifferent talent were to go on copying for two decades their superficial quality, the "Romanesque Style." It remained for the genius of Sullivan to distill from these famous buildings their true message: form follows function. This was the concept that gave sudden meaning to the struggle toward progressive architecture in which Sullivan had alawys been (although at first subconsciously) engaged, and with which he, in turn, inspired Wright. It is no accident that Sullivan did not introduce in his buildings until 1886 that curious, personal ornament, to become so celebrated and representative thereafter. Almost overnight, it seems, Sullivan decided to claim his right to express his own aesthetic, unlike Richardson's in every respect except its individuality, and to develop out of it a philosophy of ornamentation. It is a dangerous path for any but genius to follow, but, happily, both Sullivan and his foremost "disciple" had that genius in fullest measure. On the broader front of design, the exfoliation of schemes for the Auditorium is absorbing proof that Sullivan emerged under the posthumous guidance of Richardson from the overloaded romanticism of his immature work. Stage by stage, roofs and turrets, oriels and machicolations are sloughed off until there stands revealed a simple and powerful design whose purpose can be read like good prose. Wright, the gifted new protegé who watched this process in operation, felt equally the impact of Richardson's message; but it struck an inner core of previous conviction so obdurate that, like Sullivan's own effect upon him, it was reduced to a matter of the spirit. No design wholly attributable to Wright can be called Richardsonian.

Wright's career in the office of Adler and Sullivan was one of rapid rise to importance. When he first joined the firm, it was housed on the top floor of the Borden Block in Randolph Street, an Adler and Sullivan design of 1880; but upon the completion of the Auditorium in 1889, the firm moved into splendid new quarters in the loft of the great tower. Here a separate room adjoining Sullivan's and of the same size was designated as "Mr. Wright's Office." That such a privilege should be granted anyone not actually a partner in the firm, let alone so young a newcomer as Wright, is extraordinary. It gives us to understand that Sullivan had, by that time, accepted Wright on terms of equality.

Among Wright's numerous responsibilities in the office were commissions for private houses — commissions decidedly not courted by the firm,[2] but which had to be accepted in the interests of diplomacy. It is a pretty well established fact that the houses erected by Adler and Sullivan after 1887 were the work of Wright, designed at home after office-hours. This is not really surprising. Sullivan was always working at full stretch on the problem of office buildings; he had in Wright a colleague whom he obviously admired and trusted; and, furthermore, Wright had just had the advantage of working with the best "domestic firm" in town. Dankmar Adler appears to have been throughout a somewhat shadowy figure in the business of Adler and Sullivan — a man who considered himself an engineer rather than a designer, and who apparently confined his activity to this phase of the work and to the firm's finances. He certainly would have had no hand in domestic design. Lastly, the internal evidence itself of the houses turned out by Adler and Sullivan after 1887 goes far to bolster the assumption that they were Wright's work. They progressed steadily away from Adler and Sullivan's early, indifferent treatment toward a smartness and style that can be ascribed to no one but Wright and which

Note 2
Robert C. Spencer, Jr.: paper read before the Illinois Society of Architects, Nov. 28, 1939: "It is said of Louis Sullivan that a wealthy woman came to him requesting his services in designing a Colonial house, and that he replied: 'Madam, you will get just what we give you.'"

culminated in 1891 with a genuine masterpiece whose authorship is conceded. From 1887 to 1893, the period of Wright's incumbency, the firm built nine houses; of these, the two completed in 1887 do not directly concern us, since they must have been under construction when Wright came, but from the beginning of 1888 Wright was probably in control.

Prior to his assumption of responsibility, Adler and Sullivan's domestic designs were in no way distinguishable from the general run in Chicago. A drive along the old residential streets of the near South Side (now a blighted area of the city) would not reveal to any but the expert that Adler and Sullivan houses had been passed *en route*. Among the endless party-wall dwellings with high stoops, their pinched facades exuding the picturesque irregularities and mass-produced ornament accepted as fashionable in the 1880's, and so inexpressibly tawdry today, the Kohn houses (Fig. 10), the Holzheimer

Fig. 10. Adler-Kohn houses. Queen Anne Revival or "American Rococo"?

house, Dankmar Adler's own house, and others bearing the imprimatur of the firm are no less distressing than their neighbors. The sort of domestic architecture, on the other hand, to which Wright had grown accustomed at Silsbee's, although picturesque, was in a different class entirely. The unfortunate Adler and Sullivan houses, the blueprints of which must have been assigned him for study by the office librarian in the early weeks of his employment, could only have struck him as being incredibly *gauche*. He would have noted, however, some small improvement in the designs of 1887, for they showed a modicum of influence from Richardson in the treatment of wall. The Diemal house, for example, although it remains a tasteless performance, places a certain healthy reliance on areas of plain rough ashlar.

The first good Adler and Sullivan domestic design in the new Richardsonian vein was the set of three party-wall houses erected for Victor Falkenau in 1888[3] (Fig. 11). The design corresponds in its small way to its contemporary, the

Note 3
The date of 1890 ascribed by Morrison to the Falkenau houses is erroneous. The design was published by the Inland Architect, Vol. 11, June 1888, and the Chicago city building permit was issued June 2, 1888.

Fig. 11. The Falkenau houses. Observe again the draftsman's signature.

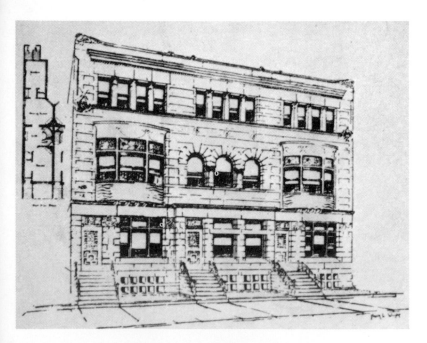

Auditorium. It is a ponderous composition accented with heavy limestone voussoirs, transoms, and squat colonnettes. But in spite of these direct borrowings from Richardson, the Romanesque norm is visibly modified in conformance with a personality that is quite different. The facades have a cultivated horizontality brought about by alternately projecting and receding masonry courses and by curiously crisp cornices and water-tables. The inevitable bay windows are neither mediaeval nor "Eastlake" in derivation; they are, instead, tailored ellipses of copper sheathing and moulded plate glass with restrained style-less detail and an interesting ornamentation of wave-lines beneath. The fine coglike enframements of the first-floor windows and the straightforward grid of square apertures screening the basement windows (although taken straight from Richardson's Glessner house) indicate a fondness on the designer's part for geometric detail. Such things as these are portents of a developing artistic mind; and in the lower right corner of the pen perspective for the Falkenau houses appears in small lettering the name "Frank L. Wright."

In 1889 the Ira Heath house was designed (Fig. 12). It is another party-wall dwelling in whose facade little is left of the Richardsonian manner but the rough-dressed masonry of which it is built — in this case, red sandstone. Its simplicity is deceptive, and it is not, despite its steep gable, a retrogression from the Falkenau design. On the contrary, it marks a stage in the designer's advance toward something new but as yet almost unglimpsed. It is a reduction to elementals of the problem of the narrow party-wall dwelling, from which to make a fresh start. There is no ornament as such, and the facade depends for its undeniably handsome effect upon only two things: intelligent proportions and rich stereotomy. In all this austerity, it is a distinct surprise to find a delicately leaded Colonial fanlight over the door under the entrance arch. Inside, there are a few areas of Sullivanesque ornament carved into the golden oak of the staircase. This is noteworthy, since it is the first example of such detail in an Adler and Sullivan house; previously, the firm had limited itself to standard wood trim in its domestic commissions.

Sullivan had not been well following the nervous strain of bringing the Auditorium to completion, and he had further depleted his strength by making continual sleeper journeys around the Far West in connection with the firm's growing business. This duty always fell to his lot, as Adler refused altogether to travel. So, in 1890, Sullivan bought property at Ocean Springs near Biloxi, Mississippi, on which to build a cottage that he could use as a retreat. A similar cottage was to be built on the neighboring property for his friends, the James Charnleys. There, in the soft air and pinewoods of the Gulf Coast, two shingle-sided buildings arose, so modest and subservient to their surroundings as to become in time, as they weathered and were eventually abandoned, almost lost to view. To followers of Sullivan's career (and of Wright's), the Ocean

Fig. 13. The Charnley cottage in a ruinous state after less than twenty years.

Fig. 12. The Ira Heath house.

Springs cottages have had a romantic and even mysterious appeal. They were restored and remodeled by new owners in the 1930's, and photographs of them in their original condition are few and unsatisfactory. Were they, like the other domestic commissions of Adler and Sullivan, left to Wright to design? Notwithstanding the inherent softness of shingle siding, the Ocean Springs cottages are little exercises in a sort of cubistic architecture, sharp-edged, crystalline. The low tower of the Charnley cottage (Fig. 13), a tapering octagon, is a motif which Silsbee might have used, but it has an unfamiliar angularity. Lily ponds are enframed in severe rectangles of railings in stained wood. Everything is handled in a consciously spartan way, and the only ornament is the interplay of crisp, geometric forms. It seems unlikely that Sullivan, if it were he who drew the plans, could have conceived of the cottages in so abstract a manner; nothing in his previous or current work could lead to such a supposition. Wright, on the other hand, as we have seen in the progression from the Falkenau to the Heath houses, had been exhibiting a marked tendency toward a tailored, geometric simplicity of design, a quality that was to be dramatically demonstrated a few months hence in the Charnley town house.

Fig. 14 (above). The Charnley house, the "lion" of Astor Street today. It was subsequently enlarged toward the south (right hand) end to the detriment of its studied composition. Fig. 15 (below). Plan of main floor.

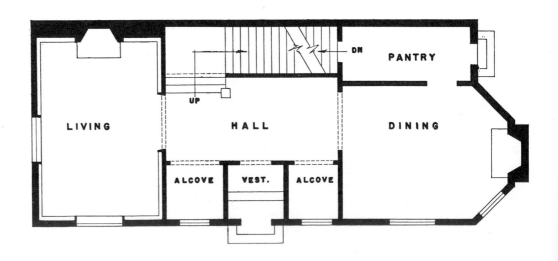

The Charnley house in Astor Street, Chicago, was built in 1891 (Fig. 14). Although it is officially an Adler and Sullivan design, it is in reality the first great monument of Frank Lloyd Wright's career.[4] It was in every sense a miraculous accomplishment. Wright justly says of it, "It is the first modern building." It stands today clean and challenging among its outmoded neighbors, a ringing statement of belief in a new future for architecture. It owes no debt to anyone but its designer, much of whose coming development it forecasts, and it carries us in one amazing leap into the spirit of the next century.

The plan of the house (Fig. 15) is simplicity itself: a stair hall in the center rising to the top of the building and flanked on each floor by two units, those of the main story being a living room to the left and a dining room (with pantry) to the right. The kitchen, as was customary in designs for cramped city lots, is in the basement. The scheme entirely avoids every whimsy so expected and admired in the late Victorian Era. The designer seems to say, "Let us begin from the beginning." It was not as if the unfortunate limitations of the row-house were, as before, a deciding factor; the Charnley property was a corner lot of average size to which an architectural caprice with bays, alcoves and turrets could readily have been fitted. Yet the building which Wright erected on it is so simple as to seem effortless. The uncomplicated disposition of interior space finds direct expression on the exterior; we feel the designer's serene confidence in his conviction that a straightforward, controlled statement of function is enough, graceful in itself. There is little ornament other than an intensification here and there, as in the balcony, of the building's self-generated rhythms. Wall-surfaces, of which we are very conscious in this house, are cultivatedly flat, unbroken by water-tables or stringcourses, given the finest texture

that Roman brick[5] and dressed limestone can supply, and sharply perforated by carefully-spaced rectilinear openings without any enframement.

The overriding effect of the house is that of quiet repose, accentuated by contrast with the hardworking pomposity of the "Period" buildings on every side. The uninterrupted dado, the long balcony, the wafer-thin brick-courses, the strong unipartite cornice, and the low chimneys are the separate elements that, together, produce a restful horizontality — the level line which, apparently, was already established in Wright's mind as the *sine qua non* of domestic architecture and which was to come to conspicuous flower a few years later in the Prairie House. We notice with some astonishment that the Charnley house is markedly lower than its neighbors, more intimately human in scale, and we realize that there can be no twelve-foot floor heights here. As much as it can, under the circumstances, the building comes to earth. Indeed, the Charnley house is both an authoritative invention, complete in itself, and a prophecy. Its inventive element is that tendency, so powerful in Wright at this moment of his life, to look upon architecture as an exercise in solid geometry, in which we can hear the clearest echoes of the principle of the Froebel "gifts," the wonderful interplay of those maple cubes as, assembled, they took on form and meaning. The prophetic element of the Charnley house is its desire to humanize architecture, to break down its pretentiousness by some means as yet not grasped. What, in essence, is so impressive about the Charnley house is that it was a first major experiment. In amazement, faced with its precocious self-assurance, we readily overlook features which, from the viewpoint of Wright's development as a whole, are strangely archaic. The Charnley house, for all its innovation and portent, has one glaring fault: it is closed, hard, impermeable. The idea of interpenetration of atmosphere and structure had not yet crystallized in Wright's imagination.

Note 4
Additional evidence for the attribution of the Charnley design to Wright was offered by George Elmslie in conversation with the author; he unequivocally stated that the first time the design was seen in the office of Adler and Sullivan was the day when Wright brought the completed quarter-scale drawings from his home in Oak Park. Elmslie himself had no doubt about the attribution.

Note 5
It may be that Wright got the idea for the use of Roman brick in domestic architecture from the published designs of McKim, Mead and White, which began to appear widely by 1885.

The quantity of exuberant Sullivanesque ornament inside the house comes as a surprise, spilling over door-panels, mantelpieces, bookcases and newel-posts. Otherwise, the rooms plainly herald Wright's later treatment of interiors. The three major spaces of the main floor open into each other with a minimum of restriction, and the staircase in its cage of thin oaken spindles (Fig. 16) is broad and of easy gradient, yet so disposed as to enrich the space by an abstract play of vertical and horizontal planes — an element of planning which, throughout the '90's, Wright was to handle with increasing delight and virtuosity. There is, however, no other sign in the Charnley house interiors of that personal decorative vocabulary of geometric forms which Wright was to bring forth within the year, fully developed, in the trim and window leadings of the McArthur house, as his response to Sullivan's declaration of independence from traditional ornament. The inner front door of the Charnley house would have offered an opportunity if Wright had been ready, or in a position, to use it for personal expression, as it has a glazed transom and sidelights; but these Wright decorated with leadings of a ribbon and heraldry pattern such as was common in the more expensive houses of the day.

Fig. 16. The Charnley house stair hall: upper levels, main floor level, and details of the Sullivanesque filligree.

Also in 1891, the so-called "Albert Sullivan house" in Lake Avenue (Fig. 17) was erected by the firm. The name is something of a misnomer, for Louis Sullivan's brother, Albert, did not acquire or live in the house until Sullivan himself had occupied it for six years. It is a small party-wall dwelling of two floors and basement, showing no departure from the standard row-house plan. There is an indication that Sullivan took a direct interest in this design; Elmslie remembered[6] Sullivan at work sketching the foliated ornament in the lunette over the front door, but, again, internal evidence, other than the extreme richness of embroidered detail inside (so much

Fig. 17. The "Albert" Sullivan house, a curious misnomer, since Louis Sullivan occupied the house for several years after its completion.

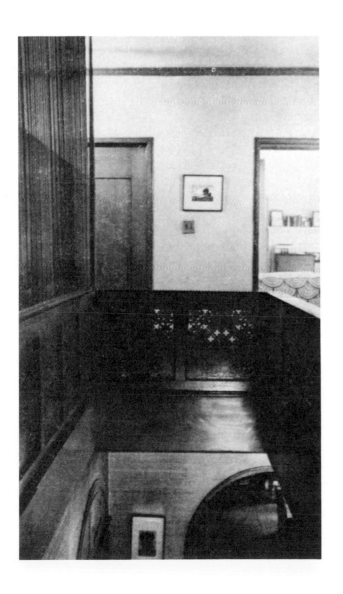

so that the little rooms have an almost "Turkish" look), corroborates the continued assumption that most of the design was Wright's. Its facade is, in some respects, a miniature of the Charnley house. It has the same tailored simplicity, clean-

Note 6
Information gained from the conversations with Elmslie referred to in Note 4 above.

cut openings, unaccented wall, and unipartite cornice with a geometrically decorated fascia; the basement window is screened, however, in the same way as those of the Falkenau houses. Certain features of interior trim are undoubtedly Wrightian: a window seat is terminated by a tall, oaken pier, oblong in section, similar to the Charnley house newel-post, and whose purpose is, although the effect is handsome, quite arbitrary except as an abstract essay in subdividing space; the staircase is set off within a cage of close-set rectangular spindles; the passage from the entrance hall, under the stair landing and into the dining room, is arched so as to interrupt the prevailing rectangularity of the interior and create counterpoint between the square and the round — all these things will appear again in Wright houses soon to come.

There was no duplicate of the Charnley house anywhere in the world in 1891. It was a spontaneous performance, the result of a radical, independent architectural vision, an unfettered mind which, as Hitchcock said, had nothing "to unlearn." But where does Sullivan, The Master, fit in? He has almost been lost sight of in the long introductory passages of this chapter supposedly dedicated to the question of his effect upon Wright, passages necessary to establishing the growth of Wright's principal interest during the years that he was employed in Sullivan's office.

Unquestionably, Sullivan, as the catalytic agent, had much to do with the materialization of Wright's vision of architecture; but he could have offered little or nothing of a specific nature. Sullivan had concentrated his whole attention upon the design of large public buildings, an occasional pure monument such as tombs, and the working out of his "philosophy of ornamentation." Apart from the evidence already set forth here, his later career confirms the inference that he had no flair for, nor did he seek, the design of private houses. From 1893, when Wright and Sullivan parted company, until his death in 1924, Sullivan built only two or three residences, and these are a curious amalgam of borrowings from Wright's Prairie Houses grafted onto a core of impersonal public architecture. There can be little transfer of inspiration from monumental to domestic design, and none in the opposite direction; the basic problems are too different, there are no common for-

mulae. He who practices successfully in both fields must have, so to speak, a double-faceted mind. Wright has, Sullivan had not. This is not to minimize the share that Sullivan could have claimed in Wright's development, but to dematerialize it. It was, to be repetitive, an affair of the spirit.

Sullivan, like Wright, was a latter-day druid. He was also a mystic and a frustrated poet. Elmslie, who knew him so well, once said: "I have in my possession some of his [i.e., Sullivan's] unpublished literary work; one of the group is a volume called The Master. It is a prose poem and a very remarkable document indeed . . . it is himself in the deepest mood he has ever expressed, his inner responses to the outer world." How revealing this information is! Wright is likewise a romantic and a poet *manqué*, drawing inspiration from a Celtic background (and, no doubt, from Walt Whitman), differing from Sullivan only in regard to his doggedness and indestructible vitality. So we are dealing, in this relationship, with an association of two highly-charged and unconventional Celts, and there is probably no hope of analyzing to a nicety what passed between them. Sullivan was given to the expression of such credos as "the artist is like an orange tree — bearing continually flowers and ripeness at every stage — pendant golden thoughts —fruits of all that sap we call imagination . . . ."[7] There are stories of conversations between Master and disciple that lasted throughout the night, discussions about Wagner, Herbert Spencer, Whitman, Richardson. "I believe," Wright says, "The Master used to talk to me to express his own feelings and thoughts, regardless, forgetting me often. But I could follow him. And the radical sense of things I had already formed got great encouragement from him. In fact the very sense of things I had been feeling as rebellion was — in him — at work." It is impossible to translate into brick and mortar the consequences of such an intimacy as this.

From about 1886 to 1890, Sullivan was undergoing his period of absorption in Richardson (whom he claimed to "hold in no very high esteem"); there is certainly nothing specifically

Note 7
Louis Sullivan: "The Artistic Use of the Imagination," Inland Architect & News Record, Vol. 14, Oct. 1889, p. 38.

Richardsonian in the Charnley design. In 1890 and 1891 he was busy with such commissions as the Pueblo Opera House, the Wainwright Building, McVicker's Theater, the Ryerson and Getty Tombs. This group of structures is as remote from the spirit of the Charnley house as the Auditorium. And, just as there was little in the result of Sullivan's struggle with the problem of progressive public architecture that could help Wright in evolving the new house, there were certain by-products of Wright's attack on the domestic problem which, for a few years, were incorporated in Sullivan's work, and unwisely. It must not be thought that Wright dealt only with house-commissions at Adler and Sullivan's; these were a small part of his duty, usually done at home out of hours and not seen by Sullivan until they were ready for bids. During the day, Wright assumed an ever-increasing share, finally as head-draftsman, of all the work which passed through the office. Consisting mostly of office buildings, hotels and theaters, this stream of work entered a new phase, about 1890, after the firm emerged from its out-and-out fascination with Richardson. Between 1890 and 1893, it is marked by an increasing reliance upon smooth wall-surfaces, oblong openings, and unipartite cornices of deep projection that have no precedent in Richardson's work but that do reflect developments taking place in the firm's private house designs. The aforementioned Pueblo Opera House, the Seattle Opera House (Fig. 18), the Saint Nicholas Hotel in St. Louis (Fig. 19), and the Schiller Building are all cases in point. Of the Schiller Building, the best-known example in the list, Wright remarks: ". . . owing to Sullivan's love for his new home in the South, [it] had been more largely left to me than any other."

These tall public buildings are all overloaded with inorganic horizontals that obstruct their rise from the ground. Wright makes an ambiguous comment about this,[8] in which he gives the impression that Sullivan had invented the jutting unipartite cornice, and expressly for use on the Wainwright Building; yet, admitting its

Note 8
Frank Lloyd Wright: "The Tyranny of the Skyscraper," Modern Architecture . . . Kahn Lectures for 1930 (Princeton, Princeton University Press, (1931) pp. 85-86.

Fig. 18 (above). The Seattle Opera House, an uncompleted Adler and Sullivan design. Fig. 19 (below). The Saint Nicholas Hotel, St. Louis.

Fig. 20. Transportation Building, World's Columbian Exposition, 1893. Detail of the Golden Gate.

complete inappropriateness to such a structure, the author goes on to say, ". . . the extension of the roof-slab says emphatically, 'finished!' The slab had no business to say 'finished,' or anything else, so emphatically above the city streets, but that was a minor matter soon corrected." Be that as it may, the roof-slab continues to speak its piece in design after design, each of which wears its crown of cornices and balconies uneasily, as if conscious of the fact that they do not belong. Morrison says of them that they are "picturesque but topheavy," and the choice of words is significant; for the picturesque was a concoction originally intended for domestic design, and that which is "topheavy" in these buildings is the porch-and-cupola motif bor-

rowed from the same source and raised to monstrous proportions.

Disturbing elements such as these in Sullivan's public architecture mark the intrusion upon the normal course of his career of another artistic personality destined to initial success in the field of domestic architecture, primarily through geometric expression of volumes and the cultivation of the long, level line. Not until Sullivan turned to the design of the Guaranty Building in Buffalo in 1894, after Wright had left his office, was he free of motifs that had no rightful place in the tall building, free to resume his uninhibited pioneering in its development. Conversely, Wright's houses from 1893 until the turn of the century are sometimes marred by elements too ambitious or impersonal in scale to suit domestic design. The conclusion is that Sullivan *cum* Wright produced, not a blend, but an emulsion, of which the ingredients foreign to each duly separated themselves out when the association was ended. Thus, we return, after a prolonged detour, to the brief and trenchant summation of the Sullivan-Wright relationship made by George Elmslie and quoted near the beginning of this chapter.

As a codicil, something should be said regarding the part each man played in the design of the Transportation Building for the Chicago World's Fair in 1893. By the summer of 1891, when preliminary drawings were published, Wright had reached the zenith of his importance in the firm. The Transportation Building was one of those commissions that come but rarely, even to large offices, and it presented problems of engineering which lay more within Adler's competence than Sullivan's or Wright's, but the great portal, the building's most memorable feature, as it turned out, was their work alone. The Transportation Building was essentially a vast, empty hall to be filled with locomotives and trains and perhaps a horseless carriage or two; the less architecture, in the popular sense of the word, there was on the inside, the better. Once the structural framing was solved, it remained for the designers, accepting the unfortunate dichotomy between structure and external appearance which still survived in those days, to clothe the building attractively. This clothing was partly prescribed by the dictates of the Commission charged with the responsibility of setting the architectural tone of the ensemble; Fair buildings must have a cornice at a ruling sixty-foot height, and, if they were not to be cast in the prevailing "Classic Style," they must at least have running arcades of some sort. It is, of course, to Adler and Sullivan's everlasting credit that, notwithstanding these limitations, they chose to deck out their building as "functionally" as possible, and in non-traditional terms. The result was that the Transportation Building alone, and engulfed by miles of Beaux Arts classicism, made a contribution to the cause of American architecture, and is remembered to this day.

Its central portal, the "Golden Gate" (Fig. 20), was a great success. The breadth of its conception, the lush East Indian touches and rich surface ornament, are all so in harmony with Sullivan's nature that it would be foolhardy to attribute them to any but The Master's hand. But the crisp geometry of the secondary forms and the triumph of the horizontal line over the powerful concentric semicircles of the entrance-way could well be due to Wright's by now articulate convictions about architectural design, and the spreading eaves of the flanking Mogul pavilions, carried far beyond any Oriental precedent, join them firmly to the composition and strike a strong horizontal right across it, investing the pavilions with an importance that, in contrast to the tremendous entranceway, they would otherwise have lacked. The box-like staircases leading up to them, making a great play of advancing and retreating planes, provide a generous introduction to the main theme, while their form and mass succeed, again, in lowering the center of the composition and attaching it solidly to the ground. Somehow, this Golden Gate called up ideas common to both Sullivan's and Wright's innate feelings and united them toward the achievement of an unforgettable reply to those who wished to use the Fair as a means of holding up to ridicule the rebellious unconventionality of the Chicago School.

Wright's association with the firm of Adler and Sullivan was formalized in 1889 by the drawing up of a five-year contract binding his services to the firm in exchange for financial advantages that would enable him to launch himself in private life. Although the contract was ostensibly a straightforward business agreement, it was prompted by paternalism on Sullivan's part. Sullivan was childless,[9] and there is a suggestion of compensatory impulse in his concern with Wright's future. Wright had found the young woman of his choice; he was on the point of getting married, and he needed funds. He wanted, above all, to build a house of his own. The contract was the answer; under its terms, Wright was able to draw advances on his salary with which to meet new obligations. Sullivan's assumption of the role of godfather was ironical in two ways: in the first place, Sullivan was only fifteen years older than his protegé; in the second

Note 9
Sullivan's one marriage did not take place until 1899; it was without issue and terminated in divorce.

place, it led to the complete undoing of their relationship.

The facts of Wright's establishment of a home and family will be found in an ensuing chapter of this book. Suffice it to say here in extenuation of what took place concerning the contract that his family, like his ambitions, grew very rapidly. It was not long before he began to experience that financial pinch which became his too familiar demon. Faced with suddenly mounting debts, it occurred to him that, if he could stretch out his nights and weekends sufficiently, he might manage to handle a few domestic commissions on the side. Such pressure of work was no novelty to him. Ever since he had been with Adler and Sullivan, he had been expected to design houses after office hours — an extra service which seems, somehow, to have been taken for granted. So, when friends and neighbors began to ask him to "plan" their new houses, he was tempted. He accepted one such commission, and this inevitably led to another; there were finally nine or ten in all, and he calls them his "bootlegged" houses. While the commissions were not a violation of the letter of the five year contract, they were certainly clandestine in that Wright never mentioned them to Sullivan, and even went so far as to arrange that some of them were announced in local contractors' journals under the name of his friend, Cecil Corwin.[10] As was bound to happen, they came to Sullivan's notice at length in the spring of 1893, and he felt bitterly deceived by what he regarded as an act of treason. There was a violent scene. Wright walked out of the office never to return, to find thereby his own sure footing in the profession. As for the contract, it was simply permitted to lapse; but it took several years for Wright to obtain the deed to his house from his former employers, and then it was not Sullivan but Adler who made it over to him. The "bootlegged houses" were thus a landmark in Wright's career and the mechanism of his release from an association that had fulfilled its destiny. Of the men with

whom he had been on good terms in Adler and Sullivan's office, only Paul Mueller[11] stood by him. As for The Master, Wright did not see him again for more than seventeen years.

Influence from Japan

In his role as privileged draftsman and confidant to Sullivan, Wright, as we have seen, was plunged into the preparations for the Chicago Fair of 1893. The design of the Transportation Building, Adler and Sullivan's agonizingly small share of the total layout of the "White City," was an important commission even though it signalized, by being so alone in a sea of Beaux Arts conservatism, the first victory of forces hostile to the Chicago School. It is safe to say that Wright made scores of trips to the Fair grounds in Jackson Park both before and after the turnstiles were in operation. It was a journey of only twenty minutes on the special trains of the Illinois Central.

Like all great expositions, the Fair of 1893 was essentially a stupendous assemblage of things — the good, the bad, and the indifferent in cheerful competition with each other for public notice. Here and there an exhibit of quiet merit stood out, and Wright, with the same unerring discrimination his mother had shown at the Philadelphia Centennial, must have found one that instantly commanded his attention and held forth the promise of significant discovery. On the "Wooded Isle," a small plot of ground set in an artificial lake and approached by a bridge, was the Ho-o-den, the official exhibit of the Imperial Japanese Government:[1] a half-scale replica of its namesake in Japan, a wooden temple of the Fujiwara Period. The Ho-o-den, together with the treasures its contained, constituted the

Note 10
Inland Architect & News Record, Vol. 17, July 1891, p. 73: the Harlan house commission is recorded in "Building News Synopsis" under the name of C. S. Corwin.
Idem, Vol. 19, June 1892, p. 66: the Blossom and McArthur houses are similarly recorded.

Note 11
Mueller was the engineer who was later to consult upon and superintend such large-scale constructions of Wright's as the Larkin Building and the Imperial Hotel.
Note 1
Okakura Kakudzo: "The Ho-o-den" (an illustrated description of the buildings erected by the Japanese Government at the World's Columbian Exposition, Jackson Park, Chicago), Tokyo, 1893.

first wholesale introduction to the Middle West of Japanese art and architecture.

For Wright, the Japanese exhibit was the confirmation of a dawning curiosity. He had already picked up some inkling of the fascination of Japanese art from his former employer, Joseph Silsbee, whose suburban house in Edgewater was filled with the sort of Orientalia that "advanced" people were beginning, in the 1880's, to collect in response to the stimulation filtering in from England and France, where the cult of Japanism had been launched by men like Whistler and the Brothers deGoncourt.

It must be conceded that there is an affinity between Wright's concept of architecture, as it was to develop, and the art of old Japan (Figs. 21 and 22). Whether this affinity amounts to actual indebtedness is a moot point, and one which Wright has always hotly debated. "No, my dear Mrs. Gablemore, Mrs. Plasterbilt, and especially, now, Miss Flattop, nothing from 'Japan' has helped at all, except the marvel of

Fig. 21. Above: Domestic architecture in Kyoto, Japan. Below: The Robie house. A similarity of the spirit.

Fig. 22. Above: Katsura Palace, Kyoto, Japan. Below: The Coonley house and driveway. Half a world and several centuries apart, yet there is an unmistakable kinship.

Japanese color prints."[2] Nevertheless, many critics and admirers, including Berlage,[3] Thomas Craven,[4] Tallmadge,[5] Behrendt,[6] and Shand,[7] have touched upon the question of Japanese influence in Wright's work as if impelled to do so by the evidence of their own eyes, and the consensus is that a debt does exist. Even Hitchcock, usually the stand-out, has been known to make a guarded reference.[8] At any rate, it is impossible to dismiss the question as cavalierly as Wright would have us do. He himself, while openly parading his Japanophilia, disposes of it as a source of architectural ideas by keeping it on a non-practical basis as something beguiling and beautiful, like music, that has simply added to his enjoyment of life — nothing more. The following passages from "An Autobiography" may be taken as a case in point:

"During the years at the Oak Park workshop, Japanese prints intrigued me and taught me

Note 2
Frank Lloyd Wright: "Recollections—United States, 1893-1920," Architects Journal (London), Vol. 84, July 1936, pp. 76-78.
Note 3
H. P. Berlage: "Frank Lloyd Wright," in special edition of Wendingen, Santpoort, Holland, 1925.
Note 4
Thomas Craven: "Modern Art," Simon & Schuster, New York, 1934, Chap. 14.
Note 5
Thomas Tallmadge: "The Story of Architecture in America," Norton, New York, 1936, pp. 228-233. Wright's debt to Japan, though he denies it, is seen in the simplicity of domestic arrangements, integrated doors and windows, and "intimate liaison between art and nature."
Note 6
Walter Curt Behrendt: "Modern Building," Harcourt, Brace, New York, 1937, pp. 134-135.
Note 7
P. Morton Shand: "Scenario for a Human Drama," Part 6, Architectural Review (London), Vol. 77, Feb. 1935, pp. 61-64.
Note 8
Henry-Russell Hitchcock, Jr.: "Frank Lloyd Wright," Cahiers d'Art, Paris, 1928: ". . . son Japonisme attardé . . ."

much. The elimination of the insignificant, a process of simplification in art in which I was engaged, beginning with my twenty-third year,[9] found collateral evidence in the print . . . Japanese art, I found, really did have organic character, was nearer to the earth and a more indigenous product of native conditions of life and work, therefore more nearly modern as I saw it, than European civilization alive or dead."

Upon arriving in Japan for the first time, in 1905, he exclaims:

"It all looks just like the prints! The quiet but gay life of the ancient modern capital is aware of Toyonobu, Harunobu, Shunso, and Shigemasa." He analyzes the style of the Japanese dwelling, not too succinctly, as a sort of index of the national tidiness: "Here you have a kind of spiritual ideal of natural and hence organic simplicity . . . the plan of any Japanese dwelling was an effective study in sublimated mathematics."

But to return to the Ho-o-den at the World's Columbian Exhibition (Fig. 23): it was an object of wonder, not only to Wright, but to his colleagues of the young Chicago School. They discussed its strange *parti*. Beneath an ample roof — a powerful expression of shelter — and above the platform on which the temple stood, was the area of human activity, an open, ephemeral region of isolated posts and sliding screens that changed its appearance according to the activity of the hour, and that, in Occidental parlance, was not architecture at all. In this space between roof and platform, solid walls were almost non-existent. The Ho-o-den opened outward and away from its one permanent partition, placed as a barrier to the prevailing wind, toward innumerable paper windows fitted into slots and only present when needed. Thus, the central hall and the flanking tearooms were in no sense boxes, but unconfined spaces existing in intimate union with gardens and air. The only element of the plan which was not subject to rearrangement was the base partition into which was incorporated the *tokonoma*, the shrine, the focus of ceremonial occasion. Daylight did not enter these spaces intermittently but everywhere

Note 9
The timing here is interesting, since Wright was in his twenty-fourth year when the Fair opened.

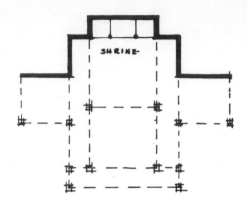

Fig. 23. The Ho-o-den at the Imperial Japanese exhibit, Chicago, 1893, a building which stood for a few months and of which nothing but vintage photographs survive.

— continuously around their perimeters, a pliant band of light — and was freed from glare by the great overhanging eaves. Because there were no solid corners, there could be no dark pockets; and, since the Japanese appeared, astonishingly, to regard their furniture, like their utensils, as things to be stored when not in use, the lack of wall-space was no objection. The fresh simplicity of these airy rooms was complemented by the materials of which they were made: unpainted wood, unadorned paper.

There was on display in the Ho-o-den a magnificent collection of seventeenth and eighteenth century prints with which to make comparison between the actual and the pictorial quality of Japanese art and customs.

What, then, could a young radical of the Chicago School learn from the Japanese Imperial exhibit of 1893? Nothing less than a highly provocative clue to a fresh concept of Western architecture: the interplay of solid structure with unprecedented quantities of light and atmosphere. Roofs, walls, and, above all, fenestration could be liberated from bondage to a rigid formalism, could be divorced from their hitherto ambiguous function, in the Western tradition, as boundary lines for preconceived canons of proportion. The Ho-o-den demonstrated that uninterrupted strip fenestration with suppressed sills under eaves restored to their proper place

as shades were the means whereby a house could be, so to speak, turned inside out. Given these new directions, the "style" would come naturally — especially to anyone already predisposed.

Two years before the Chicago Fair, Wright had designed, albeit under the flag of Adler and Sullivan, the Charnley house in Astor Street. In this design, he had stated his belief in a new simplicity of plan and structure. One necessary ingredient, however, of the still-to-come Prairie House was lacking. What Wright had arrived at spontaneously in this epochal building was a bold and prepossessing statement of faith in his personal architecture of geometry, and of disbelief in the divine-rightness of tradition. The result stopped short of total success because the building was too self-contained. A good house, Wright instinctively realized, must not be rigid; it must consciously acknowledge the earth beneath it and invite the air around it, and yet display its very human need for protection from a nature which is not always benign. In the Ho-o-den, Wright beheld an unfamiliar architectural heritage which approximated the vision in his mind. Here was the germ of continuous plastic fenestration that could be bent around corners, that need recognize no formalistic allegiance to canons of design, that could open the interior to the outdoors anywhere and everywhere, and that would produce by its inherent horizontality and by its awning-like overhangs that level domestic line which Wright intuitively admired and had determined to develop as the main theme of his house architecture.

Within a year of this event, he began to discard the sash window in favor of the casement, to prepare his work for the final change from fenestration in spots to fenestration in strips. Once done, the change automatically obliterated the severity and resistance of wall, fostered the free running treatment of sills and bases, and resulted in the victory of the horiontal as the dominant characteristic of a great style that was, indeed, to make history. The Winslow house of 1894 (Fig. 43) is a perfect example of the state of transformation at its mid-point. In it, everything is prepared for ribbon fenestration, yet it still has the widely-spaced, sharply-chiseled windows of the Charnley house and the resulting emphasis upon wall. To complete the sequence, a final contrast should be made between the Winslow house and any of the great Prairie Houses, such as the Coonley house (Fig. 126), in which all the elements of the finished style are present and fused.

Because he was endowed by inheritance and environment with a foreknowledge of such natural concepts of architecture as those embodied in traditional Japanese design, it is entirely possible that Wright might have evolved them from within if there had never been a Ho-o-den to be seen in America; but there was. If we assume that actual confrontation with a Japanese building was the necessary mechanism at a certain juncture in his career to give those concepts reality and direction, then many of the steps in the evolution of his architecture can be rationally explained. As examples: the translation of the *tokonoma*, the permanent element of a Japanese interior and the focus of domestic contemplation and ceremony, into its Western counterpart, the fireplace, but a fireplace expanded to unprecedented, animistic importance; the frank revelation of the masonry of fireplace and chimney as the one desired solid substance in an architecture of ever-increasing movement; the opening out of interior spaces away from the chimney-breast toward shifting planes of glass at their further limits; the extension of the great eaves beyond these planes to modify and control the intensity of light which they admit and to protect them from weather; the subdivision of interior space by suggestion rather than partition, acknowledging and accommodating the fluctuating human uses to which it is put; the elimination of all sculptured and varnished trim in favor of flat surfaces and natural wood — all these and more could have been adduced from the lesson of the Ho-o-den.

None of this reduces or calls to question Wright's status as a great innovator in the realm of modern architecture. He alone realized with consummate perception and insight the full contribution which Japan could make, and turned it to account. What Japan evoked in him was something far deeper than a responsive mannerism. When Wright walked round and studied the Fujiwara temple on the Wooded Isle, there was communion of like-minded men, Wright and the nameless Japanese who designed it, reaffirming in each other some very fundamental beliefs.

Doubtless, the art of the Japanese wood-block print also held an important message for him, as he tells us. He could not, at any rate, resist their beauty and appeal. He began to gather one of the Middle West's outstanding collections, and it is proof of his connoisseurship that he liquidated it, when debts mounted, for an impressive sum of money. This he repeated on at least two later occasions. The catalogue which he wrote in 1927[10] for the last and largest of these sales makes interesting reading for anyone who is curious to know the depth of Wright's scholarship and the precise nature of his tastes.[11]

In 1905, Wright made his first trip to Japan, accompanied by Mrs. Wright (his first wife), and Mr. and Mrs. Ward Willits of Highland Park, Illinois, clients for whom he had designed one of the first Prairie Houses. His Japanophilia possessed him. Leaving his companions, he put on native dress and made long, solitary trips into the interior of the Islands, collecting prints and porcelain. His acumen was respected by Jap-

Note 10
"The Frank Lloyd Wright Collection of Japanese Prints," an illustrated catalogue of forced sale by the Bank of Wisconsin (Madison) at Anderson Galleries, New York, Jan. 1927.
Note 11
A list of the masters represented is included in the Appendix, p. 215.

Fig. 24. An early photograph of the Taliesin North living room and its collection of Japanese objects.

anese connoisseurs and dealers. In 1912, he published a slim volume of critical appreciation of the Japanese print.[12] In the 1930's, when, after a long period of privation, his fortunes changed for the better, he reassembled, in so far as possible, his collection of Japanese objects, and added others, so that today the great living rooms at Taliesin, North, are once again the inner sanctum of a confessed Japanophile, as earlier photographs (Fig. 24) reveal them to have been in the years following the Oak Park Period.

During the Oak Park period, which will be introduced in the next chapter of this book, the

Note 12
Frank Lloyd Wright: "The Japanese Print—An Interpretation," Ralph Fletcher Seymour, Chicago, 1912.

stamp of Wright's Japanophilia on the productions of his drafting-room was sometimes quixotic. He was given to imitating the casual, asymmetrical arrangements of Japanese screens in his presentation drawings (Fig. 25), relegating the client's house to the status of an adjunct in the sweeping, sensitive lines of a landscape more suitable to a *kakemono* than to the client's legitimate expectations. From such aberrations as these to his more customary dealing with the problems of architecture on a practical level, something of the spirit of Yedo has continuously spilled over into everything he has done since the 1890's. Although the exact degree of Japanese influence on Wright as an architect may never be determined, and may not even be known to Wright himself, it is strongly indicated that "Japan" has been a decisive factor in his growth.

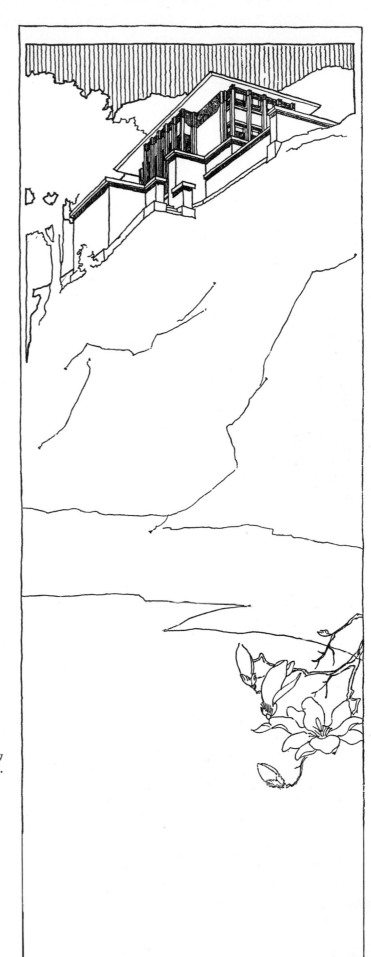

Fig. 25. A presentation drawing, taking its inspiration from Japanese screens.

3. The Studio, Oak Park

A Design for Living

The name "Oak Park" is so closely interwoven with that period of Frank Lloyd Wright's career with which we are concerned that it is very much to the point to inquire into the coincidence which brought him to Oak Park and the sort of background which Oak Park furnished for the life which he intended to live.

It is, as before in this story, Wright's mother who intervenes. Her son's precipitate departure for Chicago in the spring of 1887 left her somewhat troubled, and she presently wound up her affairs in Madison and followed him to the city. For a short while, mother and son occupied rooms in a South Side boarding-house near All Souls', but this was only an expediency until something better could be found. Mrs. Wright took the opportunity to resume an old friendship with another dedicated woman like herself: Augusta Chapin, a Unitarian minister. The Rev. Miss Chapin was then serving as pastor to the Unitarian congregation in Oak Park, and she suggested to the Wrights that they come and stay with her for a while in her "old red brick house on Forest Avenue," a gingerbread villa only a few steps from the present noisy traffic of Lake Street, the main thoroughfare.

Oak Park, then popularly referred to as "The Saintly" because of its great number of churches and rather rigid standard of conduct, was not, perhaps, the most appropriate setting for Wright's eccentricities, but it was very appealing at first to both him and his mother. In 1888 it was a small leafy suburb at the very edge of the prairie. It was almost "country," and it assuaged the nostalgia which the Wrights felt for their Wisconsin homestead. The center of the village of Oak Park was only eight miles to the west of downtown Chicago, and trains on the Chicago and Northwestern Railway were fast and frequent; Wright, of course, joined the ranks of commuters.

By this time, Wright had fallen in love with Catherine Tobin, a tall, red-headed girl whom he had met at All Souls'. The Wrights' removal to Oak Park proved to be no obstacle to the course of the romance, and in 1889 Wright asked Miss Tobin to marry him. They were both very young, and Wright was struggling for a foothold in his profession; for these reasons, Mrs. Wright's reaction to her son's announced intention was unfavorable. As she had attempted to oppose Wright's abandonment of his University program, she now opposed his engagement, but Wright again asserted his independence and the marriage duly took place. The aforementioned five-year contract with Adler and Sullivan had been drawn up for this very purpose.

Now Wright was in a position to undertake

that absorbing venture of establishing his own family and building his own house. He bought Lot Number Twenty in the new Oak Park subdivision unglamorously known as "Kettlestring's Addition to Harlem"; it lay in Cicero Township, on the corner of what were later to become Forest and Chicago Avenues. The development was so new and raw that the latter street, as yet un-named, died away a few blocks to the west in the thick hardwoods bordering the Desplaines River. Wright's corner piece was a tangle of oaks and wild vines, rough, but having the simple beauty of the uncleared prairie landscape. Here, in the fall of 1889, Wright began to build his house, the nucleus of all those future additions which were to make up the complex called "The Studio." At the rear of the property, facing on the surveyors' understanding of where Chicago Avenue was to be, there stood already a little carpenter-Gothic cottage; suitably renovated, this was set aside as the senior Mrs. Wright's home, in which she was to live for many years.

The history of the construction of Wright's residence-workshop at Oak Park could be a study in itself. Like Taliesin North and the winter headquarters in the Arizona desert (Wright's present homes), the Oak Park house was continually undergoing enlargement and improvement, leaving the historian with puzzles in chronology similar to those of the archaeologist. Many unexplained and colorful things are associated with this process of perpetual construction. Oak Parkers will never forget some of them, like the hole to permit the uninterrupted growth of a willow-tree; to this day, they refer to The Studio as "the house with the tree through the roof."

In its original state (Fig. 26), Wright's house was a modest dwelling, distinguished in the main by its unusual simplicity of form and materials. The essence of the design was a triangular prism bounded by steep roofs and set upon a low rectangular base. It comes as a surprise to one accustomed to Wright's mature domestic style to find that, in the opening years of his career, that style more often depended upon steep, prominent roofs than upon the flattened hip of the Prairie House. The pyramidal shape of many of Wright's designs in the last years of the Nineteenth Century may reflect the universal acceptance in those days of the rule of the picturesque. But in every case in which Wright embodied the steep roof, he freshened it by setting it low upon its walls and projecting it markedly at the eaves, thereby achieving, as a conspicuous sign of his emergent individuality, a calculated imbalance between vertical and sloping outlines. The result

Fig. 26. Wright's Oak Park home as it was originally built.

is as domestic in effect as it was novel,[1] for it dramatizes, in a flat scene, the idea of shelter. Despite its great gable, Wright's Oak Park house nestles into the ground.

The plan (Fig. 27) shows more compartmentation than those of his later houses, and experiments in fluid space, where they occur, are either hesitant or derivative. Polygonal bays and inglenooks were the stock-in-trade of the Shingle Style with its delight in whimsies — yet they are features that Wright was to incorporate again and again in his plans of the 1890's. There is something prophetic, however, in the relationship of sitting room, inglenook and dining room in the Oak Park house (Fig. 28), and in the tendency of these rooms to break forth from the core of the house as extruded inner volumes, demanding expression on the outside. This tendency is echoed by the advancing terrace with its low parapet, and picked up again by the pronounced overhang of the second story.

Derivative, perhaps — but the little house in Forest Avenue, as we see it in hindsight, was filled with portent. In 1889, it must have struck the citizens of Oak Park as a piece of stark but compelling architectural simplicity, and they must have speculated freely about the young couple who built it. They were soon to know, for the Wrights began to take a prominent part in village life.

For a little while, until the expanding family

usurped it, the front second-floor room was Wright's workshop. In the light from that row of casement windows, or more often in the light of a gas lamp, grew the plans for the Charnley house, soon replaced on the drafting-board by the "bootlegged houses," one after the other. It is open to surmise as to which of two motives was the deciding factor in their acceptance as clandestine commissions: the need for money, or the urgency of an impatient, creative mind to fulfill its destiny. The first of these commissions was probably the McHarg house. The one which finally provoked the quarrel between Wright and Sullivan is not definitely known. Wright says it was the house for Dr. Harlan, but, since the Harlan house was completed in 1892 and the quarrel occurred in the spring of 1893, it seems more likely that it was one of the later "bootlegged" commissions that came to Sullivan's notice. However that may be, Wright hung out his own shingle early in the fall of 1893. It is ironical that he should have commenced his independent career within weeks of the opening of the World's Columbian Exposition; the "sinister nature of its anaesthesia"[2] was, in the end, so largely responsible for Wright's tardy recognition beyond the confines of the Middle Border, and for the decline of the whole Chicago School.

From 1893 to 1909, Wright's center of activities was always Oak Park, although he maintained "fronts" for meeting prospective clients downtown in Chicago. The list of these downtown offices, now in one building, now in another, contributes valuable and occasionally unique clues to the dating of Wright's early work. Also, the offices were virtual clubhouses for gatherings of Wright's colleagues, whose contacts with him are always interesting and often puzzling.[3] The first office, appropriately enough, was on the top floor of the Schiller Building in Randolph Street, that Adler and Sullivan design in which Wright claims so large a part; he leased

Note 1
Vincent Scully has shown in his previously noted book, "The Shingle Style," that there is an undeniable similarity between the facade of Wright's house in Oak Park and a house erected a little earlier (and published) at Tuxedo Park by Bruce Price. Wright's design, however, by dispensing with the second floor, differs in proportions and in intimacy of relation with the ground. Scully's discovery serves to underscore the importance of that peculiarly native interpretation of the Queen Anne Style, now known as the Shingle Style, to the whole emergence of modern American architecture. As for Wright, it indicates that he could have absorbed the sense of freedom of the Style not only through Silsbee but through its dissemination in the architectural periodicals of the day.

Note 2
George Elmslie: "The Chicago School of Architecture—Its Inheritance and Bequest," paper read before the Illinois Society of Architects, Nov. 28, 1939.
Note 3
See Appendix, p. 215, for the list of downtown offices in Chicago rented by Wright for the period covered by this volume.

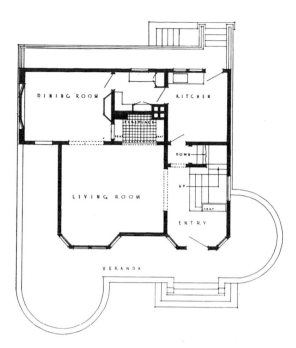

Fig. 27. Plan of the Oak Park house.

Fig. 28. Above and below: The fireplace and inglenook in relation to the living room and entry of the Oak Park house.

an office there in the fall of 1893 and kept it until 1896. He shared it briefly with his friend Cecil Corwin, who had been practicing independently since 1890. Robert C. Spencer, Jr., just out of an Eastern architectural school, came to occupy a neighboring office in the Schiller Building in 1895 and 1896; it was thus that he gained his impressive knowledge of Wright's early work and personality, enabling him to write his important article in 1900.

The description of the Schiller Building office in "An Autobiography" shows that personality, now beginning to be familiar, strongly emerging under the stimulus of independence: monotone walls, hangings of plain fabric, pots of oak leaves and sumac — it is all somehow reminiscent of the interiors of the old Gorham Street house in Madison and of the undeniable influence of his mother's taste upon him, but it adds up at the same time to a sense of decoration far in advance of its period. To this quietly furnished office in the Schiller Building came the first prominent clients: William Winslow, Nathan Moore, Edward Waller, Chauncey Williams — names which, in their association with the commencement of a career which was to be world-renowned, will find a niche in architectural history. The more it is considered, the more amazing was the courage of these men in coming to Wright for houses, with nothing other to lean upon than confidence in their own judgment. Without them, that career might never have been launched. As it was, Wright, from the very beginning, never lacked work. Soon, he was able to employ a junior draftsman, a Japanese named Shimoda, to man the Schiller Building office.

In 1893 or 1894, Wright made the first addition to his Oak Park house in the form of a large, barrel-ceilinged playroom (Fig. 29) at the back of the second floor. To symbolize the room's purpose, a scene from the Arabian Nights was painted over the fireplace, and there were fanciful chandeliers (wired, it should be noted, for electricity) composed of cascades of translucent cubes and globes.[4] The contract which Wright negotiated in 1895 with the American Luxfer Prism Company to popularize a new type of fenestration[5] gave him the necessary extra money to add to the house the complete architectural workshop along the Chicago Avenue side, the part of the establishment which gave rise to the use of the name, "The Studio," which had not been applied before.

His house thus enlarged, Wright devised a pattern for the conduct of his private and professional life which he follows to this day at Taliesin North and Taliesin West. There was the "House," the private quarters of the complex, to which he could retire quickly and easily for a rest or a change of mood, to read, to play the piano, to talk with his children. There was the "Studio," workshop proper, with its carefully-planned professional facilities, apart but connected. There were the apprentices, or draftsmen, working more or less *en famille*, taking lunch daily with the *patron* and his family. It is life in a Continental vein — paternalistic, imperious, strangely alien to American custom. Where did it come from? It is only one of many things about Wright's mode of living, such as the singular individuality of his dress, which was established at the same early date, that defy explanation.

Additions to "The Studio" continued to be made, until the original building was almost buried and the final layout almost labyrinthine; but even these enlargements could scarcely keep up with the need to provide space for a rapidly growing workshop and family. As for the latter, the six children of the union came in quick succession.[6] Wright tells good-naturedly in "An Autobiography" how his brood managed to be perpetually underfoot. True to his father's memory, Wright saw to it that each one of his children learned to play a musical instrument; and, in accord with his mother's precept, he envisioned some creative future for each of them from the day they were born. In December, 1891,

Note 4
These lighting fixtures forecast those which Wright designed in 1914 for the Midway Gardens; their source is certainly the cubes, spheres, and beads of the Froebel "gifts."

Note 5
This was a scheme to bring more intense natural light into the rear of deep rooms or stores by inserting prismatic lenses in bands in the upper registers of windows.
Note 6
The children of Wright's first marriage were, in order: Lloyd, John, Catharine, Francis, David, and Llewellyn.

Fig. 29. The playroom, added at the back of the second floor of Wright's Oak Park house. Note, in the top picture, the chandelier and the copy of the Winged Victory of Samothrace, and, in the bottom picture, the scene from the Arabian Nights over the fireplace.

on the occasion of the birth of his son Frank Lloyd, Junior (who, like his brother John, has actually followed his famous father's precedent and attained a reputation of his own in the realm of contemporary architecture), Wright sent the following announcement to The Oak Park Reporter: "A young sculptor arrived to make his father, Frank Wright of Forest Avenue, happy on the 12th inst." The mistake in prophecy was not absolute, if we grant the close relationship between the two arts.

Wright's large family was not always such unadulterated joy as this, however, and the long struggle with mounting debt soon began. But, in spite of it, Wright never questioned his privilege, as a man of fine taste and discrimination, to live life in the large. Having entered the village so unobtrusively in 1888, he began in the 1890's to cut a figure in quiet Oak Park. He kept a good riding horse; the "fine collection of palms" which was sent to decorate the chancel of the Unitarian Church of a Sunday, as recorded in The Reporter, was supplied by "Mr. Wright of Forest Avenue"; he and his wife gave parties whose "artistic" air more or less overcame their suburban acquaintances; every winter, Mr. and Mrs. Wright took season tickets for the symphony in Chicago; Mrs. Wright, no doubt inspired by her mother-in-law, sponsored a kindergarten society in Oak Park and conducted in the new playroom of The Studio an actual experiment in Froebelian training for her children and those of the neighborhood; and Wright began his collection of objects of art. "My love for beautiful things, rugs, books, prints or anything made by Art or Craft," Wright confesses, "kept the butcher, the baker, and the candlestick-maker waiting. Sometimes an incredibly long time."

After the completion of the Winslow house in 1894, an extraordinary proposal was made to Wright by the most convinced of his early patrons, Edward Waller of River Forest, a man of both means and vision. Influenced, apparently, by the counsel of his friend, Daniel Burnham, he felt that European training was an essential experience for his protegé; he offered to finance a six-year course of study for Wright abroad — four years at the École des Beaux Arts and two in Rome — and to support Mrs. Wright and the children in the interim. It was a truly Medicean gesture of patronage, empty of any genuine

value to Wright as it may have been. Quietly reaffirming his faith in a more unconventional approach to the problem of discovering a new architecture, Wright summoned the courage to reject the offer. He recalls that, after he had spoken, there was an incredulous silence in the room.

The "Bootlegged" Houses

It will be remembered that the commissions for those early domestic designs of Wright's which he has dubbed the "bootlegged houses" were accepted while the five-year contract with Adler and Sullivan was in force, and while Wright was devoting his daytime hours to the work of the firm in the Auditorium tower offices. The "bootlegged houses," therefore, by definition, were all built or projected by the late spring of 1893. Careful inspection of all available data[1] reveals that there were ten of them, of which one was unexecuted. The list of these commissions has historical interest, and is given herewith: house for Dr. A. W. Harlan, Chicago, 1891; house for W. S. McHarg, Chicago, 1891; house for George Blossom, Chicago, 1892; house for Robert Emmond, La Grange, Illinois, 1892; two identical houses for Thomas H. Gale, Oak Park, 1892; house for Warren McArthur, Chicago, 1892; house for Walter Gale, Oak Park, 1893; house for Orrin S. Goan, La Grange, 1893 (unexecuted); house for Peter Goan, La Grange, 1893. During this period, Wright also entered and won a competition in May, 1893, for the erection of the Municipal Boathouse at Madison, Wisconsin, a structure which remained *in situ* until 1928.

At first glance, the character of the "bootlegged houses" seems to retrogress from the tremendous promise of the Charnley house. Wright is conscious of this. In "An Autobiography" he makes an apology for their Sullivan-

Note 1
The data consist of: (1) Wright's dated drawings, a few of which survived the Taliesin fire of 1914 and other depredations; (2) announcements in Chicago contractors' journals; (3) Chicago city building permits; (4) personal recollections and records of Wright's and the various owners or their descendants.

Fig. 30 (above). The Blossom house, Chicago, Wright's only Palladian-"Colonial" design — but with Wrightian variations. Fig. 31 (below). Plan of the Blossom house.

ism;[2] but it is not their Sullivan-ism which is so notable or disappointing as their Silsbee-ism. Undoubtedly, the reason is that Wright could not give them his full attention. They were done, so to speak, with one eye; and Wright was too unknown to be able to assert himself with his clients or to feel that he was in a position to carry out anything really radical. One or two of these houses are undeniably banal; others have a quality that is fresh and distinctly Wright's which sets them well above the norm for domestic architecture in the area at the time; at least two make definite contributions to the advancement of Wright's style; some of them constitute Wright's one lightning-like moment of experimentation with popular eclectic mannerisms.

The Blossom house is Wright's only essay in the revived New England Colonial style, just then making its appearance in the Middle West. It is complete with butter-yellow clapboards, white trim, a classical portico, a fan-lighted doorway, and Palladian windows (Fig. 30).

Note 2
Wright, Frank Lloyd, "An Autobiography" (New York, Longmans, Green, 1932), p. 127: ". . . buildings all characterized to a certain extent by the Sullivanian idiom, at least in detail. I couldn't invent the terms of my own overnight. At that time there was nothing in sight that might be helpful."

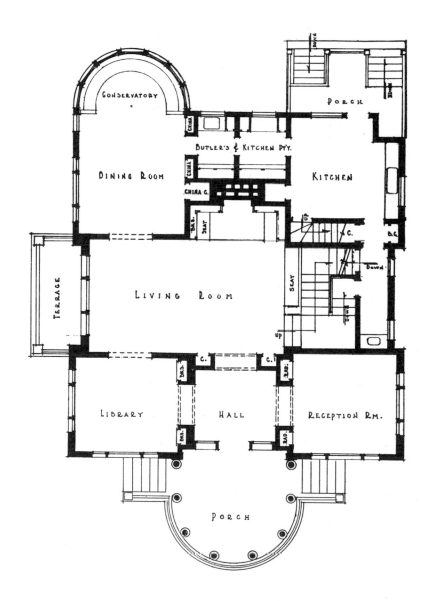

Fig. 32 (above and below). "Dutch Colonial"—the Bagley house, Hinsdale, Illinois. The octagonal library is at the left.

Fig. 33 (below). The marble-faced fireplace in the Bagley house, flanked by marble Ionic columns.

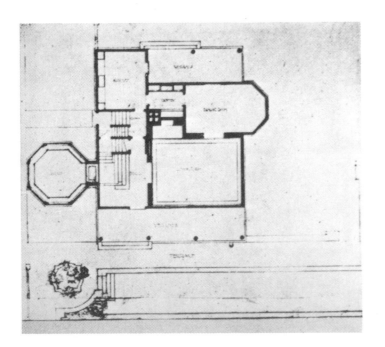

Only after careful study do we begin to see those telltale signs which add up to "early Wright": the hip roof is flatter than the Palladian canon requires, the classical cornice is replaced by a clean projection of the eaves, the sash windows are oblong, the massive chimney is of Roman brick and unexpectedly placed. To be sure, there was nothing unusual, in the 1890's, in the idea of taking liberties with the Colonial style, which was not too thoroughly understood, but in the Blossom house the liberties seem less like misconceptions than a deliberate adaptation of the style to a personal conception of architecture which had already begun to form. The plan of the house (Fig. 31), like its exterior, shows a search for change but is not revolutionary. It is essentially a nest of compartments with the various rooms interconnected by means of numerous round-headed archways, so that the effect upon entering is one of a bewildering number of short vistas. The house is difficult to furnish; there is no wall-space and every room is merely a passage to two others; the vestibule is almost as large as the library and reception rooms which flank it, while these small chambers are virtually useless. The hall-living room is an awkward but interesting space, with its recessed ingle-nook and the cage of tall spindles in which the staircase is enclosed at its northern end — these, and the semicircular prolongation of the dining room are features which have the flavor of Wright's youthful designs.

The Bagley house at Hinsdale, Illinois, is stylistically connected to the Blossom house, since it, too, is Colonial, but of that special type known as "Dutch." It is not "bootlegged," having been designed and erected in 1894; in spirit, however, it belongs with Wright's one other Colonial house. It has a big gambrel roof, gabled dormers, and an inset porch across the front. Lyman Silsbee had introduced the "Dutch Colonial" style, with modifications, to Chicago in his Jamieson house of 1889. Photographs of this house had been immediately published, and it is certainly the precedent for the Bagley house (Fig. 32). Aside from its novel Dutch Colonial appearance, the most singular feature of the Jamieson house was a circular library picturesquely protruding from one corner of the main block of the building. Perhaps Wright's client demanded a copy of the Jamieson design; but Wright could never copy. The library of the Bagley house is an extraordinary elaboration of the scheme. It is a free-standing octagonal chamber to the north of the house and connected with it by a covered passage. It has an octagonal roof of low pitch; it is lighted by means of a continuous clerestory, permitting uninterrupted shelf-space below. Although somewhat incongruous in its Dutch Colonial context, it makes a very functional library; and it is Wright's first statement of his conviction that a house should be centrifugal in plan. Elsewhere in the Bagley design there are unmistakable Wrightian touches, in the outward extension of the dining room, and in the subtly changing levels of the main floor. The long windows opening onto the porch are wider and lower than customary, and they are broken up by their muntins into an arresting geometric pattern.

The Bagley house shares another distinction with the Blossom house: they are the only executed designs of Wright's entire career which embody classical detail.[3] In the Bagley house, well-shaped Ionic columns of wood support the load over the porch, and two small Ionic columns of white marble flank the marble-faced fireplace of the living room (Fig. 33). There is an obvious explanation in this case for Wright's unwonted classicism, for his client was a marble merchant; he had the two Ionic colonettes in stock and wanted them incorporated in his house. The columns of the porch were reflections in wood of those which Wright had used, perforce, in the interior.

Note 3
To be correct, the front porch of the Warren McArthur house should be added to this brief category. It is worked out in a small-scale wooden version of the Roman arch-order. And, in the realm of unexecuted designs, there is Wright's competition drawing of 1893 for the Milwaukee Public Library (published by Henry-Russell Hitchcock: "Frank Lloyd Wright and the 'Academic Tradition' of the Early Eighteen-nineties," Journal of the Warburg Institute, No. 1-2, 1944); but the one extant drawing of this anomaly in Wright's career is so mutilated and dim, and its place as a serious and representative effort of Wright's early work so tenuous, that it has been omitted from the text of this book.

Fig. 34. The Walter Gale house, Oak Park. Above is a rare photograph showing the balustrade still in place.

But to return to the "bootlegged houses": the less pretentious of them, many of which are really cottages in scale, are mixtures, in varying proportions, of Silsbee and the dawning individuality of Wright. The pair of houses for Thomas Gale and the Goan and Emmonds houses are all plain frame structures having a modicum of features to raise them above the commonplace. The Walter Gale house (Fig. 34) is relieved by a two-story semi-circular bay (recalling the principle motif of Silsbee's design for All Soul's) and by an attenuated two-story dormer with a pargeted spandrel; these elements and the generous open verandah which precedes the house provide a certain interest. The other houses of this group share a common plan (Fig. 35). Along one flank there is a series of three rooms: the front and back parlors and the dining room. Along the other side are ranged stairs, kitchen, closets, etc. This plan offers a practical solution for the small house of the day, but it is surprising that Wright, even if we grant that these commissions were potboilers, should have retained such a degree of compartmentation. The idea of a "back parlor" must have seemed grotesque to him even as he sketched in its partitions. But there is, to compensate, the novelty of the pair of outsized, glazed corner polygons capped with tall polygonal roofs. These great bays (Fig. 36), which are further emanations

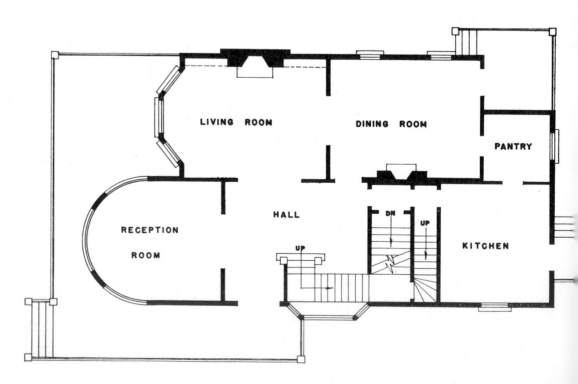

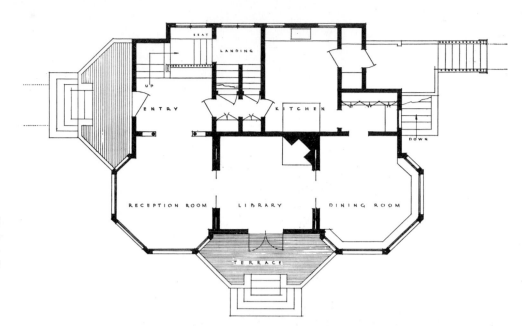

Fig. 35 (right). Plan of the Emmond house, La Grange. Fig. 36 (below). One of the twin Gale houses, Oak Park. All three of these houses have the same plan.

SEAT

LANDING

UP

ENTRY

KITCHEN

DOWN

RECEPTION ROOM   LIBRARY   DINING ROOM

TERRACE

Fig. 37. The W. S. McHarg house, Chicago. The only photograph in existence of a long-demolished and elusive building.

of Wright's desire to "bring the inside outside," are of doubtful value on buildings otherwise so small and unassuming. They unbalance the elevations, and the rooms which they contain, like goldfish bowls, have neither privacy nor useable wallspace.

Of the house for W. S. McHarg (Fig. 37), who was the consulting plumbing expert for Adler and Sullivan, there is almost nothing to write. Long since demolished, its history is buried and obscure; only one faded, broken photographic plate remains as a record, and there is no trace of the floor plans. It was a clapboarded house, of two and a half stories, covered with a high-pitched hip roof. Its only peculiarity was a surrounding verandah and balcony with balustrades composed of those attenuated spindles which Wright used so often in the 1890's for staircases and other trim.

Of all the "bootlegged" group, the McArthur and Harlan houses are the most interesting and the most significant to the progress of Wright's future career. The McArthur house, coeval with

the Blossom house and occupying the adjacent lot, might be classified as Dutch Colonial only because of its gambrel roof and dormers (Fig. 38). In plan and detail it is extraordinarily individualistic, and it embodies important innovations. Having oriented the house, due to the narrow lot, with its short side toward the street, Wright then proceeded to make a virtue of necessity and extracted from the *parti* its every possibility. There can be no doubt that Wright gave minute attention to this design. The extrusion of interior spaces by means of polygonal bays at the corners is handled in a much more mature way than in the Gale cottages. It is a quite successful attempt to break up the rigid distinction between inside and outside; and it is noteworthy that here Wright has adopted the casement window wholeheartedly to further the attempt, although it is still to be several years before he discards the sash window altogether. Corner bays were, of course, derived from Silsbee's practice, but Wright used them in the McArthur house not as any deliberate courting of the pic-

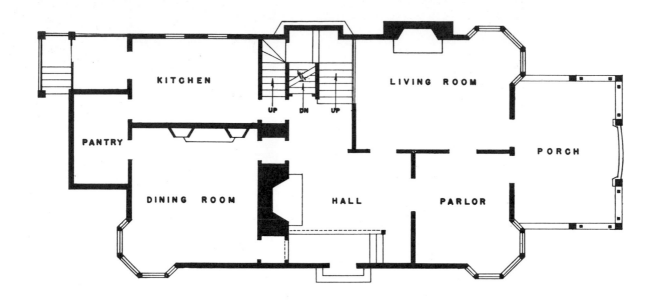

KITCHEN

PANTRY

DINING ROOM

UP DN UP

HALL

LIVING ROOM

PARLOR

PORCH

Fig. 38. Plan and exterior of the Warren McArthur house, Chicago.

turesque, but from some inner necessity; and, in any case, they are very freshly handled, with a geometric crispness which was generally unknown to the Shingle Style. The external walls of the McArthur house are unusual: they are composed of a dado of Roman brick, a sort of continuous sill, above which there is a band of brown plaster in which the casements are set. As he was, in this design, feeling his way toward plastic fenestration, Wright was also laboring to arrive at a correspondingly plastic articulation of wall. The resultant banded effect in the walls of the McArthur house plays its part in producing horizontality. The round-headed entrance door, too low for comfort (an error in scale which Wright continued to make, in his wish to bring houses down to earth, for decades), let in to the banded composition of the south

wall, acts as a foil to its prevailing horizontality; this is the decorative sense in which Wright, customarily and with caution, employed the circle in his early career.

It was Wright's privilege, in the McArthur house, to design all of its trim and fittings and some of its furniture. Thus, he was able, for the first time in his life, to put into practice his belief that it is the duty of the unconventional architect to carry his design to its ultimate conclusion and not to leave the client with the hopeless task of trying to equip his house with what he could find in the open market. He was also able to materialize in wood and glass ideas for the decorative arts which had been obviously stirring in his mind for a long while. The trim and fittings of the McArthur house (Fig. 39) constitute another miracle in Wright's career.

Fig. 39. Details of the hall woodwork, built-in buffet, and glazed interior doors in the McArthur house.

As in the case of the elevations of the Charnley house, these additional manifestations in the McArthur house of his emergent personal conception of design appeared full-fledged and complete. The woodwork of the hall and dining room, the built-in buffet, and the glazed interior doors are brilliant examples of what Wright could do once he had freed himself of the influence of Sullivan's version of ornament. There is absolutely no trace of Sullivan here — or of anyone else, for that matter. The leadings of the doors and buffet are as distinctive, though they are Wright's first, as those of, say, the Robie house some fifteen years later. The only evolution is from the exuberant richness of the early designs to the restraint of the later. The leadings of the McArthur house, tightly interconnected patterns of rectilinear shapes alternating with

relatively unbroken areas of clear glass, sparkling with insets of milky, green, and golden hue, are so dense in places as to have the texture of carpet; then this richness gives way to the long simple lines that fall to the bottom rail of the sash. It is remarkable that Wright was able to find, in those days when the horrors of "art glass" were coming into vogue, a craftsman capable of understanding and executing his crisp, geometric designs in which color was subservient to linear pattern. He may already have discovered the glassmaker Orlando Giannini, his indispensable co-worker for many years, to whom further reference will be made.

The oaken woodwork of the McArthur house is equally remarkable. The planes of the wainscoting and of the built-in furniture have no carving and very little ornament other than a few

Fig. 40. Exterior and plan of the A. W. Harlan house, Chicago. The living room was later bisected at the insistence of Dr. Harlan. The style of the clothing of the group in front is the major clue to the building's age.

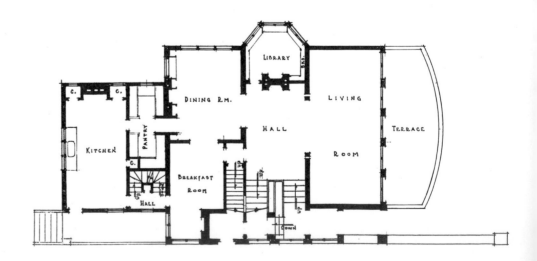

simple beadings. They rely for their interest upon the play of intersecting geometric forms. The little polygonal end motifs of the buffet are reproductions in miniature of the structural polygons of the plan of the house. The horizontal boards of the wainscoting are channeled along their joints to emphasize the level line of the dado; this is a device which Wright frequently used in the 1890's.

The Harlan house (Fig. 40) is the most radical of the group in elevation and plan. It has none of the high, pyramidal quality of most of the other "bootlegged houses." Its low hip roof is characteristic of the next period in Wright's career, while its over-all effect is one of unbroken horizontality. This effect is heightened by the single low dormer, the ribbon fenestration, the balcony and the advancing terrace. And yet it is a curious fact that, although the Harlan house looks more like its descendant, the Prairie House, than any other in the group, it is tightly planned; it is contained within a long rectangle, there are no extrusions of interior space. The house is built of wood, but it is sheathed with flush siding in order to achieve those tailored areas of smooth wall which had been produced in the more expensive Charnley house by walls of finely-jointed Roman brick. The elements of the facade reflect the placing of the principal rooms across the front of the house. It was only because of the client's inalterable determination to have twin parlors that the architect later bisected this large front space with an inner partition. As in the McArthur house, the main entrance is at the side, and this element of *parti* is even more radically handled here: access to the door is by means of a passage incorporated into the general design of the facade.

The chief interior feature of the Harlan house is its monumental stair hall, a two-story well of open design with the staircase ascending at one corner (Fig. 41). A high balustrade, made up of the by now expected comb of spindles, runs around the upper level and increases the quality of an exercise in abstract space which the room purveys. On the tall, oblong newel-post, and in the panels of the solid parapet which extends behind it to the south wall, are areas of Sullivanesque ornament, plexi of spiky foliage and curling tendrils against arabesques of braided lines; this is the unique case of its use in the "bootlegged houses." The chief exterior feature

of the Harlan house is the bold, striking balcony which originally graced its facade, running straight across at the level of the second floor and having a canopy suspended from above on thin stanchions. The panels of the balcony had Sullivanesque motifs in their centers, but they were without the usual foliage and greatly simplified. The single dormer in the center of the roof is eccentric in design, forecasting the capricious dormers of the Winslow and Williams houses three and four years later.

The Municipal Boathouse on the shore of Lake Mendota at Madison was the only public building which Wright erected independently during the period of his affiliation with Adler and Sullivan. The competition for its design was sponsored by the Madison Improvement Association in February, 1893; as $4000 was the modest sum

Fig. 41. Newel post and stair well in the Harlan house. The ornament carved into the wood is Sullivanesque. The "lightolier" atop the newel post cannot, needless to say, be ascribed to Wright.

allotted by the Association for the structure, the competition was local, and Wright must have heard of it through connections in Madison. The wording of the announcement of the award in Madison newspapers in May of 1893[4] sheds light on Wright's youth and relative obscurity at the time; the award, one of them said, went to "Frank Wright, a former Madison boy, now a Chicago architect." The design which Wright submitted, a frame structure with shingle siding (Fig. 42), is arresting in two respects: it is based upon a semicircle, and it is the progenitor of two of his later designs for similar projects on a magnified scale, the Wolf Lake and Cheltenham Beach resorts. In all three designs, a semicircle terminating in square pavilions embraces the central feature, a boat-well and marina. In the Madison Boathouse, the second-story promenade is functional; it is the principal means of access, as the site slopes abruptly and the visitor enters the enclosure at the upper level, to descend to the boat landings by staircases. The resulting semicircle of the *parti* is echoed in the archway which spans the boat-well. This, too, is a scheme that Wright was to use again, as in the Fred Jones house and the George Gerts cottage. The end pavilions are very Wrightian for their day; the round-headed doors interrupting the high dado, the smooth rise of walls from dado to cornice, the low-pitched roofs, the heavy overhang of the eaves, the absence of familiar mouldings, and the simplified Sullivanesque arcades all add up, in the 1890's, to Wright's signature.

Independence and Transition

After Wright set himself up in independent practice in 1893, and until the turn of the century, most of his designs incorporated elements so strongly reminiscent of Louis Sullivan that the seven years of this period might be called the Sullivanesque phase of his career. This derivative quality in Wright's early work had been submerged in the "bootlegged houses," but, once the break with Sullivan had been made, it blossomed forth. Nor was Lyman Silsbee wholly

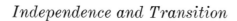

Note 4
Wisconsin State Journal, Vol. 82, No. 57, May 12, 1893, p. 3. Madison Democrat, Vol. 50, No. 113, May 12, 1893, p. 5.

forgotten; we still see echoes of his picturesque style in an occasional high roof or polygonal bay. At times, too, there is a dimming of Wright's intuitive feeling for the domestic in architecture through use of elements too impersonal for a house; this marks a temporary deflection of the course of his genius which puzzles us until we remember that he had just experienced the closest contact with a man whose great gift was for public architecture.

In the main, however, the buildings designed between 1894 and 1900 are first of all Wrightian, no matter how noticeable the trace of Sullivan, and Wright at once began to concentrate upon and develop the principles of a new architecture

Fig. 42. The Municipal Boathouse on the shore of Lake Mendota, Madison, Wisconsin. A competition design that was built!

which he had outlined in the Charnley, Harlan and McArthur houses. There was little immaturity in Wright's career. Some of his designs for the period now in question are patently experimental, but they are seldom awkward and never trite.[1] The driving purpose behind them gives to each a dignity that often rises higher than the sum of its component parts; we see that these experimental buildings are genuine

Note 1
There is, perhaps, one exception to this statement: the Francis Woolley house in Oak Park, a design of late 1893, which is truly commonplace.

evolutions, obeying a new set of laws. It is an exciting experience for students of Wright's architecture to come upon them today, often in outworn, by-passed sections of Chicago, old, as things go in the Middle West, yet triumphant over time and circumstance.

With the same amazing leap into the future which brought the Charnley house into being, so the first of the group of buildings done in independence is the finest of the lot.

Soon after Wright and Corwin had established themselves as co-lessees of the Schiller Building office, William H. Winslow came to Wright to place the commission for a new house in River Forest, the next suburb to the west of Oak Park.

Winslow was a business man of artistic bent; he was the president of a large firm of ornamental ironworkers. By nature he was a craftsman, although, in the American way, he had made his craft pay him handsomely. His hobbies were typography and printing, and he and Wright were later to collaborate in a modest publishing venture.[2] He stipulated that a workshop and pressroom be incorporated in the stables behind his new River Forest house. To William Winslow goes great credit for recognizing genius in Wright long before his praises were sung. In 1893 Wright was, at the age of twenty-four, father of a new architecture not yet discovered.

Winslow had acquired a large piece of property in Auvergne Place, a private street which had been cut through the Waller Estate. River Forest was more remote and quiet in those days than Oak Park, and it was zoned (although the word would not have been recognized or understood in the 1890's) for larger holdings. The Waller Estate was wooded, its terrain was flat, and the lazy little Desplaines River flowed through it along the western edge of the lots in Auvergne Place. This was the perfect setting for the ancestor of the Prairie House, which the Winslow house was to be; and Wright's singular ability to do it justice is apparent in the effortless masterpiece with which he graced it. Like the Charnley house, it was without precedent and its first impression upon the observer is that of tremendous simplicity.

The *leitmotiv* of the Winslow house design is the harmony of the restful horizontal line with its level woodland setting (Fig. 43). Every element in the design conspires to engender a sense of ease and tranquility: the low hip roof, strongly projecting over walls composed of a lower band of Roman brick and an upper one of softly-colored tiles, the widely-spaced oblong windows, the broad chimney, the suppressed basement, the ribbon of thin-risered steps leading to a low terrace with no punctuation other than a pair of flattened urns. It is all so straightforward that we feel we know this house at once — that it can have no complications inside or

Note 2
William C. Gannett: "The House Beautiful," Auvergne Press, River Forest, 1896-97, page decorations by Frank Lloyd Wright.

out to baffle us — yet we are prepared to find, for we sense them, endless subtleties.

To enhance the quality of simplicity in the Winslow house, the value of plain surfaces is carefully cultivated. From a short distance away, the band of tiles becomes only a neutral tone differentiating the second story from the first; and, as the door and windows have only slight enframement, the great shadow of the eaves is the principal decoration — an ornament so moving and uncomplex that the eye finds particular pleasure in following the fall of its shadow into the little valleys and interstices of the tilework. The perfect proportion of the openings to the oblong plane of the facade and the light, decorated plaque in which the entrance is set complete the harmony of house, shadow, and level lawn. A design based upon such studied elementals as these might well be stark; but the Winslow house is not. It improves with familiarity. Mrs. Edward Waller, who lived opposite for nearly a half-century, told the author in 1939 that she never grew tired of looking at it.

The most important innovation in the Winslow house is its roof. Here, in unambiguous form, that low, generous hip with wide eaves that is to become the keynote of the Prairie House makes its appearance. Suggested by the roofforms of traditional Japanese architecture, perhaps, it was the answer to an urgent inner need on Wright's part to bring the house to earth — to lower its center of gravity, to underscore its function as shelter, to make the horizontal dominant. That it had other happy results, as byproducts, is more significant sociologically than aesthetically. It precludes any thought of using attic space as living space; ushering household domestics out of cramped, airless quarters under the rafters was Wright's most humanitarian contribution, in an age when domestic service was still taken for granted, to the progress of the American dwelling.

Despite the beauty and the marked forward strides of the Winslow design, it is a house in a state of transition. Its isolated, clean-cut sash windows, its corresponding reliance upon the effectiveness of smooth areas of wall, its curious treatment as a unit of entrance and flanking windows within a specially demarcated plane of different material, its over-all feeling of self-containment all hark back to the Charnley house. As for the much-disputed influence of Sullivan's

Fig. 43. The William Winslow house, River Forest, Illinois. The picture above shows the original terra-cotta roofing tiles. Below is a closeup of the entrance.

Fig. 44. South, east, and north facades of the Winslow house. The composition roofing was added at a later date. The polygonal element is a stair-tower.

work in the design, it is confined to certain spots of pure decoration.

The north side of the Winslow house is encumbered with a huge *porte-cochère,* a feature which was apparently indispensable to elegant living in the days of the horse-drawn carriage. The east, or back, facade is in strange contrast to the utter simplicity of the west (Fig. 44). There is a projecting wing, and the whole composition is made restless by many sharp-edged, prismatic extrusions of inner volumes; nevertheless, each in itself is a bold and uninhibited experimentation in the dawning concept of the centrifugal plan and the space-block. The prolongation of the dining room away from the great chimney toward a semicircular terminal fitted with a ribbon of leaded casement windows is progressive, as is the tall, polygonal stair-tower, almost free-standing, and lighted by attenuated, casemented oriels fitted into narrow slots in the brickwork. Where, in Sullivan's work to this date, could we find precedent for such features as these?

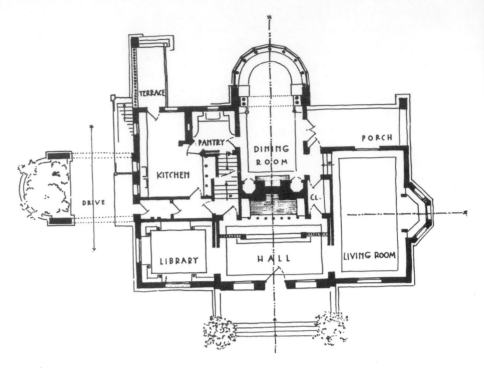

Fig. 45 (right). Plan of the Winslow house. Fig. 46 (below). The attenuated arcade in front of the hall fireplace.

Fig. 47 (right). The Winslow stables.

The plan of the Winslow house (Fig. 45) arrives at a nice balance between wall and openings; it is only semi-fluid. The concealed staircase is a very rare departure from Wright's customary method of treating vertical circulation as an ornament within a house, in full view. As carried out, the Winslow plan contains none (except for the external stair-tower) of those polygonal elements for which Wright had such a predilection in the 1890's, but the original drawings[3] show that there was to have been an outlying octagonal porch to the south, connected with the living room by a covered gallery; this would have been a sort of counterpart of the Bagley house library.

Out-and-out Sullivanesque ornament is very limited on the exterior of the Winslow house. The spandrels of the arched *porte-cochère* are

Note 3
Robert C. Spencer, Jr.: "The Work of Frank Lloyd Wright," Architectural Review (Boston), Vol. 7, June 1900: plate of drawings and plans for the Winslow house.

carved in a leafy Sullivanesque design. But the tilework of the second story has decidedly undergone the discipline of Wright's decorative geometry. Inside, bursts of Sullivanesque ornament are carved in the woodwork of the principal rooms. The strange, spindly arcade (Fig. 46) that stands, like a screen, in front of the hall fireplace is a cabinetmaker's interpretation of the arcades of the Schiller Building, and its spandrels are adorned with Sullivanesque cartouches and foliage.

The Winslow stables (Fig. 47) are just as fascinating and prophetic, in their way, as the main house. The incorporation of a carriage-yard gave Wright the opportunity to use the wall-enclosed form for the first time, and it is amazing how closely the resultant design tallies with the disposition of the walled "barns" and "stables" of the Froebel textbooks. The design is not to be dismissed as a commonplace treatment of carriage-yards for suburban houses at the time; coach-houses in the Middle West were customarily quite exposed or merely screened by planting. The cautious use of the curve over

the entrance of the Winslow stables to relieve the prevalent rectangularity is also in keeping with the Froebelian attitude toward the curve as part of the self-contained sphere; round-headed openings and ceilings are exceptions (until lately) to Wright's normal idea of good structure. One wing of the spacious Winslow stables was given over, as has been indicated, to the Auvergne Press, Winslow's hobby and relaxation.

The polychromy of the Winslow house and stables must have been an essential part of their original effect. Dark orange brick, bronze-glazed tiles, buff limestone, and terra-cotta roofing[4] composed a warm autumnal palette which Wright was to use again and again in masonry houses. In frame houses, external walls are stuccoed in deep yellow or sienna tints with wood trim stained a very dark brown. Then, from embrasures in these chromatic walls gleam forth the myriad insets of the casements — gold, green, buff, henna, and white. The interiors of the more ambitious houses, after 1900, are worked out in the same subdued colors.

The Winslow house is, incontestably, another of the miracles of Wright's career. Hitchcock said of it in the Museum of Modern Art (N.Y.) catalogue of 1932: "There was nowhere in the world at the time any precedent for the effect which he attained. 'Prairie Architecture,' as it was to be known, sprang suddenly into being..." But the Winslow house is not to be considered, any more than the Charnley house, as an end in itself; taking the broad view of Wright's career, both are seen as steps along the way. We are, in this particular period of his work from 1893 to 1900, in a transitional passage characterized by intense searching and experimentation. The other major domestic designs of the period show an astonishing divergence from what the public has come to consider Wright's norm, although, in hindsight, we can see that, generally, they share a common sense of direction. The McAfee, Devin, Furbeck and Husser houses are all in the direct line of descent leading, through the Winslow house, to the mature Prairie House. The Williams and Heller houses, because of strange experimentations with roof-forms, are sports in

the genetic sense, leading nowhere except to that handful of gable-roofed Prairie Houses that appeared very briefly in the first years of the twentieth century, only to be discontinued. The Foster cottage, at the very end of the period, is undisguisedly Japanese. And there was to be yet one more short moment of playing, by command, as it were, with the historical styles — this time, the Tudor. All of these developments will be investigated in this chapter, using the houses already mentioned — a short list selected from the much larger total — as examples.

All of Wright's clients in the 1890's would not, of course, accept revolutionary designs. Those who knowingly did had not only the courage of their convictions, but had occasionally to suffer for it. Wright relates how William Winslow underwent a form of mild persecution from his hidebound friends after his River Forest house was completed. For a few months he avoided the popular morning and evening expresses on the railway to escape the banter of the scores of commuters who knew him well enough to speak their minds. It is, in fact, amazing that Wright found such a steady succession of clients willing to experiment and to try the uncharted; but he, like his Uncle Jenkin, has always had the power of persuasion. Occasional remarks, not untinged with envy, appeared in the press concerning this. In 1905, one writer said[5]: "He [i.e., Wright] also must have had the sort of client who wanted a mediaeval castle; and it may be well to pause and consider for a moment how he has been able to reconcile the uncompromising rigour of his style with the satisfaction which he has evidently given to a large number of clients . . . and we surmise that Mr. Wright is able to command the confidence of his clients by a certain vivid emotional interest which the man imparts to his work."

However that may be, there was one important early client who did want the mediaeval and was not to be persuaded by any vivid emotion other than his own. Wright was thus projected into the (for him) uncharted seas of the Tudor. Nathan Moore of Oak Park came to Wright late in 1894 with a commission of con-

Note 4
The roofing tiles were replaced at a later date by mottled asbestos shingles.

Note 5
"Work of Frank Lloyd Wright—Its Influence," Architectural Record, Vol. 18, July 1905, pp. 60-65.

siderable interest to which a proviso was attached: he would have "nothing but an English house." As it turned out, this meant half-timbering and all that goes with it. The story of the resultant Moore house, the only black-and-white Wright ever designed, is a complicated one. At first, Wright and Moore toyed with the idea of remodeling Moore's old nondescript frame house in Forest Avenue, diagonally opposite The Studio, giving it a new face of the required Englishness. The idea was abandoned, but not before elaborate plans were drawn; these plans, subsequently lost, are still referred to as "Moore house I." "Moore house II" was built by Wright, without any reference to the old building, from the ground up and completed in 1895. It was gutted by fire in 1922. Moore again got in touch with Wright (who had just returned to Chicago from Tokyo), and a wholly new and enlarged "Moore house II" was built on the same foundations. It is this structure, with its really compelling mixture of Tudor and the Wright of the 1920's, that today's visitor to Oak Park sees. To complicate the story, the original frame Moore house whose remodeling was contemplated in 1894, was moved to the south edge of the Moore property to make way for the new building and then, at last, remodeled by Wright in 1900; this building still stands, and is known as "Moore house III." Exactly why Mr. Moore came to Wright in the first place, when Wright had had no experience whatever in the Tudor style, and set all this elaborate chain of events in motion, is not too clear; as an old man, he told the author in 1940 that he did so "just because Wright happened to be a neighbor."

It is not possible to say much about the original Moore house II, as it exists only in the form of photographs (Fig. 48); but it *was* Tudor, with a half-timbered second floor, enormous mediaeval roofs, moulded brick chimneys, and good Period accessories. It was a reasonably capable "English" design for the time and place, from which Wright, with what must have been heroic effort, excluded all personal expression. It is important as the prelude to the second Moore house II, which is instinct, although it retains the outward semblance of the Tudor style, with personal expression, and is a thoroughly fascinating curiosity of Wright's career. For many years, both of these buildings enjoyed a wide acclaim, and there was a time when Wright had

regularly to fend off prospective clients who wanted "another Moore house."

The first Moore house II was important for yet another reason: experience with the English mediaeval style led Wright to try his hand at it once again in another design of the 1890's unrelated in all other ways to the Moore house. This is the set of four party-wall Roloson houses — an executed design which had been lost to memory until 1940.[6] So far as is known, this is the unique example of the standard row house

Note 6
The author happened upon the Roloson houses while driving along Calumet Avenue looking for some early Adler and Sullivan buildings.

Fig. 48. The first Moore house II, executed in the Tudor style.

Fig. 49. The four party-wall Roloson houses. Lost to memory until 1939.

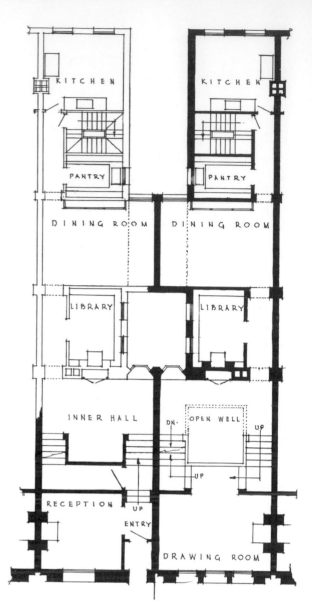

Fig. 50. Plan of the Roloson houses.

in Wright's entire *oeuvre* (Fig. 49), if we discount those he did as a draftsman for Adler and Sullivan. The commission to design the houses was brought in to Wright's Schiller Building office in 1894 by Robert Roloson, a son-in-law of Edward Waller, who had some property on the South Side of Chicago which he wanted to improve. The idea of erecting four identical row houses quite naturally suggested itself, both as an adequate means of return on the investment and as the expected thing to do in that crowded section of the city. Wright's contribution was to design a set of party-wall dwellings in a modified Tudor style, but with great freedom and distinction and plenty of individuality.

Even the plan (Fig. 50) of the Roloson houses shows a fresh approach to a tired and difficult problem. It is conceived on the mezzanine principle: that is, there is a break in floor-level at the central stair-well, and the rooms to the rear of it, on each floor, are several steps lower than those in front. There are also some minor variations in floor heights, so that the interior spaces constantly shift in relation to each other as one moves about. The great stair-well is really majestic in scale for houses of this type, and all of the main rooms are separated from each other by secondary or introductory rooms generating rich spatial effects. In spite of some Sullivanesque ornament here and there, the interiors have a crisp geometrical quality, decidedly fresh and Wrightian. But the facades are the triumph of the Roloson design. Essentially, they are four great English gables set contiguously, resting upon a basement of dressed limestone, and enclosing a panel of superimposed mullioned windows. From that premise onward, however, all is Wright. Everything seems to conform to some geometric principle which stills the customary clamor of so rich an historical style; we are conscious only of a very disciplined composition of squares surmounted by the single triangle of the gable. The only applied ornament is the set of three foliated spandrels of each facade, beautifully controlled and adapted to their square shape. In front of each house is a paved terrace approached by a low flight of three steps and guarded by a limestone balustrade of simple spherical members whose nether halves are decorated with Sullivanesque patterns in relief. The Roloson houses are an extraordinary manifestation of Wright's power to transmute what he touches into something peculiarly his own, even when he starts with an unfamiliar borrowed style.

It is little to be wondered at, therefore, that the series of truly experimental houses whose design punctuated the years immediately following the erection of the Winslow house should show aggressive innovations and changes. But before going on to these, there is one design contemporary with the Winslow house that, eccentric as it is, demands attention: this is the Chauncey Williams house in River Forest, one short block to the east of Auvergne Place, but still within the old Waller Estate. The Williamses had moved to Chicago from Madison, where they had been acquainted with Wright's family, and were taken into the charmed circle of the Waller-Wright-Winslow côterie. It was to be expected that they should presently want a house in the vicinity of their friends, and one designed by Wright. The Williams house arose simultaneously with the Winslow house, and both were supervised by Wright as one job — but they are strikingly dissimilar in design.

The Williams house, from every angle, is sharp-edged and complex, like an irregular growth of crystals. It is one of those occasional designs of Wright's which depends for its effect upon a conspicuous, steep-pitched, widely overhanging roof (Fig. 51) set upon a low, flowing base. In a puzzling way, the design is derived from Silsbee's picturesque style; but that there is no actual resemblance to Silsbee's work is due to the same transmutation of precedent which made the Roloson houses so Wrightian. The house hugs the ground in a remarkable manner, and from a distance the shadow of the great eaves engulfs the verticals beneath down to the

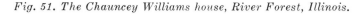

Fig. 51. The Chauncey Williams house, River Forest, Illinois.

Fig. 52. *The Williams house entrance door, framed and leaded with Sullivanesque ornament and flanked with mounds of boulders.*

projecting brick dado, so that the composition seems to consist only of roof and foundation, tentlike. The roof itself is unclassifiable; it is neither gable, gambrel, nor hip. In the sense that, in places, it terminates in a flat deck at the summit, it is a mansard, but a mansard stylized by Wright's touch into an utterly novel form. It, and the weird dormers which intersect it, are abstract arrangements of geometric solids. They verge on caprice, yet there is no denying that the total effect of the Williams house is agreeable and stimulating. The two chimneys, stalwart pylons of Roman brick, are magnificent extensions into space of the inner core of the house, whose massive strength is thus dramatized. Immediately below the eaves there is much to recall the McArthur house of 1892. The supporting walls are subdivided into longitudinal bands, the lower of brick, the upper of stucco, and their planes are slightly differentiated by a watertable over the brickwork; these bands enhance the lowness of the design by their pronounced horizontality. The casement windows, let into the stucco band, tend to cluster in jutting oriels and corner bays, their frames, when open, just clearing the heavy overhang above.

The Williams house, for all its eccentricity, is an early example of Wright's growing tendency to regard the house as consisting of three layers: the platform, the roof, and the area of human habitation between, and close-guarded; of these,

the middle space only is without definite boundaries, a shifting region of glass and other materials of light appearance. It is the working-out, in Wright's mind, of the lesson of the Ho-o-den.

There are some spots of Sullivanesque ornament in the Williams house. A ribbon of it enframes the arched entrance door (Fig. 52), an uncomfortably small aperture, and the glazed inner door is leaded in Sullivanesque patterns. To the left of the entrance is a decorative window composed of interpenetrating circles and a square which we immediately compare with the extraordinary terra-cotta cartouche over the entrance of Sullivan's bank in Grinnell, Iowa — but that came years later. To each side of the Williams house door is a mound of boulders set into the brickwork, a distracting and inexplicable touch until we learn that it was prompted by sentimentality. The boulders were gathered on summer weekends by the Wrights, the Williamses and the Wallers from the bed of the Desplaines River, and they were incorporated into the Williams house to symbolize the Illinois prairie's era of glaciation — a fact which furnishes an insight into the youthful enthusiasm of these people for a new, indigenous architecture growing from the native landscape and expressing its innermost meaning.

Even at this early and sanguine moment of Wright's career, he began to taste the disappointment of commissions which never pro-

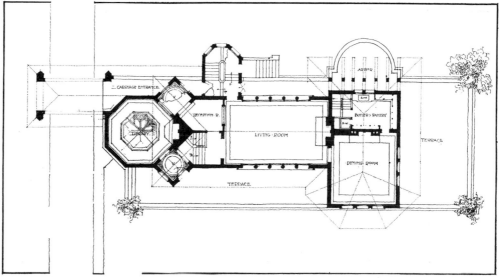

Fig. 53. The C. H. McAfee house rendering and plan. The house was never built.

gressed beyond the paper stage. Edward Waller was a friend and client with large ideas in which he involved Wright, many of which died in gestation. It is a curious fact that Wright never built a house for the Wallers; though schemes were often contemplated, the only domestic commission which Wright executed for Waller was the remodeling of the interior of his large old house in Auvergne Place and the addition of a stables. There were other clients in the same category. Warren Furbeck, Jesse Baldwin, Henry Cooper, C. H. McAfee, and Mrs. David Devin were among those who sought him out in the Schiller Building days, and for whom much was projected and nothing built. Of these fiascos in the domestic realm the latter two are highly important as records of those steps-in-

progression toward the mature Prairie House which is the principal subject of this chapter. The McAfee and Devin designs have much in common, both as to setting, date, and *parti*, and they are well-known due to their inclusion in the Wasmuth monograph of 1910.[7] They were both to have occupied narrow sites on the flat, sandy shore of Lake Michigan at what was then the northern edge of Chicago.

The McAfee house (Fig. 53) was to be placed upon a paved platform a step or two above the

Note 7
Frank Lloyd Wright: "Ausgefuehrte Bauten und Entwuerfe von Frank Lloyd Wright," Wasmuth, Berlin, 1910.

Fig. 54. The design and plan for Mrs. David Devin's house — never built. The plan at left is of the first floor; the plan at right is of the mezzanine. The second floor plan is not shown.

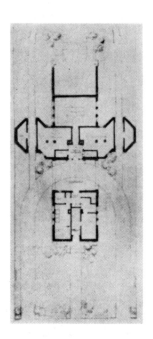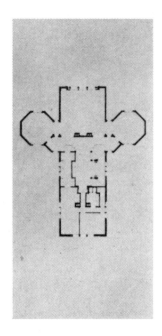

sandy ground. This pavement at once provided the house with a broad and handsome base and gave it an unwonted air of formality. But it must be realized that lawns and forest trees could not be made to thrive at the windy margin of the great lake and upon such soil. Since natural greenery was out of the question, Wright substituted earth pockets for vines and urns for flowers, and made them an integral part of the composition. Wright's first use of the urn in this manner, a motif later to become almost like a trademark of his developed style, was in the mysterious, unexecuted Goare house design, the immediate forerunner of the Winslow house, where they appeared again. In these earlier cases, the urns were not genuinely integrated with the architecture and they were of fairly conventional profile. It was in the McAfee design that the familiar Wrightian urns, very low and geometrically stylized, made their sudden debut.

In many ways, the McAfee house is a review and summation of the designs which had just preceded it, although not by much.[8] In plasticity it marks a decided advance. Sills, as such, are non-existent; they are synonymous with the stringcourse that demarcates the second story from the first. All parts of the house are now freely subject to the play of the architect's

Note 8
The Winslow and McAfee designs, for example, may have actually been on the drafting boards at Oak Park at the same time in January 1894. The earliest known sketch for the McAfee design bears that date; in June the "Oak Park Vindicator" announced commencement of construction on the Winslow house.

imagination as elements of a reasoned but arbitrary horizontality. The survival of isolated sash windows on the first floor is one of the indications of the transitional stage to which the design belongs; but fenestration at the second level is largely by means of grouped casements, turning corners where desired, as in the front bedrooms giving onto the lake. The openness which these casements give to the design is strangely negated elsewhere. The tripartite dining room window is cumbrously divided by columns and encased in a rigid rectangular enframent of Sullivanesque derivation; the entire motif and its vernacular are too grandiose for a private house. The plan of the house moves further toward the ultimate centrifugal goal, the main rooms advancing from the core of the building in long arms with unbroken flanks toward ephemeral areas of glass at their tips; the resultant movement and fluidity goes far beyond the resistant cube of the Charnley house or the serene single plane of the west front of the Winslow house. The octagonal, skylighted library contained within blank walls at the rear of the house is typical of the work of the transitional period, with its constant references to the circles and polygons of the old picturesque school of design. It recalls the Bagley house library, but its tight incorporation into the general scheme is more sophisticated. The low hip roof is by nature superbly adapted to following the plastic flow of the supporting walls, to extend over and shelter them, to unite the house closely with its site, and to mirror the wide, uncomplicated horizon of the lake.

But although the McAfee house shows such progress toward the Prairie House, and might have been admirable if executed, it is less ingratiating than the Winslow house because it is less easy. Both it and the Devin design (Fig. 54), which is in the same vein, work too hard and have too many superficial complications. It is as though at this juncture Wright were trying to compress and assimilate into his personal vision of domestic architecture too many recollections of the rich fare of Sullivan's style and the picturesqueness of Silsbee's. The same remarks could apply to the last two important domestic commissions of the period: the Heller house of 1897 and the Husser house of 1899.

The Isidore Heller house, like so many of Wright's houses of this period, is long and narrow (Fig. 55); it adapts itself to a cramped

Fig. 55. The Isidore Heller house. Note the monitor roof and loggia with sculpture by Richard Bock.

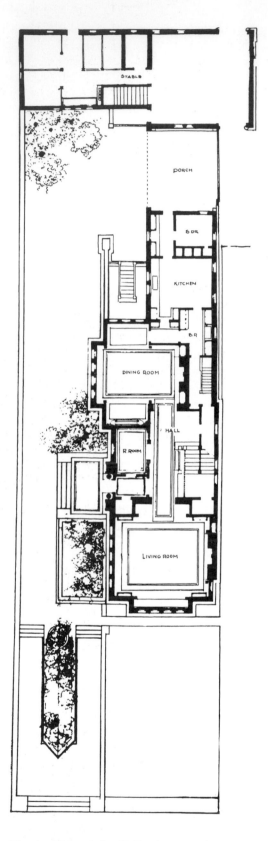

Fig. 56. Plan of the Heller house, built on a long, narrow city lot.

city lot on the South Side of Chicago by presenting its end to the street. Because of its roof it represents a small inner category of domestic design in that part of Wright's career which this book covers: it is of a type known as a "monitor," that is, a third story is added above the main eaves, smaller than the others, and capped with its own hip roof. In the Heller house, the walls of this extra third story, which is only partly enclosed, are elaborately worked with a frieze of Sullivanesque ornament interrupted by open arcades. The human figure in high relief which is the central feature of each panel of the frieze was the work of Richard Bock, an Oak Park sculptor who collaborated with Wright in many of his commissions. This sculptured loggia, which is what the third story largely is, cannot be explained in any other way than as a compulsion on the designer's part to recapture something of the florid exuberance of Sullivan's work just before and after 1890. It is out of place as an element of private house design in a Chicago city street. It is monumental rather than domestic, and the observer struggles to find justification for such an architectural debauch at the top of a moderate-sized dwelling. There is certainly no prospect to be enjoyed from its arcades.

The main door of the Heller house, in the middle of the south flank, is a square-headed opening with engaged Romanesque columns at each side, the whole surrounded by a great paneled motif of remotely Arabic appearance, while over it, at the second floor level, is an inset porch with a row of elaborately filligreed terra-cotta colonettes supporting the load above. Necessarily enough, the Heller house elsewhere is plain almost to the point of monotony. In plan (Fig. 56), it embodies none of those polygonal spaces so characteristic of the period. The two principal rooms, living and dining room, assume that cruciform shape which Wright was to use so frequently in the Prairie Houses; this is hesitantly revealed on the outside of the house by short rectangular projections of wall corresponding to one arm of the cross within.

There is nothing hesitant about the Helen Husser house (Fig. 57), which reveals its interior disposition with frank abandon. It is the first truly centrifugal plan of Wright's career, forecasting those pinwheel and windmill plans of later date, while in ornament and richness it is the last flare-up of Sullivanism, glowing most

Fig. 57. The Helen Husser house. The last stop before the full-fledged Prairie House, and the author's first introduction to Wright's work.

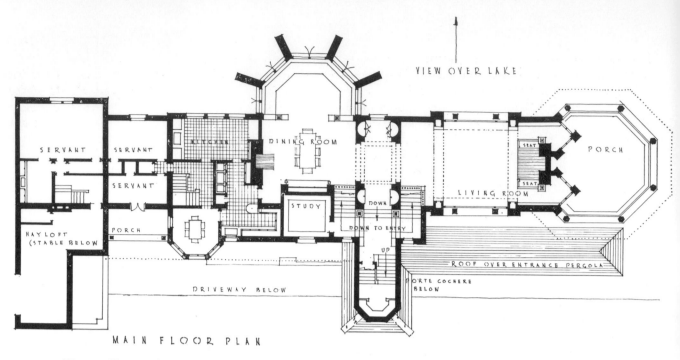

VIEW OVER LAKE

SERVANT   SERVANT   KITCHEN   DINING ROOM   PORCH

SERVANT

SEAT

SEAT

LIVING ROOM

STUDY

DOWN

HAY LOFT
(STABLE BELOW   PORCH   DOWN TO ENTRY

UP

ROOF OVER ENTRANCE PERGOLA

DRIVEWAY BELOW   PORTE COCHERE
BELOW

MAIN FLOOR PLAN

Fig. 58. Plan of the Husser house, forerunner of the "windmill" and "pinwheel" plans of later work.

brightly and illogically just before it expired. The containment of the second story windows within encrusted arcades that can only be recollections of the Transportation Building, and the monumental tripartite windows of the living room with their squat Romanesque columns, are the Sullivanisms of the Husser house which leap instantly to the eye and brand it as transitional. But there are innovations which, although they are less salient at first glance than the decorations, are deeply significant. In two respects, the Husser design ranks second only to the Winslow house as a milestone of progress toward the houses of the First Golden Age: first, the above-mentioned centrifugality of plan; second, the scheme of the raised basement. By placing the basement floor at ground level, it ceases to be a cellar; it becomes a fitting area for such secondary needs and activities of the house as servants' rooms, entries, vestibules, grade-rooms, childrens' playrooms, as well as heating equipment and laundries. Automatically, by this scheme, the living, dining and relaxing spaces are lifted above their former level into a quieter region, and from their elevated position, in this reinterpretation of the Continental concept of the *piano nobile*, they enjoy wide vistas across the flat landscapes of the Middle West (in the Husser house, it was Lake Michigan, just to the east, which gave purpose to the scheme). The

bedrooms, now, are even more delightfully located on the third level, roughly corresponding to the former attic. There was no burden of additional height to be coped with in this wonderfully simple arrangement, for Wright, as compensation, had done away with the attic (as he had also done away with an excavated cellar); and he had at his call the cultivated, developed horizontality of his new architecture by which he could easily make a three-story house seem lower than the standard two-and-a-half. By 1899, Wright had gone very far toward obliterating the rigid preconceptions of the traditional American house and had replaced them with something so flexible that it could be bent to serve a new code of architectural law as unprecedented as his.

Continuing that *parti* which had been intimated in the McAfee design, the Husser house is a pronounced cross in plan (Fig. 58) with the shorter arms composed of the great dining room bay, with its dramatic buttresses, and the boldly-projecting stair-tower. Consequently, the cluster of windows at the far ends of the arms is very noticeable and contributes greatly to the centrifugality of the design. The attachment of the garage (originally, of course, a coach-house) to the main block of the building is a highly prophetic act for which there could have been little or no example in 1899; this feature and the long covered passageway at ground level leading to the entry stress the main axis. The whole effect is thus dynamic and directional in a way that is a far cry from the classic unity of the Winslow house, and that will culminate in the shiplike Robie house of 1908.[9] The centrifugal plan, such as that of the Husser house and many of the great Prairie Houses, provides a luxury of light and air and vista that demands a generous setting and that Wright's clients were not always able to afford. A house thus extended is twice as costly to construct and maintain as a compact house of equivalent volume.[10] Wright's genius is never at home in the realm of the merely economical, as will be pointed out again in varying contexts in this book. The charge is often brought against him that he does not know how to be practical. This is an absurdity. It is the result of the mistaken belief that practicality and cheapness are one and the same.

The Rollin Furbeck house in Oak Park (Fig. 59), built in 1898, bears some resemblance to

Note 9
For an analysis of the increasing directionalism of Wright's plans, see H. de Fries: "Die Grundriss-Gestaltung des Architekten Wright," in "Frank Lloyd Wright, Aus dem Lebenswerke eines Architekten," H. de Fries (ed.), Pollak, Berlin, 1926, pp. 70-73.

Note 10
Walter Curt Behrendt: "Modern Building," Harcourt Brace, New York, 1937, p. 137: "Jacob Burkhardt, the justly famous historian of Renaissance architecture, used to say that one must have money as well as luck and humour for the pleasure, so questionable to him, of creating an unsymmetric building. This pious prescription has been fulfilled for Wright insofar as he has almost always been able to build for the more affluent, who have placed at his command large, and even unusual, means."

Fig. 59. The Rollin Furbeck house, Oak Park.

Fig. 60. The Francis Apartments, Chicago. A landmark in Mid-West apartment-house design.

the Heller house in its crowning loggia and obtrusive Sullivanesque detail. It has a soaring height which its low roofs and wide eaves can do nothing to mitigate, and is a type of house, to be repeated at least twice in the Prairie House period,[11] which is an aberration in Wright's work that seems to deny all those principles toward which it was leading. The diagonal buttresses at the corners of the house and the splayfooted piers, prismatic in section, of the porch are noteworthy. Rollin Furbeck commissioned another house in Oak Park the following year;[12] the architect in this case was George Maher, an interesting figure in the Chicago School — in some respects a rival, in others an imitator of Wright's. Of all the house designs which Wright executed between 1893 and 1900, the Winslow

house was the most influential in the Chicago area, and the one which was most copied. It was certainly the inspiration for many of Maher's houses.

Perhaps the second most influential Wright design of this transitional period was an apartment house, the Francis Apartments, erected in Chicago in 1895 (Fig. 60) for the Terre Haute Trust Company of Indiana. Consideration of this design leads us, for the time being, out of the field of domestic architecture into Wright's early dealings with the problems of mass-housing and public buildings.

As Hugh Morrison points out, the Francis Apartments is a design which continues the principles involved in the Charnley house, applying them across a broader front — a legitimate procedure, since both buildings fall within the wide definition of domestic architecture. This apartment-house established a new high level for such buildings in the Middle West, as the Charnley house had done in its turn. That it was much admired is attested by the frequency with which it was imitated. Like the rest of

Note 11
The Fricke and W. E. Martin houses.
Note 12
See Construction News, Vol. 8, March 29, 1899, p. 439.

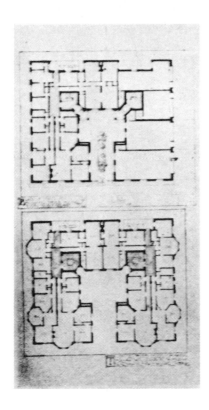

of camouflage. What such buildings were unable to achieve despite the results of their architectural larceny, Wright encompassed by a simple statement of function plus reliance upon good proportion and cultivation of the quiet horizontal line. He also proved that tenants were not as insistent upon fancywork as had been imagined, and that good apartment-houses could be built and rented with far less ornamental outlay.

The Francis Apartments is a design which has a reasonable, domestic look. Wide sash windows and equally broad vertical rows of bays stress that dependence upon ample air and sunlight which the routine of domestic life demands. Also, this form of fenestration leaves large areas of smooth wall which lend dignity and suggest generous interior wall-surfaces for the placement of furniture. But the resultant self-containment of this kind of construction, as well as the rich bands of ornament across cornice and basement-course and the very Sullivanesque iron gates at the entrance, place the building stylistically in the transitional period.

The other multiple dwelling designed and erected in this period was Francisco Terrace (Fig. 61), also in 1895. This was an Edward Waller project, located in the low-income, densely-populated part of Chicago known as the "near West Side." It is in quite a different class from the Francis Apartments. It was, in fact, a model tenement behind whose construction lay a modicum of philanthropy. Being of only two stories throughout, it spreads over a corner property considerably larger than that occupied by the Francis Apartments, and is far less com-

Wright's best work, its greatest novelty, and its appeal, is its directness of approach. There is no effort to disguise the fact that the building consists naturally of layers of identical requirements, floor upon floor; in this alone it stood apart from the regulation apartment-house designs of the 1890's, which were frenzied mounds

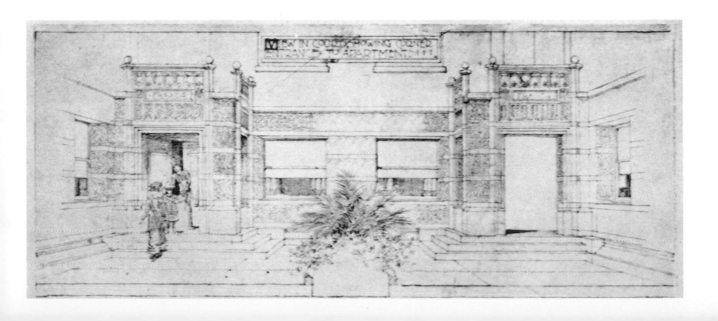

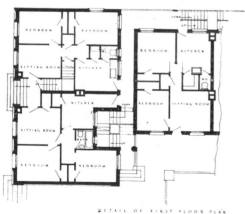

DETAIL OF FIRST FLOOR PLAN

Fig. 61. Entranceway and plans of the Francisco Terrace, Chicago. On the facing page are views of the open courtyard and stair towers.

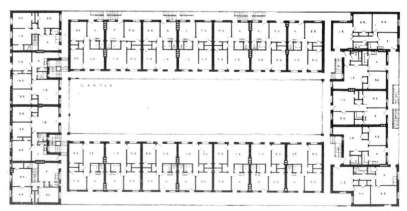

pact. It is built around the four sides of a rectangular central courtyard, and is doubled in thickness along the two street fronts. The controlling idea is that every pair of flats shall have direct access to the outdoors, doing away with all inner public corridors. The street-front flats are approached directly from the sidewalks; the courtyard flats are accessible only through a single wide archway opening into the court, at its narrow end, from the street. Open towers with elevated roofs are located at each corner of the block; these contain the public stairways, and from them circulation to the front doors of the upstairs courtyard flats is by means of an overhanging gallery running continuously around the court. The high, close-set spindles of the gallery railing is a typical "early Wright" touch; its incongruous use as outdoor trim, however, was duplicated only once, in the "bootlegged" McHarg house. The spandrels of the arched courtyard entranceway are filled with Sullivanesque foliage. But the extraordinary bit of ornament in the design is the open terra-cotta fretwork of the stair-towers: a piece of Gothic tracery.

The scheme of Francisco Terrace is more inventive than rational; yet it was imitated several times. There is a certain nice independence in entering one's flat directly from the outdoors; but the price that is paid is surrender of privacy in the front rooms. Also, the advantages of an inner court, when it is bare and narrow, are dubious. Children race and pound around the wooden gallery, and the court reverberates constantly with their cries. No doubt the secret of the initial success of Francisco Terrace is that it was first inhabited by young childless couples; this is indicated by the fact that it was popularly known as "Honeymoon Court."

Wright undertook five projects for public structures, two of them of immense size, during the seven years of his career now under consideration; none of them was built. These projects were: the Wolf Lake and Cheltenham Beach resorts, the Mozart Gardens, the competition bank design for the magazine "Brickbuilder," and the office building for the American Luxfer Prism Company. Compared with the impressive number of houses which Wright designed before 1900, the public buildings do not bulk large in his total accomplishment; this is a disproportion which continues to characterize his work for

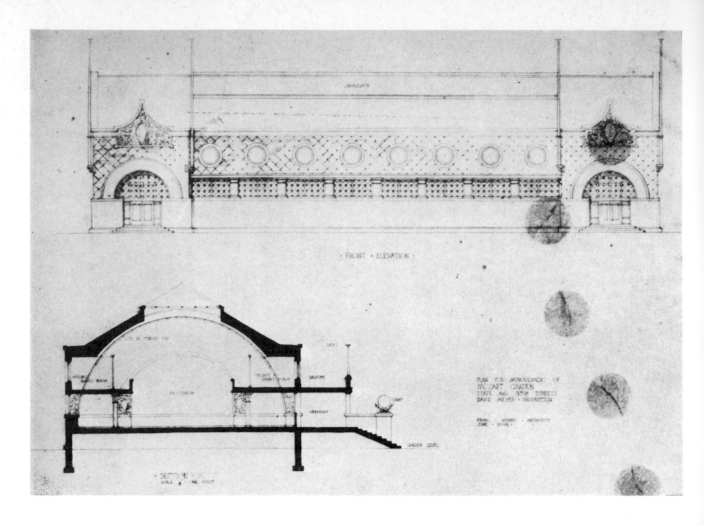

Fig. 62. *Elevation and section for the remodeling of the Mozart Gardens — an early project with strong reminiscence of Sullivan. The five dark circles are due to gummed wafers with which the torn paper is held together.*

many years to come. In the beginning, when the design of a public building came his way his thoughts reverted to the practice in Sullivan's office, where the proportion of domestic to public commissions was just the reverse. He had not yet formulated his own conception of public architecture. The unexecuted design of 1898 for remodeling Mozart Gardens (Fig. 62), a popular road-house on the southern fringe of Chicago much frequented by parties of cyclists, shows great dependence upon Sullivan. The sheltered part of the Gardens was to be a large barrel-vaulted room whose design closely resembled the top floor dining room of the Auditorium Hotel, ornament and all.

The Wolf Lake resort (Fig. 63) was to have been a large public pleasure ground along the shore of a shallow body of water straddling the line between Illinois and Indiana a few miles to the southeast of Chicago. It was then open prairie; it is now a dreary industrial waste. The great bird's-eye perspective of Wright's design (1895) shows an organized complex of buildings arranged upon a semicircular plan, partly extending into the lake, and replete with architectural motifs calculated to induce a carnival feeling. The project was on the grandest scale, and if it had been erected it would have made history in America as the first such establishment conceived as a unit and controlled by a single taste. While the *parti*, so dependent upon the swinging lines of the circle, is a decided anomaly, the parts of the composition are the strangest amalgam of Sullivanesque and Wrightian elements. The various buildings of the semicircular plaza are all linked by a succession of triumphal arches, of which the most conspicuous is the central one, the keystone of the design. It is as though a dozen "Golden Gates" of 1893 had been torn from their context and forced to stand in a sort of giant cromlech along a boardwalk. Then all is interwoven and interpenetrated by a maze of low horizontal planes, mostly structural but partly arbitrary; where roofs are called for, they are the flattened hip of the proto-Prairie House, but they are supported by running arcades. Rising at uniform intervals from this enormous spread of busy architecture are towers — fascinating pylons of abstract geometric shapes, strictly rectilinear and sharply prophetic of that sort of Wrightian architectural sculpture which was to characterize the Midway Gardens of 1914 and the Imperial Hotel in Tokyo. While the Wolf Lake resort is backward-looking in many ways, particularly in the Beaux Arts grandiloquence of its *parti*, it is also a catalogue of rough sketches of things to come.

Fig. 63. The Wolf Lake resort — an impressive design that would have made history if built.

Fig. 64. Perspective of "Cheltenham Beach" — one of the many uncompleted Waller projects.

Cheltenham Beach was a projected development (Fig. 64), similar in spirit to Wolf Lake, for the shore of Lake Michigan at 79th Street, about where the South Shore Country Club now stands. These resorts, before the day of the automobile, were appreciated in ratio to the ease of reaching them, and were often used as weekend retreats. Cheltenham Beach was another of Edward Waller's schemes, and was designed to outclass Manhattan Beach, an existing nearby resort patronized by the humbler residents of Chicago. The great perspective drawing of the design, published in Spencer's article of 1900, carries the names of Cecil Corwin and Hugh Garden as well as Wright's, but the precise degree of their collaboration is not clear. Corwin's contemporary buildings for Rush Medical School in Chicago and Garden's modified traditionalism of the time indicate that these men could not have offered much of value to the pronounced individuality of the design.

The "Village Bank" for "Brickbuilder" was first published in that magazine in August, 1901,[13] but stylistically it belongs in the transitional period. This assumption is confirmed by the set of drawings still on file at Taliesin. While the finished drawings bear the address "1106 Steinway Hall," which is the downtown office that Wright shared with some colleagues for a

Note 13
Frank Lloyd Wright: "A Village Bank," Brickbuilder, Vol. 10, Aug. 1901, pp. 160-161.

few years after 1900, a small pen-rendered perspective of the identical design is labeled "Study for Concrete Monolithic Bank, 1894." The building (Fig. 65) is an uncompromising cube, largely sealed and lighted by two sets of clerestory windows. This, as we have seen, was a favorite device of Wright's for rooms which required uniform light, continuous wall-space, and no view, as in the Bagley and McAfee libraries. The walls of the building are necessarily massive, for it is a monolith of unreinforced concrete. It is almost Egyptian in appearance. Nothing relieves the severity of its form but the single area of decorative richness contained within a rectilinear panel on the facade, generally Sullivanesque in vocabulary. Here, the motif is appropriate, whereas, on a smaller scale, it was too monumental in feeling for the Devin, McAfee, Husser, and other contemporary domestic designs. In its frank expression of inner volume and cubical handling of it, the "Village Bank" leads to those great public designs of the First Golden Age: the Larkin Building and Unity Church. But in the interim, Wright was to learn how to state his instinct for ornament wholly in his own language. It is worth noting that, inasmuch as Sullivan spent many years of his professional life building such small banks as this, Wright's solution of the problem is characteristically rectilinear while Sullivan's is more often the semicircle inscribed within a square. The two men had the same radical approach in that they allowed the function of the small bank, as they saw it, to dictate the *parti;* discarding

Fig. 65. The "Village Bank," a design in unreinforced concrete with a puzzling set of conflicting dates.

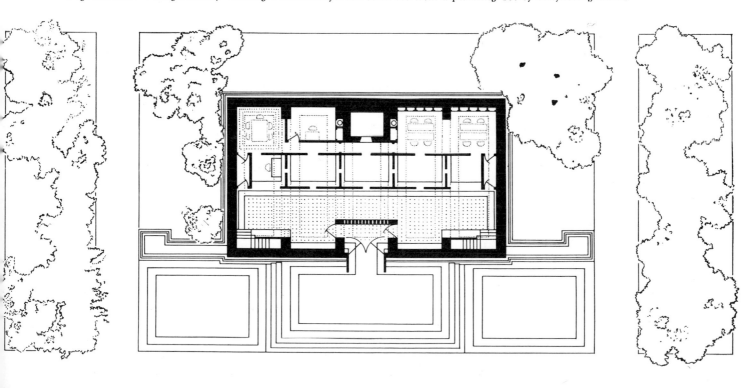

precedent, they relied upon their inner conviction in this, as in all problems.

The date of the projected office building in Chicago for the American Luxfer Prism Company is fixed by a document at Taliesin: 1894. This was just a few months before Wright negotiated a contract with the company to act as their architectural consultant. The company wanted to launch an ambitious program for popularizing their prismatic glass bricks as replacement for ordinary glazing of windows in commercial structures; the idea was that they focused light

Fig. 66. Projected office building for the American Luxfer Prism Company, Chicago. This unsatisfactory half-tone illustration is the best record that remains of a very significant design.

upon the rear areas of a room or store. Their headquarters was to be the ten-story building which Wright designed. Pevsner[14] characterizes the design (Fig. 66), in comparison with the Larkin Building, as an immature Sullivanesque work. This is partially true. The design does lack finesse, and there is obvious dependence upon Sullivan for surface enrichment. Otherwise, it is a simple, direct statement of essentials: a rectangular grid, stressing neither the vertical nor the horizontal (and thus respecting the neutrality of the supporting steel framework within), is filled with forty-eight squares of prismatic glass; the whole is set upon a horizontally disposed basement of ground floor and mezzanine, and enclosed within an uninterrupted envelope of mouldings. It comes surprisingly close to being the glass-fronted box of modern practice; change it a bit in detail and increase it to heroic proportions and it becomes the prototype for, if you will, the United Nations Secretariat in New York. If, on the other hand, we think of the American Luxfer Prism design in terms of Sullivan's accomplishment, we must wait at least four or five years, for the erection of the Gage Building, or, better, the Schlesinger-Mayer Building, to find anything as clean and as prophetic as Wright's essay. As for Wright's own career, that essay will lead to others in the realm of the glass-sheathed skyscraper: St. Mark's-in-the-Bowery, the National Home Life Insurance Building, and, ultimately, to the Price Tower in Bartlesville.

It was the proceeds from the Luxfer contract that, it will be recalled, enabled Wright to carry out some needed alterations and extensions of his own home in Oak Park. In 1895 he added those offices and drafting-rooms along the Chicago Avenue side of the house which were to constitute The Studio proper (Fig. 67); only one interior door connected these new spaces with "the House." The Studio successfully fulfilled two functions: workspace and a discreet form of advertising — for it was an arresting design, and an object of continuing interest to the people of Oak Park and the adjacent suburbs.

Note 14
Nikolaus Pevsner: "Pioneers of Modern Design from William Morris to Walter Gropius," 2nd. ed., Museum of Modern Art, 1949, p. 117.

Fig. 67. The Studio, Oak Park. This addition of a workshop to Wright's house officially inaugurated the "Oak Park Period."

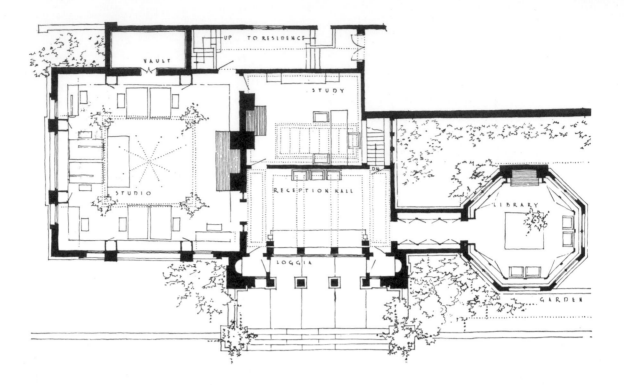

Fig. 68. Above: Plan of The Studio. Below: Entrance, showing the loggia, the octagon of the drafting room, and the pitched roof of The House behind.

The chief elements of the plan of The Studio (Fig. 68) are an anteroom, a drafting-room, a library, and a private office. The library and drafting-room are octagons with clerestory lighting. In spite of the unusual height of one of these rooms, the effect of the building on the outside is uniformly low and horizontal. The roofs are nearly flat, and partly concealed behind parapets; rectangular, jutting cornices take the place of the more customary eaves. So as to harmonize with the older parts of the structure, siding is a mixture of shingles and brick. The most notable features from the street are the polygonal superstructure of the drafting-room and the entrance portal, a handsome unit of brick and ornamental terra-cotta quite similar to the motif of the facade of the "Village Bank," but drastically lowered. This portal (Fig. 69) is an early expression of Wright's belief that access to a building should not be too direct — some complications must introduce the carefully cultivated

spatial experiences that await the visitor inside. In front of The Studio portal is a low brick wall around one end of which one must pass to reach the door. Entrances in many of his buildings lie thus concealed behind a screen or fold of external walls or balustrades. In a sense, such arrangements also play a part in breaking down the old preconception of the inside and outside of a building as two distinct entities. From the moment that we step upon the introductory terrace we are, spiritually, in the building and enjoying its spatial organization.

The plan of The Studio is a long stride toward Wright's ultimate goal of free-flowing interiors. There are few partitions, the various functions being defined by bearing walls, chimneys, and other isolated supports. Once again, however, as in the Bagley house, the library is semi-detached, and reached by a passageway lined with books. Interior trim is heavy, bold, and dark (Fig. 70). Skylights here and there, long, plain rectangular

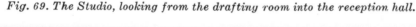

Fig. 69. The Studio, looking from the drafting room into the reception hall.

Fig. 70. Above: Reception hall, looking toward the drafting room. Below: Library of the Studio.

openings, emphasize the main directions of the plan, and are leaded in tight and intricate geometrical patterns. There is really no reminiscence of Sullivan. Whether or not the terra-cotta decorations on the outside of the entrance motif are Sullivanesque is open to debate. The sculpture of the four piers is still too naturalistic for Wright's architectural style. The symbolic male nudes on their pedestals at each side are by Bock, the sculptor of the Heller house friezes, and the artist who is to continue to collaborate with Wright for many years. The comic, bespectacled secretary birds worked into the design of the

Fig. 71. The windmill built for Aunts Nell and Jane and their Hillside Home School, Spring Green, Wisconsin.

piers of The Studio portal are, of course, his. Their presence there is explained by Spencer: "The solemn birds have their meaning to the designer, who in these 'caps' has enjoyed taking a quiet fling at the reactionary spirits who dominate the 'Arts and Crafts Movement.' "

While we are, so to speak, on the subject of family matters, there is something topical to say at this point about the developments of the Hillside Home School back at Spring Green and the expanding establishment which was the lifelong enthusiasm of Wright's maiden aunts. What is to be discussed is the celebrated windmill (Fig. 71) which Wright built for them in 1895, which takes up such an inordinate amount of space in his autobiography, and which was, for reasons never fully understood by the author of this book, referred to as "Romeo and Juliet."[15] The windmill was a very practical mechanism which raised water faithfully for many decades, but it is also a beguiling piece of abstract design whose section closely resembles the modern airfoil. It is a turret sixty feet high, capped by a disc, and containing within it a circular staircase. Fused to the basic octagon of the structure is a diamond-shaped spine upon whose oaken core the metal wheel at the summit is actually mounted. It is the sum of the cylinder and the triangular prism which approximates the basic shape of aeronautics and other fields of engineering concerned with the problem of wind resistance. Originally sheathed in gray shingles, the tower now has a siding of horizontal boards, their joints accented by battens. The successful completion of "Romeo and Juliet" seems to have given its designer a feeling of personal triumph which none of his other accomplishments of the 1890's quite equaled.

Note 15
In a letter about the windmill written, just after its construction, to his aunts Nell and Jane ("An Autobiography," New York, Longmans, Green, 1932, pp. 132-33) Wright speaks of the diamond-shaped spine of the tower as "Romeo," the surrounding octagon as "Juliet." "Romeo, as you will see, will do all the work and Juliet cuddle alongside to support and exalt him . . ."

Fig. 72. River Forest Golf Club, with the octagon added.

The long-since demolished River Forest Golf Club (Fig. 72) of 1898 was the only clubhouse design of the transitional period, but it was the forerunner of several to come. The central feature of the Golf Club was its great octagonal common room,[16] from which wings extended forward and to the sides, turning back upon themselves swastika-like and enclosing two small green courtyards. Very low to the ground, with widely overhanging hip roofs, ribbon fenestration, three broad chimneys in banded masonry, a soft brown monotone with shingle siding, no trace of Sullivanesque elements — these things

Note 16
The club was extensively enlarged in 1901, at which time the octagonal room was added.

add up to a very progressive design which, despite its semi-public function, comes closer in effect to the ideal of the Prairie House than any which had preceded it. The River Forest Golf Club is a clear demonstration, as the old century and his period of minor dependence upon Sullivan ended, of how little Wright had deviated from his precocious, personal vision of architecture first glimpsed in the Charnley and the Winslow houses. We may seriously question whether there had been anything in the interval to alter it other than the influence from Japan.

As if to underwrite this thought, there was a brief period in the months just after the opening of the twentieth century when Wright designed some houses with undisguised Japanese details. They belong neither to the transitional period nor to that which followed; they are sports, in

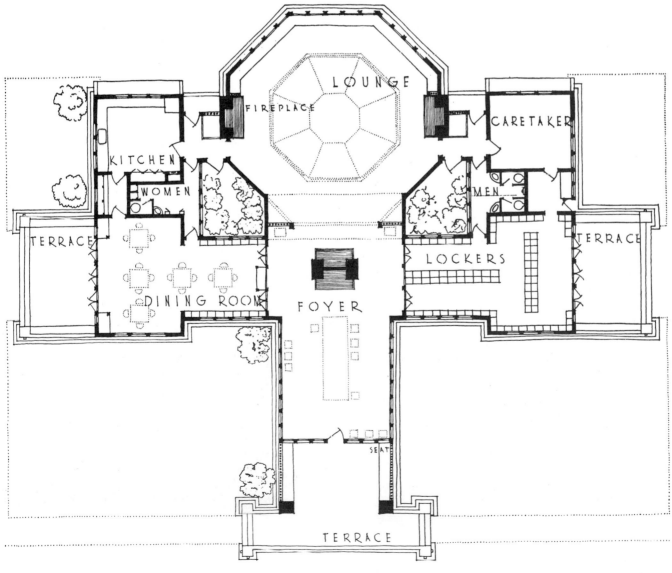

LOUNGE

FIREPLACE

CARETAKER

KITCHEN

WOMEN

MEN

TERRACE

LOCKERS

TERRACE

DINING ROOM

FOYER

SEAT

TERRACE

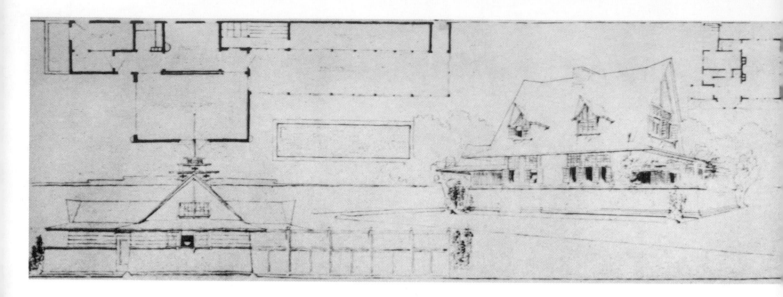

Fig. 73. Above: Plans for the Judge Foster house and barn. Below: A photograph of the Foster house taken a few years ago.

a class by themselves, but very revealing. The major design of the group is the house and barn for Judge Foster (Fig. 73) built in 1900 on a prairie in the remote regions of southwestern Chicago then known as West Pullman. The buildings have Japanese roofs, with rising ridgepoles and flaring eaves, and there is a little wooden *torii* through which one enters the grounds. The Pitkin cottage on an island near Sault Ste. Marie, Michigan, and the Fred Jones boathouse on Lake Delavan, Wisconsin (Fig. 74), complete this short but significant list.

Fig. 74. The Fred Jones boathouse, Wisconsin — the spirit of Yedo on the shores of Lake Delavan.

THE FIRST GOLDEN AGE

1. The Prairie House Unveiled

The period of Wright's career which we now enter, the first decade of the twentieth century, brings to a sudden end those transitional, often reminiscent, and occasionally unproductive qualities in his work. Henceforth, he is supremely sure of himself and of what his destiny calls upon him to do. It is the First Golden Age, the triumph of that new form of domestic architecture toward which he had been concentratedly making his way: the Prairie House.

There was a time when it was fashionable to attack the term, "Prairie House," as arbitrary and meaningless. A critic writing in 1912[1] remarked: ". . . Mr. Wright will pardon us if we do not wholly follow him in what he will not mind our calling his Rhapsodie Prairiale." As late as 1928, yet another, writing for a French magazine,[2] spoke of ". . . l'absurdité et le provincialisme du nom de guerre: 'prairie architec-

ture.'" But the term is here to stay. It has, in fact, a long, well-documented history. Robert Spencer first hinted at it in 1900[3] by the following words: "A younger man, who has scorned this easy and popular route [i.e., the Beaux Arts tradition], swinging easily along amid the beauties of the forests and flower-sown prairies of his own country, has shown a more intelligent grasp of what architecture means today." In 1908, the term was twice approached and explained in print: Thomas Tallmadge, in his pioneer article on the Chicago School of architecture,[4] declared that a strong horizontal treatment in distinction to the vertical was "an absolute result of the inspiration of the prairie"; in the same periodical,[5] editorial comment was made to the effect that "western architects are working in a style

Note 1
Montgomery Schuyler: "An Architectural Pioneer; Review of the Portfolios Containing the Works of Frank Lloyd Wright," Architectural Record, Vol. 31, April 1912, p. 247.
Note 2
Henry-Russell Hitchcock, Jr.: "Frank Lloyd Wright," Cahiers d'Art, Paris, 1928.

Note 3
Robert C. Spencer, Jr.: "The Work of Frank Lloyd Wright," Architectural Review (Boston), Vol. 7, June 1900, pp. 61-72.
Note 4
Thomas E. Tallmadge: "The 'Chicago School,'" Architectural Review (Boston), Vol. 15, April 1908, pp. 69-74.
Note 5
"Publisher's Department," Architectural Review (Boston), Vol. 15, April 1908.

that they consider appropriate and inspired by the broad stretches of the western prairies, where all the horizontal lines are often strongly and unduly accented." Later, Lewis Mumford[6] drew the obvious conclusion: "Mr. Wright's low-lying houses with their flat roofs which seem about to dissolve into the landscape are an expression of the prairie; it is no accident that these forms have been so readily appreciated in The Netherlands and on the plains of Prussia."

The most convincing evidence that Wright and his pupils of the Oak Park days constantly had in mind the ecology of the region in which they were working is afforded by the close cooperation which they sought with certain Chicago landscape gardeners who were spreading the doctrine of letting the modest beauty of the prairie speak for itself: Jens Jensen, Walter Burley Griffin,[7] Wilhelm Miller and others. In a resumé of what had been accomplished in prairie gardening up to 1915, Miller wrote:[8] "The Middle West is just beginning to evolve a new style of architecture, interior decoration, and landscape gardening in an effort to create the perfect home amid the prairie states. The movement is founded on the fact that one of the greatest assets which any country or natural part of it can have is a strong national or regional character." He then proceeds to analyze one of Wright's designs as a successful "prairie house"; it is consciously harmonized with its setting by its low lines, its brown siding and green roof, and the forest trees, carefully preserved, are allowed to brush against the walls and eaves.

Note 6
Lewis Mumford: "The Social Background of Frank Lloyd Wright," from "The Life Work of the American Architect, Frank Lloyd Wright," Mees, Santpoort (Holland), 1925 (published as seven numbers of "Wendingen").
Note 7
Griffin is better known as an architect, town-planner, and ex-pupil of Wright's; his greatest single work was the plan of Canberra, the Australian Federal Capital.
Note 8
Wilhelm Miller: "The Prairie Spirit in Landscape Gardening," University of Illinois Press, Urbana, 1915.

In January, 1900, Wright faced the new century with optimism and a sense of high purpose. Activities at The Studio in Oak Park were in top gear, and the "front office" downtown was now a suite of rooms in Dwight Perkins' Steinway Hall, where an informal clubhouse of progressive architects had come into being. Here were the offices of Perkins, Robert Spencer, Myron and Jarvis Hunt, George Dean, Hugh Garden, and Webster Tomlinson. They were all members of the Chicago School, each in his own way determined to do something "new"; the atmosphere of Steinway Hall must have been extraordinarily stimulating. With Tomlinson, Wright was shortly to enter a one-year partnership, the only one of his career. But although he took part in the give-and-take of this group, Wright was never really one with it. Perhaps the fact that, unlike the others, the true center of his operations was elsewhere gave to his appearances in Steinway Hall the quality of merely visiting; in any case, albeit he kept an office there until 1908, he imperceptibly withdrew from the group after his experience with Tomlinson came to an end in 1902.

The Studio, as the aftermath of the panic of 1893, had felt a decided lull in its activities during the last four years of the old century; but there was magic in the coming of the new to which everything in the creative world responded — at once, in 1900, commissions began pouring in to The Studio. Wright's prosperity grew for a while to outstanding proportions, even though it took increasing bravery, in an era when well-bred eclecticism in arts and manners was sharply on the rise, to place one's self in his hands as a prospective client. No doubt those who observed him were affected by Wright's abounding confidence in his ability to transfer his new doctrine of architecture into physical material. He said so, openly, in public addresses: the much-quoted Hull House lecture of 1901, "The Art and Craft of the Machine," in which he spoke in behalf of technology as an indispensable partner in the evolution of new architectural attitudes; and the less well-known paper entitled "The Architect"[9] which he read before the second annual convention of the

Note 9
See Construction News (Chicago), Vol. 10, June 16 and 23, 1900.

Architectural League of America at Chicago in June, 1900, in which he sounded a call to architects to bring forth a new architecture for a new land and new materials, to avoid commercialism and "archaeological dry bones bleaching in the sun." Of course, he was not entirely alone. Other disciples of Louis Sullivan were rallying to the battle cries of "Form Follows Function" and "Progress before Precedent,"[10] as the published articles by George Dean and Elmer Grey[11] attest. But these were words. The series of wholly radical buildings that flowed from Wright's drafting pencil was the best proof that there was something more in the air than slogans.

In the welter of commissions which filled The Studio from the beginning of 1900, the actual debut of the Prairie House is difficult to determine. The Willits house in Highland Park has a certain claim to the honor, but one that is hard to substantiate[12] since it is based upon personal recollections. There can be no argument, however, about the date of the two model houses which Wright drew up sometime in 1900 for the Curtis Publishing Company of Philadelphia, and which received nationwide publicity in the Ladies' Home Journal in February and July, respectively, of 1901. In these designs, Wright officially unveiled the Prairie House, and the title of the first of the two presentations was "A Home in a Prairie Town."

The sudden linkage at this moment of Frank Lloyd Wright of Oak Park, Illinois, with a publishing house in Philadelphia is sufficiently unexpected. It was due to the interest in the field of small house design actively taken for a few years around the turn of the century by Edward Bok, then head of the Curtis Publishing Co. After some travel in the Middle West which convinced him of the low level of taste in American housing, Bok decided to use his publications as a medium for acquainting the American public with the possibilities of better design. His scheme was to buy designs from representative American architects and then to resell them to his readers (complete working drawings) for five dollars a set. While he did not propose to dictate to his architects, he had a few rules which had to be observed, among them the stipulation that the "parlor" be replaced by a "living room" (a new phrase then) and that servants' bedrooms be increased in floor-area and have cross-ventilation. Bok found the strongest opposition to his scheme on the part of the architects themselves; most of those with whom he put himself in touch refused to participate. Nevertheless, he launched his campaign in 1900 in the Ladies' Home Journal, and Wright, who eagerly accepted the opportunity and saw no loss of dignity therein, was among the first to submit designs.[13]

His Ladies' Home Journal designs are full-fledged Prairie Houses (Fig. 75), and have all the characteristics which we have learned to expect except for the absence of Wrightian leadings in the casements (cost, in this case, was an object); it is interesting to speculate upon their impact on readers conditioned for so long to think of model houses in terms of the traditional styles. Wright's two houses were scaled to a definite price, and an itemized budget was included with each design. The first was to cost seven thousand dollars, the second somewhat less.

There is not a single remaining trace of Louis Sullivan in either design, outside or in.

The plan of the first is loose and flowing, with interior partitions reduced to a minimum and replaced, where possible, by head-high screens that merely serve to indicate without

Note 10
See Robert C. Spencer, Jr.: "The Chicago School of Architecture," paper read before Illinois Society of Architects, Nov. 28, 1939.
Note 11
(a) George R. Dean: "A New Movement in Architecture," Brush & Pencil, Vol. 5, March 1900.
(b) Elmer Grey: " 'Indigenous and Inventive' Architecture for America," Inland Architect, Vol. 35, June 1900, pp. 36-37 (reprint of paper read before the second annual convention of the Architectural League of America, Chicago, June 1900).
Note 12
Mr. Willits told the author unequivocally in 1939 that there had been "a couple of years' delay" between the design of his house and its construction.

Note 13
The author is indebted to Miss Jessie Poesch of Winterthur, Wilmington, Del., for this précis of Edward Bok's campaign.

Fig. 75. Wright's first design for the Ladies Home Journal. A Prairie House priced at $7,000 but never put to the test. The second-floor plan shown on the facing page is with the two bedrooms over the living room; the cutaway perspective shows the scheme with the extra bedrooms removed and replaced by the balcony across the fireplace end.

compartmentalization the direction of circulation and the nature of use. On the ground floor, it results in the concept of a single space for common use and enjoyment — a space embracing the functions of living room, dining room, and library. Although there is an alternate sketch which substitutes in its place a pair of bedrooms, the preferred plan shows a balcony over part of the unified living area, serving to enrich and subdivide space without sharply containing it. Wright explains the balcony in the accompanying text: "In a house of this character, the upper reach and gallery of the central living-room is decidedly a luxury. Two bedrooms may take its place . . . The gallery feature is nevertheless a temptation because of the happy sense of variety and depth it lends to the composition of the interior."

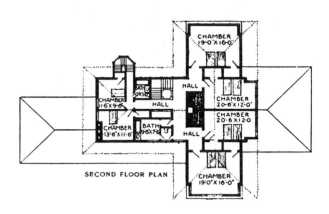

SECOND FLOOR PLAN

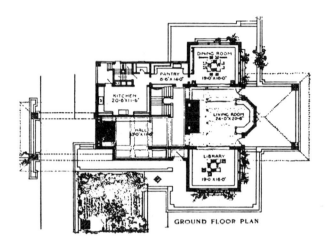

GROUND FLOOR PLAN

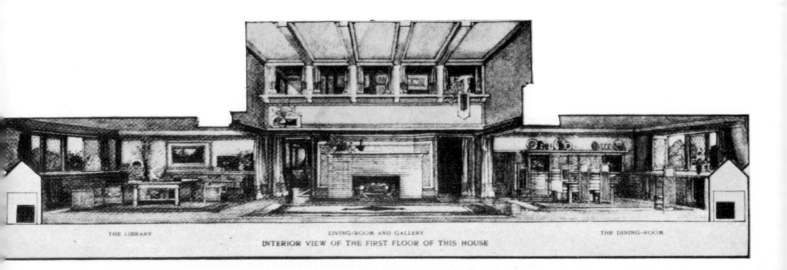

THE LIBRARY LIVING-ROOM AND GALLERY THE DINING-ROOM
INTERIOR VIEW OF THE FIRST FLOOR OF THIS HOUSE

The second design, which was called "A Small House with 'Lots of Room in It'" (Fig. 76), was for a building costing fifty-eight hundred dollars. Its effect outside depends upon a complexity of low gables instead of the more customary hips. This predilection for gables in Prairie Houses, which had been noticeable in Wright's transitional work, will continue sporadically to mark their design until 1906, when it dies out. Wright explains it as follows, quoting again from the text of the Ladies' Home Journal articles: "The average home-maker is partial to the gable roof . . . The gables in this design are slightly modeled, making the outlines 'crisp.'" Of the general *parti* he says: "The plan disregards somewhat the economical limit in compact planning to take advantage of light and air and prospect, the enjoyable things one goes to the suburbs to secure . . . The dining-room is so coupled with the living-room that one leads naturally into the other without destroying the privacy of either."

These two original and revolutionary Prairie Houses, accorded the widest publicity then pos-

sible among American homeowners, had no immediate effect in the nation at large. They may have motivated some prospective clients in the Chicago area, but, with one exception, the Sutton house at McCook, Nebraska, no commissions came to The Studio as a direct result of the publication of the model houses. Generally, the American public was too convinced by the various eclectic styles in vogue; furthermore, it was about to embark upon its period of enthusiasm for the so-called "Mission house" and "California bungalow," both of which passed for contemporary architecture and successfully clouded the issue of a genuine, indigenous domestic style. For the period which this book covers, the circumference of Wright's activity was virtually limited to "Chicagoland" and Buffalo.

The Ladies' Home Journal designs are Prairie Houses that have come down to us only on paper. If we discount the Willits house claim to primacy, the first Prairie Houses to be erected were those in Kankakee, Illinois, for Harley Bradley and his brother-in-law Warren Hickox, in 1900

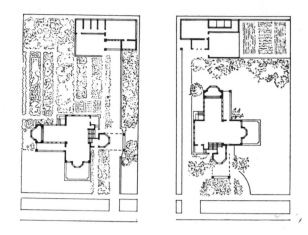

Fig. 76. "A Small House with 'Lots of Room in It' "
— priced at $5800. Wright's second design for the
Ladies Home Journal.

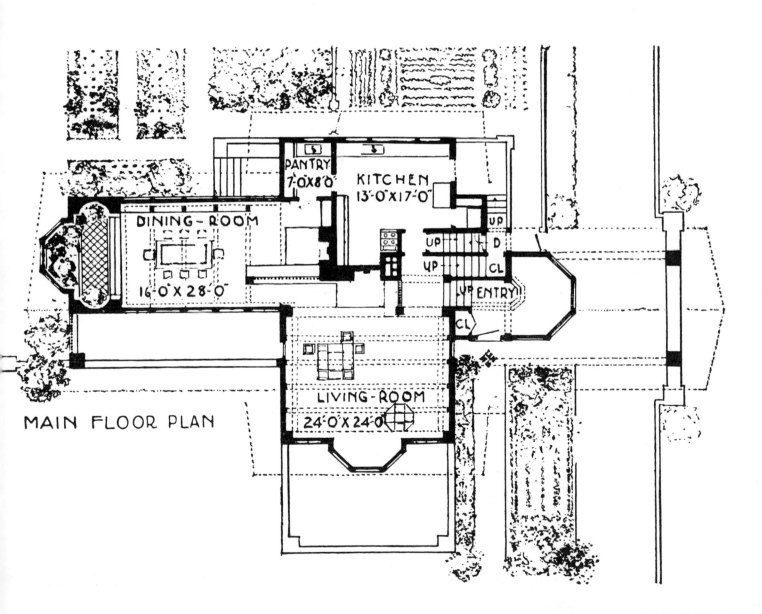

PANTRY
7'-0"X 8'-0"

KITCHEN
13'-0"X 17'-0"

DINING-ROOM

16'-0"X 28'-0"

UP

UP   D

UP   CL

UP ENTRY

CL

LIVING-ROOM
24'-0"X 24'-0"

MAIN FLOOR PLAN

(Fig. 77). These houses, featuring low, broad gables with "crisp" edges, are similar in external appearance to the "Small House with 'Lots of Room in It,'" and probably preceded it in inception. They were both (but especially the Bradley house) more tailormade in details and fittings than the budgeted model houses. Following in quick succession upon the Kankakee buildings comes a host of completed Prairie Houses — the Willits, Wallis, Fricke, Henderson, Daven- port, Thomas, Dana, Heurtley, W. E. Martin, Little, Beachey and Walser houses, to mention only a characteristic sampling — all finished by 1904. Sharing the broad principles upon which the mature Prairie House is based — the flowing plan, the directional or centrifugal lines, the generous, low roofs with pronounced overhang, the broad chimneys, the reduced floor-heights, the suppression of sills, the ribbons of case- ments, the geometrical ornamentation, the inti-

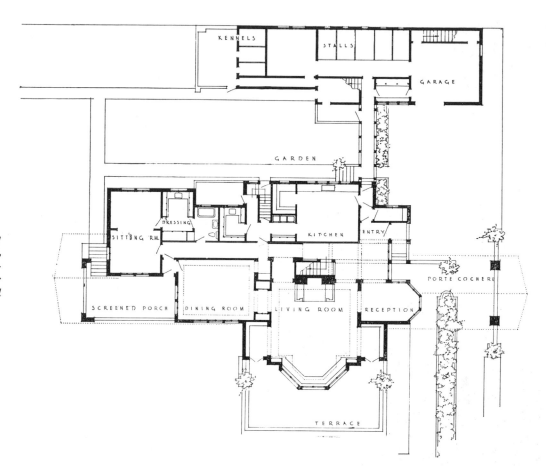

Fig. 77 A. The Harley Bradley house, Kankakee, Illinois. This, the Hickox house, and the Willits house are contenders for the title of First Erected Prairie House.

Fig. 77 B. The Warren Hickox house, Kankakee, Illinois.

mate liaison of house and site — they also fall
within secondary classifications. Some are gable-
roofed, at first thin-edged, later more massive,
as in the Dana and Beachey houses; others are
hip-roofed, the more customary procedure. The
Heurtley and Thomas[14] houses continue in their
raised basements the principle first enunciated
in the transitional McAfee and Husser designs;
the others have the usual relationship between
grade level and first floor. The Willits house

Note 14
*Sometimes referred to as the "Rogers"
house; the house was built for James Rogers,
but upon completion it was presented by him
to his daughter and son-in-law, Mr. and
Mrs. Frank Thomas; Mr. Thomas knew be-
forehand that he and his wife were to occupy it and took an active interest in its
construction.*

(Fig. 78) established the precedent for Prairie Houses with symmetrical wings. There might likewise be a classification by materials. The evidence that Wright preferred to work in solid masonry is persuasive; whenever the client could afford to give him *carte blanche,* he thought in terms of brick and stone, but he had, more often, to work out his ideas in wood and stucco. These things are all, however, variations on a single theme.

The reception accorded the unveiled Prairie House was scarcely different, on the part of the general public, than was that given the houses of 1893 and 1894. The following commentary inspired in a writer in 1905 by his first acquaintance with a Prairie House is characteristic:[15] "One summer I spent some little while in Oak Park, Chicago, and daily passed the Rogers [i.e., Thomas] residence by Mr. Wright. The neighbors called it 'The Harem,' and it does have a sort of seraglioic appearance, quite Oriental in its high encompassing blank walls . . . That sort of thing is simply exotic." This man failed to

Note 15
F. W. Fitzpatrick: "Chicago," Inland Architect & News Record, Vol. 45, June 1905, p. 47.

Fig. 78 A. Plan for the Ward Willits house, Highland Park, Illinois.

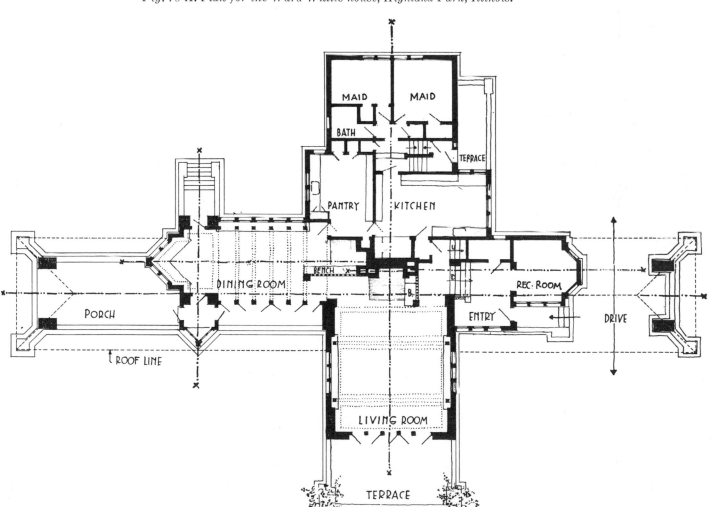

Fig. 78 B. The Ward Willits house.

raise his eyes enough to take in the extraordinary openness of the house (Fig. 79), with its terraces and sparkling casements, above the basement walls. This kind of half-arrived adverse criticism lay at the bottom of much of the misunderstanding of what Wright was trying, in these houses, to do. The public damned him out of hand. When, at length, Wright's personal life took dramatically unconventional and tragic turns, it was somehow felt that both the architect and his misguided clients were justly tarred by the same scandals.

Many of those clients, nevertheless, had the complete faith in Wright — and sometimes the means — to entrust him with all the furnishings of the house, including carpets, draperies, lighting fixtures, bric-a-brac, upholstered and case furniture, etc. Notable examples of this wholesale reliance upon Wright, prior to 1905, are the Bradley and Dana houses. Indeed, such a trust in his taste was highly advisable against the prevailing background of fumed oak, cutglass, encrusted wallpapers, and *kaiserzinn*. Wright always hoped for the best, but he was

Fig. 79. The Thomas house, Oak Park, Illinois, sometimes known as the Rogers house, and known to the neighbors as "The Harem."

relieved when his clients gave him at least partial supervision of the decorations. "As for the objects of art in the house — even in that early day they were 'bêtes noires' of the new simplicity . . . Better to design all as integral features . . . I tried to make my clients see that furniture and furnishings not built in as integral features of the building should be designed as attributes of whatever furniture *was* built in." It required not only a wealthy but a tractable client to accept so fixed a scheme of decoration to which he could hardly add a single item of his own selection; but, if he were willing, it worked for his ultimate protection. Except for "Mission" pieces and those bulky examples of oak-joinery produced by Elbert Hubbard's Roycrofters, there was nothing to be bought that even approximated the lines of Wright's new architecture. Wright despised Mission furniture; even so, he occasionally had to recommend

it for want of anything better. When he exercised no supervision whatever over the decorations of a Prairie House, the results were disastrous: ". . . when the building itself was finished, the old furniture they already possessed usually went in with the clients. Very few of these houses were anything but painful to me after the clients moved in and, helplessly, dragged the horrors of the Old Order along after them." Thomas Tallmadge, who had witnessed such scenes, went so far as to accredit part of the eventual stalemate of the whole Chicago School to obstacles experienced by owners trying to furnish houses of the new order.[16]

Wright's first chance to design fittings for one

Note 16
Thomas E. Tallmadge: "The Story of Architecture in America," Norton, New York, 1936, pp. 228-233.

Fig. 80 A. The living room of the Willits house is strongly impressed with Wright's personality.

Fig. 80 B. Above: Wright designs in solid oak for the Bradley house, bringing to the heaviness of the times a vigorously fresh flavor. Facing page: Dining room of R. W. Evans house, Chicago. Wright's incisive geometric patterns are very evident here.

of his houses came with the Warren McArthur commission of 1892, and his ideas on the subject were even then so crystallized that they very accurately forecast the sort of furnishing which he carried out, when possible, for the Prairie House. His deep respect for the nature of wood, glass and textiles caused him always to strive for "functional" handling of designs for the applied arts; it often resulted, none the less, in a mannerism because his personal, curiously geometric vision of form got in the way (Fig. 80). His case-pieces of the Prairie House days are complex, and were probably uncomfortable; but they are never made to assume shapes unnatural to wood. In designing dining room furniture, his

constant aim was that chairs, table and lighting-fixtures should make a compact unit, but, no matter how reasoned the aim, such units were frequently cumbersome and did not lend themselves to flexibility in seating varying numbers of people. Sideboards and buffets were miniatures in cabinetwork of the house elevations, obeying the same principles of horizontality and crisp definition of planes; so as to achieve a trim, uninterrupted base for the greater elaborations above, drawer-fronts were made without rabbets, mouldings or handles, just as they so often are today, albeit for different reasons. Wright usually sidestepped the problem of designing fully-upholstered furniture by relying upon

padded benches, window seats, and settles with scatter-cushions to provide an element of comfort. Plain wall-surfaces and simple fabrics, serving as background for the studied placement of objects of burnished copper or plaques of metallic tesserae, unified the whole restrained effect. The charge is often heard that Prairie House interiors were gloomy and cavernous despite the long rows of casements that took the place of wall over half the room's perimeter. It is true; but it was not due to the overhang of the eaves, whose soffits were usually distempered a creamy white, but rather to a pervading brownness of tone which was the one characteristic which the Prairie House shared with any average American dwelling of the early twentieth century. All the same, a carefully designed and furnished Prairie House interior was aesthetically excellent, sometimes beautiful, and extraor-

dinarily in advance of anything that could then be called "contemporary."

In all truth, Wright, despite the power and originality of his ideas about the role of the minor arts in his houses, could not stand alone in executing them. The debt which he owed to clever craftsmen who, to their eternal credit, understood in those unsubtle days of house-furnishing what he was driving toward must be acknowledged. Chief of these, perhaps, was the Milwaukee cabinetmaker and decorator, George Niedecken. Wright relied upon Niedecken through the entire Oak Park Period and well past it for the actual fabrication of everything that went into the custom-built Prairie House or club or public building. In the sense that what they contributed became physically integrated with the architecture, certain glassmakers, too, were of immense importance to Wright's early

Fig. 80 C. The padded cushions on the straight-line chairs flanking the fireplace in the Heath house, Buffalo, soften the lines of the chair for the sitter. The lettering of mottoes over fireplaces and elsewhere is characteristic of both Wright and the times.

Fig. 81. Above: The old Lawrence house as the Dana house begins to rise around it. Below: The completed Dana house.

Fig. 82 A. The Dana house, Springfield, Illinois —a showplace and a focus of civic pride.

success. The leaded casements and interior doors, without which Wright's structures of the time would have had a blank, unfinished look, were usually the work of Orlando Giannini of the firm of Giannini and Hilgart — more rarely, of the Linden Glass Company. It is no exaggeration to say that Giannini was indispensable to Wright in bringing to completion his famous, personal vision of architecture.

The Dana house (or, sometimes, the "Law-rence house," after Mrs. Dana's family) at Springfield, Illinois, was Wright's most extravagant commission to its date, and, like the slightly later Darwin Martin house at Buffalo, was an architect's dream-opportunity. It was completed in July, 1904, after a two-year building-campaign. The Lawrences had been pioneers in the settlement of central Illinois, but by the twentieth century they were off the land, living in affluence at the State capital. Only "Mother

Lawrence," kindly remembered in "An Auto-biography" for her home-made blackberry jam and salt-risen bread, retained the simple tastes of pioneer days. Her daughter, Susan Dana, was a woman of ambition and far wider outlook. She came to Wright to place the commission for a new house at Springfield which would be not merely a residence but a family memorial and a setting for the suitable discharge of her obligations as a social leader of the community. The house was to be built on the site of the old Lawrence residence and to incorporate it as a sort of shrine. Actually, in the enthusiasm of working out the design, client and architect whittled away at the old house until only a sentimental vestige of it remained at the core of the new establishment. A rare photograph of the Dana house in the early stages of construction (Fig. 81) shows Mother Lawrence's house being engulfed by the rising walls of her daughter's.

Fig. 82 B. Above: Entrance to the Dana house. Facing page: Dining room with painted frieze.

The Dana house (Fig. 82) is roofed with gables — low, broad, thick, modeled, and elaborately flashed with copper. Its plan is a rough letter T, the long arm being extended by a pergola to a detached building containing a gallery for objects of art and exhibitions. Part of the house is designed on the raised-basement principle. At the entrance, a broad flight of low steps leads from the vestibule at grade level to the series of principal rooms above, each flowing into the other with minor variations of level, creating vistas of impressive length. The visitor is conscious of space that invites but cannot be exactly defined. Everything within and without the building is obedient to a prevailing autumnal tonality. Inside — tawny oak complemented by fabrics of gold, brown, and russet. Outside — Roman brickwork of warm buff, topped by a band of bronze-lustered tiles in which the leaded casements are set. There is the bright verdigris of many weathered bronze and copper adjuncts, and the glint of prisms of colored glass. The long, straight parapets and balconies are equipped with earthpockets and flattened urns

from which vines trail and soften the hard edges of precision masonry. The total effect of the building is one of great mass in movement, ponderous structural forms flowing slowly over the level ground, yet a mass whose profiles have knife-like sharpness and definition.

In its heyday, the Dana house was Springfield's showplace, though one which, we can safely assume, was more wondered at than understood. Wright lavished upon it every facet of his creative skill, collaborating with his favorite craftsmen. Richard Bock and the Linden Glass Company contributed pottery, tilework, and the intricate leadings of the casements, in which prairie flora, such as sumac, were used as the inspiration for abstract design. Bock made the fountain and the semi-stylized statuette of the vestibule, "The Flower in the Crannied Wall." Not only decorative accessories, but furniture, fixtures, carpet and hangings were custom-made to Wright's specifications (Figs. 82 B and 82 C).

In contrast to the Dana house, the Arthur Heurtley house, erected in Oak Park in 1902, has an almost classic unity and directness (Fig.

Fig. 82 C. Below: Breakfast alcove in the Dana house, showing the straightback chairs and leaded casements. Facing page: Leaded French doors flanked by Wright draperies.

Fig. 82 D. Gallery in the Dana house — an element of spatial luxury in a luxurious Prairie House.

83). It is often considered the gem of the early Prairie Houses, and makes, for several reasons, the third milestone of progress in the development of Wright's domestic architecture; we think of the Charnley, Winslow, and Heurtley houses as the great triumvirate, each so clearly stating in relation to the other the steps by which that architecture reached maturity. When, later, we add to the list the fourth item, one of the terminal masterpieces like the Coonley or Robie houses, the story of the Prairie House is essentially complete.

Like the two predecessors named above, the Heurtley house is a simple rectangle in front elevation with no wings or major projections.

Its studied horizontality differs from the Winslow house only in degrees of subtlety; in plasticity, relation to site, openness to atmosphere and assimilation of Japanese precedent, it goes far beyond the Winslow house and immeasurably beyond the Charnley house; yet all three are unmistakable examples of the personalized geometry of Wrightian design, the constant recall of the wonder of those maple cubes and prisms and spheres of the "gifts." The *parti* of the Heurtley house is that of the raised basement, with all principal rooms on the second level above grade; there is no third floor. This is a scheme which, as has been mentioned, is in beautiful harmony with the objectives of the Prairie House. From elevated living spaces through rows of casements, the occupants look out over the landscape with that sense, so agreeable in a flat country, of having a vantage-point; yet the distinction in levels is so manipulated, in accord with the other principles of the Prairie House, that intimacy with the site is enhanced. Inside such a house (Fig. 84), the ceilings of the main living spaces and the undersides of the roof are the same, permitting incorporation of overhead structural planes as part of the spatial and decorative ensemble; inside such spaces, one is always aware of the great sheltering roof above.

Within the strict confines of its rectangular plan (Fig. 84), the arrangement of rooms in the Heurtley house is such as to sacrifice nothing of the dynamic, flowing quality that we associate with the Prairie House — it is just condensed. Only two elements are allowed to extend beyond the envelope: the diamond-shaped bay at the north side, with its oriel above; and the advancing entrance terrace with its low parapet and urns partly screening, and forming an introduction to, the arched portal. The red brick walls are laid in alternately projecting bands, grace-notes to the all-pervading horizontality interrupted only by the arch of the door. The great hip roof adapts itself without effort to the span of the house beneath, and, at its apex, the broad pylon of the chimney reflects the general

Fig. 83. The Arthur Heurtley house, Oak Park, Illinois — the Prairie House classically self-contained.

Fig. 84. Plan of the Heurtley house and its living room, whose design takes its cue from the great roof above.

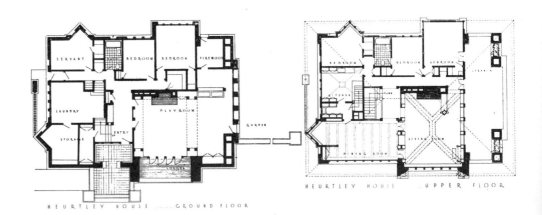

HEURTLEY HOUSE ...... GROUND FLOOR

HEURTLEY HOUSE ... UPPER FLOOR

mass. The balance of the design is occult, with buttresses to the right offsetting the door and terrace to the left of center. And from the shadowed area beneath the eaves comes the expected brilliant glitter of variegated bits of glass worked into the geometric leadings of the casements.

The endless adaptability of the Prairie House formula was perhaps its greatest miracle. It could be simple or complex in plan; it could follow the standard relation of house to grade, or it could substitute the raised basement; it could have one story or two or more; it could be made to serve the requirements of a palace or a cottage; it could be built of durable masonry or of light frame, it could be sided in stone, brick, stucco, or brown shingle; it could be set in manicured lawns — it was equally at home in the wild forest or on the dunes. And in the period of Wright's career which we are discussing, every

4. 85. The Charles Ross house, Delavan, Wisconsin, is a Prairie House in the simplest materials to express the simple summer life.

one of these conditions, singly or in combination, was fulfilled by the Prairie House. It was to be found not only in Chicago's suburbia, or the small towns of the prairie states, but in cities, and in the northwoods of Wisconsin and Michigan (Figs. 85 and 86), and all around the edges of the Great Lakes.

The second group of buildings for Hillside Home School at Spring Green, built by Wright in 1902 (Fig. 87), while not a domestic commission in the strict sense, was designed within the Prairie House formula, and further illustrates its elasticity. The original school buildings of Silsbee's — and, possibly, Wright's — had, by this year, been altered beyond recognition and become outgrown. A new, up-to-date plant was necessary, and the Misses Nell and Jane Lloyd-Jones turned, this time without any hesitation, to their nephew with the commission. This was

to be Wright's first major construction on the family land, the precursor of Taliesin North and, in some respects, its prototype. Characteristically, in keeping with his reverence for the place, Wright decided that Hillside School II should be made of the local sandstone, in rough ashlar. Consequently, he aimed at more rugged effects than he had attempted hitherto. It was not to be any spurious rusticity, but a real communion of structure and site in the oft-told Lloyd-Jones spirit of forthrightness and hard work. Another factor which he carefully included in his calculations was the fact that the Wisconsin River valley, with its bluffs and ravines, has a certain simple majesty of landscape that is more insistent than the quiet prairies of Illinois, and that a building must not only reflect but actually compete with it. Hence, the lines of Hillside School are very primal and strong.

Fig. 86. The summer cottage for Walter S. Gerts is a Prairie House reduced to an incident in the Michigan forests.

Fig. 87. Part of the second group of buildings built for Hillside Home School, Spring Green.

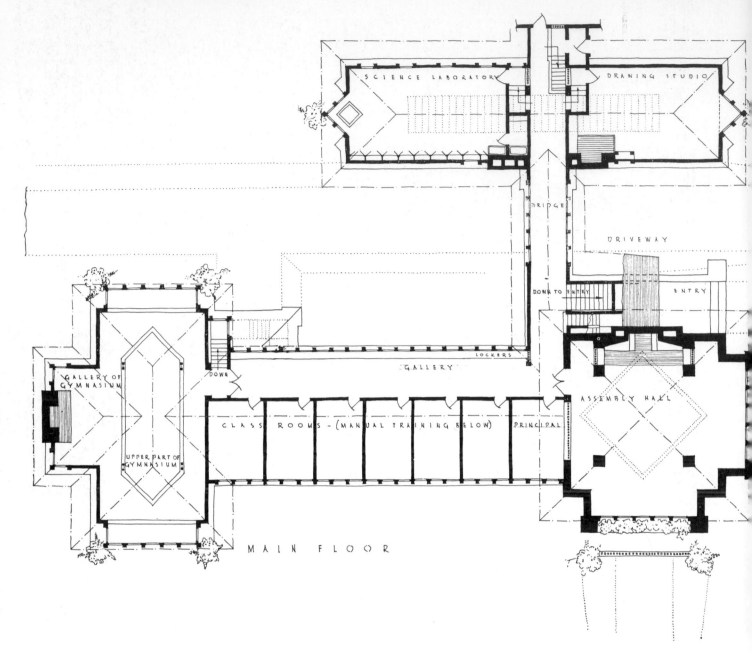

Fig. 88 A. Hillside Home School II.

The plan of Hillside School II is complicated, but it is ordered in accordance with Wright's concept of its function. It is very similar in this way to the later Taliesin complex, which is such a miracle of suitability. The School buildings spread out over the rolling ground with many re-entrant angles, incidents, and breaks in profile and floor-level, their flattened hip roofs following without any sharp discontinuity the rich variation in volumes which they cover. The pre-vailing Prairie House horizontality is dramatized by Prairie House chimneys and the gleam of grouped and slotted casements. But we know it is not a Prairie House because its main feature is a series of tall, cross-shaped pavilions with two-story bays that read at once as class or assembly rooms, and the semi-public nature of the buildings is revealed. The application of the dynamic, free-flowing Prairie House plan to the functions of a school was a revolutionary

thing, looking forward to today's pinwheel and fragmentized solutions of the same problem.

With the unveiling of the Prairie House formula, Wright's personal concept of architecture was fully defined and ready for judgment. By 1905 he was no longer the "former Madison boy" who had entered and won the competition for the Municipal Boathouse on Lake Mendota, but a man of mark in the Chicago architectural world. Against the resistance of the ridicule and reactionary-ism of the Phillistines, his initial success had been remarkable; but, looking at it from the professional point of view, that success might have been more enduring had it been less brilliant. By its very brilliance, it alienated those Chicago colleagues who understood, at least partly, what his architecture meant, and who might have rallied to his support when, after the first scandal, he returned from Europe in 1911.

The catalogues of the Chicago Architectural

Fig. 88 B. The library in the old Hillside School.

Club's annual exhibits[17] have a significant story to tell. In the last years of the old century, Wright had been a modest exhibitor, usually under the aegis of the American Luxfer Prism Company; but he stepped into the spotlight, with eleven exhibits under his own name, in the show of 1900. Every one of his entries was illustrated in the pages of the slim catalogue, which could thus favor only the smallest minority of the exhibitors. In the catalogue for the show of 1901, Wright enjoyed a prominence of a different but equally effective kind: he had entered none of his current work, but the entire transcript of his Hull House lecture, "The Art and Craft of the Machine," was printed. At this juncture, it seemed that his colleagues, especially those in the Steinway Hall "club" and other young followers of Louis Sullivan, were eager to cheer on the disciple with the facile pen and the gifted tongue and the impressive list of completed buildings. Yet, in spite of all this, Wright never became a member of the Architectural Club. Was it due to the same diffidence that made him draw away from the gatherings in Steinway Hall — or was it a sort of lingering wariness on the part of the Club itself?

In 1902, a contretemps occurred. Perhaps because Wright's most confessed admirer, Robert Spencer, was on the Hanging Committee for the Club's exhibition that year, twelve of Wright's designs were selected and arranged in a special, centrally-located alcove of head-high partitions built and supplied by The Studio at Oak Park; and by far the greater part of the catalogue, never a bulky affair, was given over to what amounted to a monograph on Wright's career. It was an unwise move on somebody's part, and it was too much. The Club members themselves did not go on record with their opinions of the exhibit of 1902, but the eloquent fact remains that Wright did not participate again until 1907. An anonymous voice was allowed to speak for the architectural fraternity of the city. The critic who wrote for The American Architect as their Chicago correspondent, who had unstintedly praised Wright's more modest display in

1900, had this to say concerning the exhibit of 1902:[18]

"Collected under the banner of Mr. Frank L. Wright, doubtless, most of the designs bearing his hallmark, one of the smaller galleries is given up entirely to his exhibit. From the standpoint of professional ethics, it seems questionable whether such a pronounced personal exhibit should have its place in a general architectural exhibition, as it certainly smacks of advertising more than anything else. Having selected one of the small rooms, with a door for entrance and one for exit directly opposite each other, a low partition is run across from one door to the other, forming a distinct room. The color-scheme of this small division is very charming. Warm light browns and grays are combined, the walls being some brownish burlap banded with strips of some soft-finished wood. The exhibited designs on the walls are all framed to harmonize with the general color-scheme. Brown leather covers stretch across desks and tables, on which dull copper vases hold effective bunches of gray milkweed pods, brown grasses, teazles, etc. Tall copper and bronze vases in the style of 'L'Art Nouveau'[19] hold slender brown seed-cups of some last year's plants; bits of colored and leaded glass, a marble font of good design, a bronze figure, chairs and tables from Mr. Wright's own house, all have a place in this room. This is all very well as far as it goes, and it certainly is *pretty*, almost 'too pretty,' as Mr. Raffaeli has put it, for such a place as this. Why in an architectural exhibit, the chief one for the year, why should Mr. Wright's tables and chairs, and his teazles and milkweeds and pine-branches cover so much space? When one sees the seri-

Note 18
"Chicago," American Architect & Building News, Vol. 76, April 26, 1902, p. 29.
Note 19
The anonymous writer here mistakes Wright's mannerisms for the lines of the Art Nouveau, whose backwash had not yet penetrated to Chicago except in the form of book decorations and illustrations. There is no actual influence of l'Art Nouveau upon Wright anywhere or anytime. Its whiplash curves and nervous sinuosities were totally opposed to the geometry of his style.

Note 17
A compendium of Wright's exhibitions for the Chicago Architectural Club is included in the Appendix, p. 216.

Fig. 89. The Davenport house, River Forest, Illinois, officially ascribed to the firm of Wright & Tomlinson.

ously beautiful work, even [sic] in domestic architecture, that is being done in other parts of the country, notably in the East, one is ashamed of the trivial spirit that is abroad here among us. There is a set of younger men here in Chicago who foster all this sort of thing. They have among them men with the artistic spirit and feeling, but their aim seems to be always to strive for the semi-grotesque, the catchy. Their compositions lack the best principles of honest design. Their aim seems to be to impress upon the beholder the belief that they are so filled with artistic inspirations and ideas that the flood cannot be held back for a minute, and must be dashed down on to paper as fast as ink and lead can carry it. There *is* a certain dash about it. These men treat the world like one huge studio, but how will these look, say, even twenty years from now? Like a dusty studio from which the life has gone. There certainly will be no acquired dignity born of time. The designs hardly amount to designs, and the execution is usually so extremely cheap that one questions the honesty of the whole thing ... There have been two notably fine houses finished this year on the North Side in Chicago, one a beautiful Colonial on Wellington Avenue, the other an equally good French Renaissance on North State Street. Only one of these houses appears at the Exhibition, and that only in one form, somewhat overshadowed in spirit by teazles and pine-branches ... The works

of different men are placed in the catalogue in groups in the reproductions of drawings and photographs of actual buildings and details. This is generally done quite unostentatiously, but when Mr. Frank Wright's portion is reached, we are introduced to his fourteen pages with a title-page effect in which is the inscription 'The Work of Frank Lloyd Wright.' A Wright chair, vases, and the bronze figure before alluded to, and the usual architectural jetsam compose the material of the title-page composition."

This long, heated passage is given here almost in full for its vintage quality, and for, despite itself, its fine description of a long-past event in Wright's career. The trenchant observation of the mysterious Mr. Raffaelli leaves us wanting more. It is all a wonderful insight into what progressive architects, and Wright in particular, were up against in the first years of our century. The "bronze figure before alluded to" was, of course, one of Bock's — a winged *putto* for which Wright's son Llewellyn posed. The teazles, no doubt, were gathered by Mrs. Wright and the children in the wild vacant lots to the north of The Studio. It was a production in which, again in a Continental vein, everyone in the family and entourage took part. It was handsome but it was too ambitious. It not only fired the Philistines into a fine rage, but, what was really serious, it transformed friendly colleagues into antagonists.

It is appropriate to speak here of Wright's one brief experience with formal partnership, an event which coincided with the period of his prominence as an exhibitor in the Architectural Club annuals. Wright and Webster Tomlinson worked as a team from some time before February, 1901, to some time after March, 1902.[20, 21] The first commission accepted by this partnership, the Davenport house in River Forest (Fig. 89), is officially dated in the former month by a construction notification and by a few blueprints still preserved at Taliesin. Neither Wright nor Tomlinson kept any actual books of their association. Apparently, the partnership was for business purposes only. Tomlinson had nothing to do with the work of designing at The Studio, and he, presumably, was occupied right along with his own independent commissions.

Note 20
These dates were arrived at by means of notices in Construction News (Chicago) and those blueprints extant at Taliesin which bear the name of Tomlinson as "collaborator."
Note 21
A complete list of the buildings upon which Wright and Tomlinson collaborated is included in the Appendix, p. 216.

His part in the association was confined to handling, in the Steinway Hall offices, the various practicalities which arose. A student poring over local construction periodicals of the time realizes at once the effectiveness of the scheme, for Wright. Whereas, before, Wright's commissions and contracts were only sporadically reported, for the few months of the partnership every contract is entered punctually and in a business-like way. These notices[22] are revealing in their phraseology. At first referring to the partners separately, they progress toward the use of the word "associates" until eventually the phrase "Wright and Tomlinson" appears. In July, 1902, Wright is again referred to independently, with his address at Oak Park instead of Steinway Hall. In view of the unusual status which Tomlinson had in the strange partnership,[23] there can be little question of stylistic influence passing between them.

Note 22
See Construction News (Chicago) and The Economist (Chicago) for the months in question.
Note 23
His status as a managing partner only is confirmed by letters from Mr. Tomlinson to the author.

2. The Buffalo Venture

In 1903, Wright designed (and Walter Griffin supervised) a narrow three-storied Prairie House in Oak Park for W. E. Martin, president of the Martin and Martin Stove Polish Company in Chicago. The design was not one of the most successful of the period, for the Prairie House does not thrive on cramped lots, but the repercussions of this commission were of immense importance for Wright's career. They started the chain of circumstances that led to Buffalo and the Larkin Building.

Mr. Martin was a brother of Darwin D. Martin of Buffalo, an active and progressive man with an eye for the fresh and original. When, on a visit to Chicago he saw his brother's new house, he in turn was captivated by Wright's style. He soon presented himself at The Studio to meet the young architect of whose genius he seemed to have had no doubts, and, before the W. E. Martin house was completed, Wright found himself one summer afternoon in Buffalo inspecting the large property in Jewett Parkway upon which Darwin Martin proposed to erect two new houses.

Darwin Martin's principal business was the Larkin Company, a mail-order and wholesale concern dealing mostly in soaps and grocery staples, with affiliations throughout the country. The officers of the Company were related not only by common business interests but by mar-

riage ties. The co-founders were John Larkin and Elbert Hubbard, whose sister was Mrs. Larkin; another sister was married to W. R. Heath, attorney to the company. The Heaths and Martins were intimate friends. Elbert Hubbard retired in the 1890's to East Aurora, some thirty miles southeast of Buffalo, to establish his monkish group of craftsmen, the Roycrofters, and to devote his time to writing his series of quasi-philosophical books. Darwin Martin stepped into his place, bringing Alexander Davidson as advertising manager. Martin, aside from his Buffalo interests, was co-owner with his brother of the factory in Chicago, previously referred to, which made the "E-Z" brand of stove polish. All in all, Wright designed and built nine buildings for the Martin brothers and their connections: six houses, an office building, an exposition building, and a factory.

The Jewett Parkway property was perfectly flat and commodious enough to permit considerable development. Wright's design, as it finally stood, consisted of three separate but related parts: the main house, a garage and conservatory, and a secondary house. The secondary house, fronting on Summit Avenue, was for the occupancy of Darwin Martin's sister and brother-in-law, the George Bartons; it is known and published always as the Barton house. It was this smaller house on which Wright actually

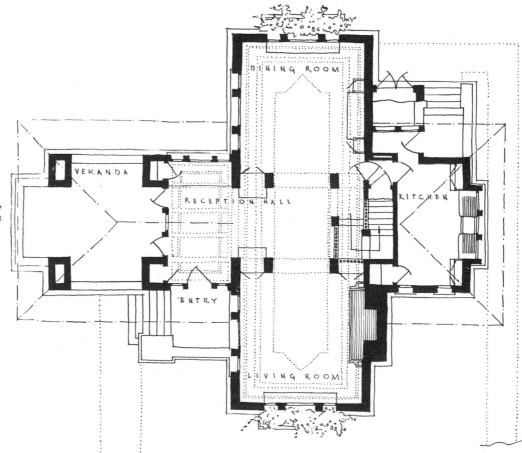

Fig. 90. The George Barton house, Buffalo. This was the first event in the Buffalo venture.

began his work in Buffalo in the fall of 1903; the building permits for the other two units were not applied for until nearly a year later. The Barton house (Fig. 90) is built of the same russet Roman brick, with deeply-raked joints, and the same flat red roofing tiles that were used in the other two structures, but in *parti* it adheres closely to that of the just-completed Walser house in Chicago — a reduction of the Prairie House formula to a tight, symmetrical plan with side-entrance and street elevation made up of a self-contained tripartite window for the living room on the first floor, a continuous strip of casements above, and the capping eaves. The pinched, topheavy effect of the design is partly compensated for by low wings to the rear and by short lengths of garden wall forward to the right and left. The Walser-Barton *parti* was a scheme which, despite its shortcomings, Wright often used as the answer to the problem of fitting a Prairie House to a narrow lot and a limited budget; but, since neither of these conditions existed in Summit Avenue, it is puzzling why he used it there except as an expediency, so as to get to work as soon as possible upon the main house.

The arrangement of the entire complex of the Martin and Barton houses, with their adjuncts (Fig. 91), is even more ambitious than the Dana house in Springfield, but the lowness of the

Fig. 91 A. Darwin D. Martin house, Buffalo — one of the "great houses" of the Oak Park days.

buildings coupled with the uniform employment of the hip roof makes for a less overwhelming effect. The Barton house and the communal greenhouse and garage (not a stable — Mr. Martin was, of course, a believer in the automobile) are all disposed along a secondary axis toward the rear of the property; the main, or Martin house, fronts on the Parkway, parallel with the line of buildings behind it and joined to them by a long, massive pergola. The whole scheme is laid out on two sides of a square, open toward the corner where Summit Avenue and the Parkway intersect. The pergola has four functions: it unifies the arrangement; it offers protected access to the greenhouse; it divides the gardens from the kitchen and drying yards; and its basement passage is a conduit for steam pipes coming from the furnace in the garage. Its long line is given interest by means of little sculptured towers at intervals — small editions of those geometrical pylons used in the Wolf Lake resort, and, here, designated by the architect as "stone bird-houses." The greenhouse shows that Wright's personal conception of architecture was not swayed by the traditionally sinuous form of conservatories; it is rectilinear and thoroughly Wrightian in detail; its focal niche is occupied by a marble replica of the Victory of Samothrace, Wright's favorite Classic statue, copies of which, big or little, are fre-

Fig. 91 B. The conservatory and pergola for the Martin house. The pergola connects the conservatory with the main house, as shown in the plan on the facing page.

quently seen in or around Prairie Houses. Flooded with light from the glass roof over it, this statue is in direct line of sight from the front door of the Martin house, over one hundred feet distant, like an object seen through the bellows of a camera (Fig. 92).

The main house is a low, two-story block with standard relation to grade, terminated at the left by a *porte-cochère* and at the right by a covered porch. The plan, quite aside from all those innovations which we have by now come to expect, is remarkable. The entrance hall bisects the house. To its right is the great unit-room, its separate functions flowing imperceptibly into each other and suggested only by truncated partitions and portières. The central portion, with an enormously wide fireplace, is the living room, advancing toward the glazed doorways leading to the porch. The two flanking spaces are a library and a dining room; these are well-lighted by long rows of casements, but the living room is dark, its source of daylight over-shadowed by the roof of the porch. As an after-thought,[1] a small skylight was inserted through the floor of the bedroom gallery overhead, but it is inadequate, and the room remains cavernous. To the left of the hall are the "south room," a secondary living room, Mr. Martin's private office, wardrobes, lavatories, and the kitchen premises. (Wright apparently had no qualms about locating the kitchen at a considerable distance from the dining room, and detached from it by the hall.) The main staircase is typical of Wright's treatment of the spaces of vertical circulation in a house; in its web of spindly balusters and rectangular newels, it surrounds a large square well, dimly skylighted. Disseminated strategically throughout the plan are six ex-

Note 1
Mrs. Darwin Martin, with whom the author had conversations in 1940, is the authority for the statement that the living room skylight was an afterthought.

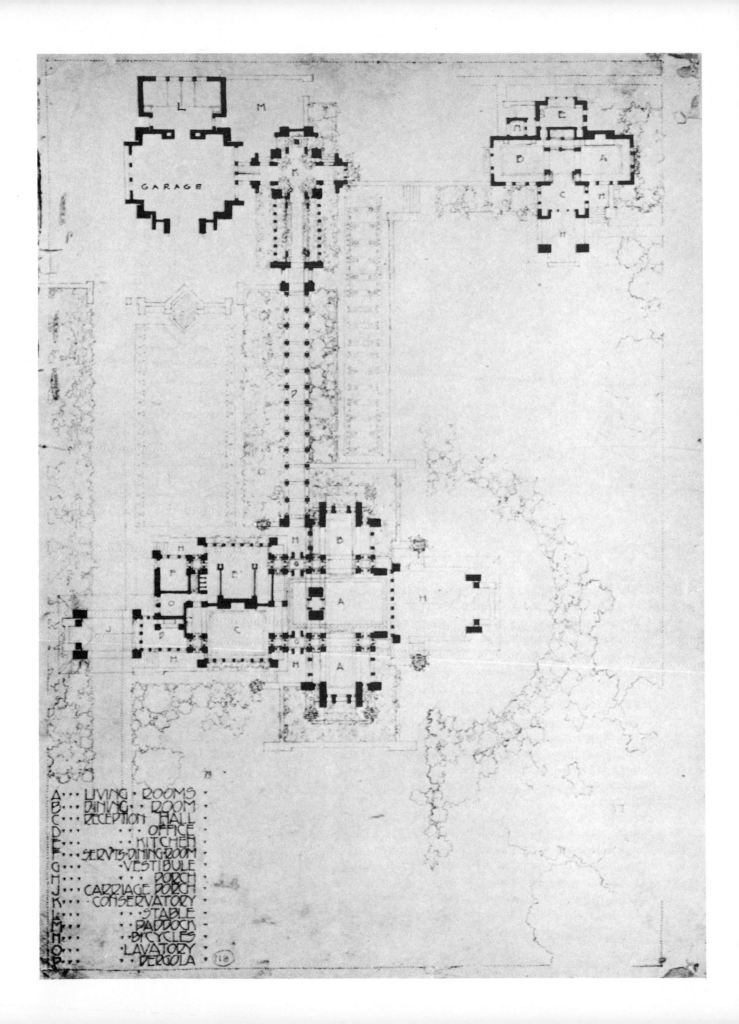

GARAGE

A····LIVING·ROOMS·
B····DINING·ROOM·
C····RECEPTION·HALL·
D····OFFICE
E····KITCHEN
F····SERV'TS·DINING·ROOM·
G····VESTIBULE
H····PORCH·
J····CARRIAGE·PORCH·
K····CONSERVATORY·
L····STABLE·
M····PADDOCK·
N····BICYCLES·
O····LAVATORY·
P····PERGOLA·

Fig. 92. This majestic vista through the hall and the pergola of the Martin house greeted the visitor at the front door.

traordinary features: rectangular areas devoted to an archaic form of radiant heating (Fig. 93). The bank of radiators within each is covered at shoulder-height by perforated oaken boards, and into the space remaining under the ceiling little groups of leaded casements open from the various adjoining rooms. From the hall, a concealed stair descends to the ball room in the basement, roughly corresponding in floor area to the unit-room above it; it is a fantastic place, seemingly filled with piers and chimneys of Roman brick whose deeply-notched profiles form the chief decoration, as well as the only boundaries, of the room.

Like the Dana house, the Darwin Martin house was unbudgeted, allowing Wright to indulge his most extravagant ideas about the fittings and furnishings of a Prairie House. Lighting-fixtures, lamps, rugs, hangings, and all furniture, including a grand piano, were designed by him. The wood of both trim and furniture is

a honey-colored oak, and the fabrics are all in tones of gold, lemon, and russet (Fig. 94). Apart from some good Japanese decorative objects, always harmonious with Wright's style, there was almost nothing in the Martin house that was not a product of his own fertile mind. He was assisted by some excellent craftsmen, such as the brickmasons who executed the magnificent arched fireplace of the "south room." The Chicago glassmaker, Gianinni, made the celebrated mosaic of glass tesserae[2] for the chimney-breast

Note 2
The design for the mosaic facings of the main fireplace in the house was probably the work of Blanche Ostertag, an artist then working in Chicago; a very similar mosaic overmantel in the Husser house was attributed to her in a Chicago Architectural Club annual catalogue.

Fig. 93 (left). "Radiant" heating unit in the Martin house. Fig. 94 (below). As usual in the largest Prairie Houses, Wright designed house, furniture, and fittings as one unit.

Fig. 95. Fireplace between the hall and the living room in the Martin house. The wisteria mosaic is a theme continued from the overmantel of the Husser house.

Fig. 96 A. Preliminary sketch for the Larkin Building, Buffalo, as seen from Seneca Street.

between the hall and the living room (Fig. 95). Its design is patently Japanese: cascading white wistaria blossoms against a gold background whose metallic sheen is echoed in the fitful reflections of the gold-leaf pressed into the horizontal mortar joints of the interior brickwork. Gianinni also made the exquisite leadings of copper for the myriad casements of the house, their geometric patterns picked out with bits of white, green, and gold glass. The Martin house, with its use of casement windows and brickwork both outside and in, was the most striking example to date of that determination of Wright's to demolish the hard-and-fast distinction between the exterior and the interior of a house. Walls must not exclude and define the surrounding world of nature, nor continue to serve the old belief that the outside of a house must be treated in one way and its inside in quite another.

The houses for W. R. Heath and Alexander Davidson were the result of the admiration which the members of the Larkin entourage felt for the Jewett Parkway buildings. The Heath house was built in 1905, the Davidson house in 1908. The latter design properly belongs with the later group of Prairie Houses; stylistically, it belongs with the Roberts and Baker designs rather than with the Barton, Heath and Martin houses. Like the Martin house, only much smaller, the Heath house is carried out in the massive terms of brickmasonry, and is likewise faced with red Roman bricks and roofed with russet tiles.

The commission for a new administration building for the Larkin Company came shortly on the heels of the Darwin Martin commissions. There is a set of working drawings at Taliesin labeled "Revised, April 1, 1904"; for a building of such magnitude, the revised plans must have been preceded by many weeks of labor. The construction permit was issued in July, 1904.

The way in which Wright approached this task is suggested by a little booklet of preliminary sketches[3] for the Larkin Building, also preserved at Taliesin. The general *parti* of the building (Fig. 96) seems to have occurred to him at once, in that intuitive way which characterizes the inception of most of Wright's major successes. It was to be a central, skylighted well

Note 3
It was Wright's practice in the Oak Park Period to present clients with a little square booklet containing a sheaf of preliminary pen-sketches. A few survive. Their format and insignia, as well as the delicate drawings which they contain, make them delightful and informative items of Early Wrightiana.

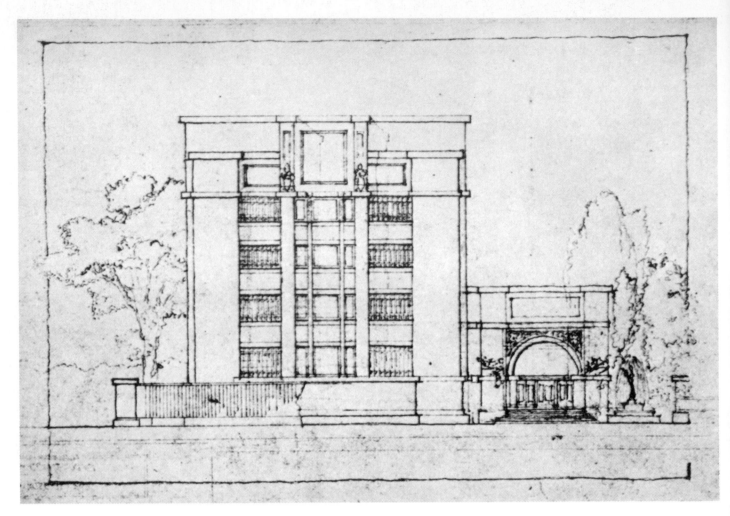

*Fig. 96 B. Seneca Street elevation (above), longitudinal section (below), and plan (facing page) for the Larkin Build-
ing — all in a preliminary stage.*

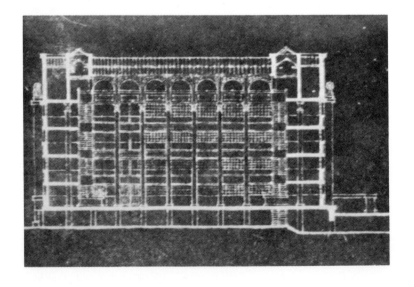

surrounded by several levels of subsidiary
spaces, like balconies. It was to be attached to
a smaller space along its flank containing entrances, private offices and reception rooms. Its
superstructure was to be a composition of space-
blocks, the projection into the surrounding atmosphere of the disposition of volumes within.
There would be no facade, in the ordinary sense
of the word, any more than the Great Pyramids
have a facade, or that there is a favored aspect
in an exercise of solid geometry. It was a revolutionary concept of architectural expression for
which Wright could have found no precedent in
1904.

The odd feature of the preliminary sketches
is that, despite the radical nature of the con-

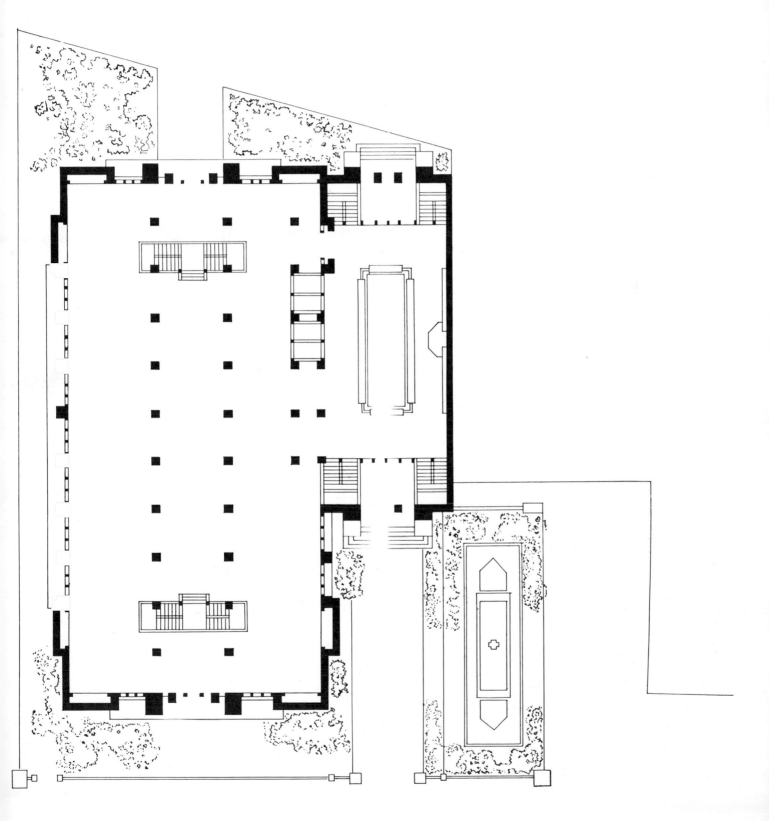

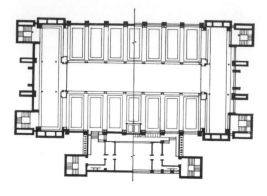

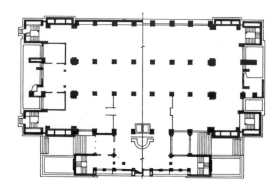

Fig. 97. The final plans for the Larkin Building.

cept, the decorative vocabulary was Sullivan-esque. The piers of the central well were to terminate in arcades with spandrels carved in foliated designs, as in the Winslow house *porte-cochère,* or the interior of the Mozart Gardens; the main entrance portal was a sort of triumphal arch like those of the Wolf Lake resort, preceded by a heroic statue of naturalistic forms support-ing a fountain. As always, the Sullivan tradition in public architecture was so compelling that Wright's vision, even in 1904, automatically sur-rendered to it at first. But swiftly his design was transformed in all its details into something personal to himself, and Sullivan was forgotten. Amazing changes took place around the portal from the moment that it was conceived to the time that it took form in brick and mortar.

The problem involved in designing the Larkin Building was very special. Unlike an average office building, the Larkin Building was to be used for a single purpose: the efficient operation of a vast mail-order business. Wright material-ized this function in terms of a great central space, dominating the structure and lying at its core. He immediately saw that the principles of the Prairie House, in which a solid core is sur-rounded by spaces, were of no use to him; he dismissed them from his mind.

Having established the scheme of a dominant central well in a generally oblong form, in the final plan (Fig. 97) the bony framework which enclosed the well was relegated to the outside of the well, and in its interstices were placed many of the subordinate volumes and functions of the building. Staircases, which had risen through the well itself in the preliminary sketches, were moved into this outer area and encased in corner bastions, identical with the fire-stairs, and the bastions were enlarged into huge rectangular prisms of brick, given further salience by the narrow glazed slots inserted be-tween them and the main block of the building (Fig. 98). At the narrow ends of the oblong, and between these fire-towers, the dimensions of the central well found expression in a grid of but-tresses and lintels corresponding to the well and the web of balconies which surround it. But because the balconies were subsidiary spaces, the horizontal members of that web which sug-gested their floor-levels were subservient to the vertical members. The resultant verticality of this part of the design was a marked break from the previous horizontality of Wright's style. Then, a simple massive attic, demarcated top and bottom by a unipartite cornice, surmounted the whole, re-stating with the directness of building-blocks the cubic volumes within and their interrelationships. That the power of this cubistic architecture should not be impaired by piercing it with portals in any obvious manner,[4] entrances were concealed in the re-entrant an-gles of the joint connecting the main block with the subsidiary block on its flank. This subsidiary block was a sort of miniature of the main block into which one half of it was merged; the re-maining half was again defined by blank towers at its two corners containing additional sets of

Note 4
The early drawings for the Larkin Building featured a Sullivanesque arched portal in the center of one street elevation.

stairs leading to the private offices on its second level. The entrances were unadorned square openings over which were large rectangular windows screened by closely-spaced brick mullions, recalling the vertical buttresses of the short ends of the main block.

This was the scheme. Once established, it was not deviated from nor compromised. That the result is not stark is due to Wright's enormous skill in organizing the volumes and planes at his disposal and making of them a structure which commands attention both for the fascination of its volumes and the sculpturesque quality of its majestic surfaces. There is applied decoration, but it is highly disciplined and concentrated at the upper levels of the design, producing an effect of richness in excess of its amount. The great buttresses of the end elevations, of that oblong section which Wright has loved from the earliest moments of his career, are capped with a geometric design of coping-stones and fillets surmounted with a huge globe symbolizing the world-wide scope of the Larkin Company's affairs. These globes are the only curvilinear elements in the entire composition. At their bases are some rather unfortunate little human figures, seriously out of scale, designed by Bock. Along the flanks of the main block and just under the attic, open loggias are inserted; their supporting piers are continuations of the mullions which rise from the base and articulate the windowed walls below, and they are ornamented with bands of carved relief.

Finally, there is a square plaque of low relief to the right of each entrance (Fig. 99) and against the base of the stair-towers of the secondary block. These plaques are pleasantly vague in subject. From beneath them there issues a long

Fig. 99 (above). The Larkin Building entrance is designed as an introduction to the spaces inside.

Fig. 98. The exterior of the Larkin Building is dictated by the disposition of its inner volumes.

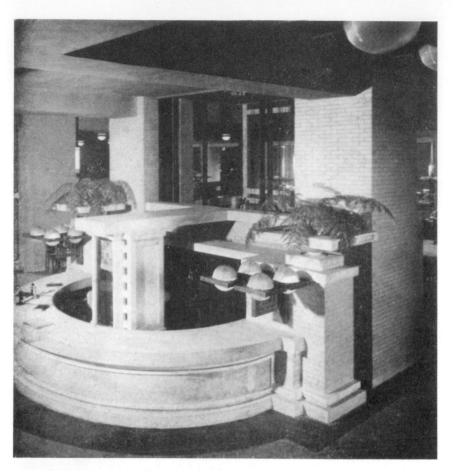

Fig. 100 (above left). Information desk in the lobby. Fig. 101 The central well (above right), lit by skylights (below and facing page).

sheet of water falling into simple rectangular tanks, and they are lettered in their centers with mottoes whose sentiment suggests that they might have been contributed by Elbert Hubbard.

Passing the portals and entering the lobby of the Larkin Building is an experience in the beauty of simple forms and spaces. The doors are unbroken panels of plate glass with no hardware other than a bar of bronze against which to push; the side panels and the transoms are also sheets of clear glass, so that upon ascending the outer steps the whole lobby comes into view. The focal point of the lobby is the semicircular information desk (Fig. 100) with a Wrightian composition of piers, shelves, and square urns as a backdrop. Access to the central well of the building is at either side of the desk. This impressive space reaches upward through five floors to a glass roof, and it is bounded, as the exterior has led us to anticipate, by a rectangular grid of voids and solids (Fig. 101). It is flooded with daylight. The brick piers which support the balconies stretch unbroken from floor to ceiling, the flat spandrels masking the floor slabs hung between them. The effect is one of powerful rising movement. The piers terminate in dense masses of geometrical ornamentation, and the spandrels of the topmost balcony are painted with Wrightian motifs and lettered with more of the mottoes. The floor of the well and the three balconies above it are given over to business. The fourth balcony is a restaurant for employees, and its different function is indicated by screening with planting-boxes from which vines fall over and descend several feet into the well.

An early form of air-conditioning was installed in the building, and all the window-sash are fixed. The working floors are equipped with wonderful innovations in metal furniture, filing cabinets and lighting-fixtures, all designed by Wright (Fig. 102). In the much-published photographs of the interior, taken at the time of its completion, it is only the costumes of the Gibson-girl stenographers that remind us that the date is 1905.

Although the Larkin Building was presently to become one of the beacons for a new architecture in Europe,[5] it was indifferently received in this country. Wright tells that the Larkin officials were irritated by the length of time it took in building, in consequence of the many untried features which it embodied, and this mitigated their satisfaction. An occasional voice rose in praise, however, in the American press. In 1908, The Architectural Review of Boston declared it "about as fine a piece of original and effective composition as one could expect to find . . . absolutely in the line of creative architecture," but these words were buried away in the monthly review of current periodicals. A more prominent and studied contemporary criticism was that of Russell Sturgis:[6] he admitted that, inasmuch as traditional architecture had reached an impasse the finality of which was hardly realized by American architects, Wright had accomplished a brave and progressive feat of design in the Larkin Building, but he concluded with the opinion that it was "an extremely ugly building." Even more interesting were the reactions of those few European critics who penetrated to the Middle West before 1910 to see the architecture of Sullivan, Wright, and the Chicago School of which they had read a few accounts. H. P. Berlage, the father of modern Dutch architecture, visited the Larkin Building a few years after its completion and became one of its outstanding champions. He later wrote a long analysis of it,[7] in which he marveled at the simplicity and unity of its *parti*, especially the great central correspondence room. He saw in the arrangement of furniture there a plain example of American democracy, for bureau chiefs were not, he noted, separated from their staffs by walls. He deplored the fact that no one in Europe had given any constructive thought to the possibility of turning the new *mores* of commerce to a thing of beauty in its own right, as had been done with the mail-order activities of the Larkin Company. "I went away," he said, "with the conviction of having seen a genuinely modern work, and with respect for the master able to create things which had no equal in Europe."[8,9]

Wright was to design another building for the Larkin Company, which had acquired space at the Jamestown Tercentennial of 1907 and called upon Wright to follow through with the necessary architectural display. The spirit of the Exhibition was fiercely traditional, not only because it took place upon the soil of the "Old Dominion" and celebrated its first colonization, but also because the final flare-up of eclectic taste in America was just then gathering force. Amid the pompous "Magazine-Colonial" porticoes of the Virginia fair, Wright's low, severely geometrical little building looked lost and out of place, although a carnival note was struck by a lot of Japanese-looking vertical banners on poles. It seems to have attracted little attention.

It is tempting to try to draw conclusions from the propinquity, during the time of the Buffalo venture, of Wright and Elbert Hubbard. Al-

Note 5
Both H. P. Berlage and C. R. Ashbee (the English architect who wrote the appreciation of Wright's work in the small Wasmuth monograph of 1911) saw the building before 1910.
Note 6
Russell Sturgis: "The Larkin Building in Buffalo," Architectural Record, Vol. 23, April 1908, pp. 311-321.
Note 7
H. P. Berlage: "Zu Einigen Bauten des Architekten F. L. Wright," in "Frank Lloyd Wright, Aus dem Lebenswerke eines Architekten," H. deFries (ed.), Pollak, Berlin, 1926, pp. 74-75.

Note 8
"Ich ging weg mit der Ueberzeugung ein echt modernes Werk gesehen zu haben, und mit Achtung vor dem Meister, der solches zu schaffen vermochte, dasz in Europa seinesgleichen sucht."
Note 9
Unfortunately, the foregoing passages on the Larkin Building must, for the record, be changed to the past tense. Berlage and a whole world of admirers notwithstanding, and with remarkably little outcry, the Larkin Building (abandoned and ruinous) was torn down in 1950. As this book goes to press, another great monument of the Oak Park Period is threatened: the Frederick Robie house (see pp. 198-200)—but now, in 1958, the outcry is astonishing and there is some hope that the building may be saved by popular demand.

though Hubbard was senior by thirteen years, the two men have many traits in common. They both affected (Wright still does) long hair, flowing ties, and informal, individualistic attire; they were both born in the Middle West of strongly religious pioneer stock; they shared a worship of Lincoln and Whitman; they were both interested in the Arts and Crafts Movement — Hubbard wholeheartedly, Wright ambivalently; they suffered from scandal and irregularities in their private lives; and, lastly, Hubbard was a co-founder of the Buffalo organization for which, in various capacities, Wright worked for over four years. Each man must at least have been aware of the other as a public personality and an artist; yet there is no evidence of their having met.[10] David Balch, Hubbard's biographer,[11] makes no mention whatever of Wright. In 1892, after an epochal meeting with William Morris in England, Hubbard retired from active participation in the Larkin Company and became absorbed in his Roycrofters; when he was not making one of his "Little Journeys," "Fra Elbertus" was at East Aurora. This probably accounts for the otherwise in-

credible indication that he did not seek out the brilliant architect who was creating such history in Buffalo, and who, in many ways, resembled him. Of course, that resemblance was superficial. Wright's work was vigorously addressed to the future, Hubbard's to the past. Only rarely did Hubbard rise to the level of genuine creation, as in the celebrated "Message to Garcia." Still, a haunting similarity remains, and a possibility that, long before the Buffalo venture if not during it, the two men influenced and reinforced in each other that streak of sentimental, self-conscious American primitivism which they both have.

Note 10
Mrs. Darwin Martin (see Note 1, p. 142) made a canvass of people in Buffalo who knew Hubbard intimately and would have known of any such meeting had it occurred; she discovered no evidence whatever.
Note 11
David Arnold Balch: "Elbert Hubbard," Stokes, New York, 1940.

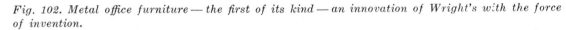

Fig. 102. Metal office furniture — the first of its kind — an innovation of Wright's with the force of invention.

3. Unity Church

If we discount that first published sketch, "A Unitarian Chapel for Sioux City," there are only two ecclesiastical designs in Wright's work to 1910: a project which went badly astray, and an executed design which ranks with the Prairie House and the Larkin Building as the third major success of the period. In many ways, the project which went astray is a prelude to the one which didn't, and should properly be discussed at this point in the narrative although it necessitates going back a few years in time.

It was about 1897[1] that Wright's uncle, the Rev. Mr. Jenkin Lloyd-Jones, his congregation having outgrown the curious edifice, All Souls', that Silsbee had built for it, approached Wright with schemes for a new building even more radical than the first. The congregation had acquired a large corner piece in Oakwood Boulevard diagonally opposite All Souls', and here the Rev. Mr. Lloyd-Jones envisioned a tall, multi-storied structure, with room for all the variegated activities of his flock including the auditorium for services, schoolrooms, assembly-rooms, kitchens, gymnasia, and living quarters

Note 1
The source of much factual information about Lincoln Center, included here, is information supplied the author by Mr. Dwight Perkins in 1939.

for himself. There could even be a few shops at ground level to help along with expenses. For this agglomeration of functions, he had chosen a new name: "Abraham Lincoln Center." Aesthetically, his chief concern was that his new building should have "no nonsense about it" — apparently the same instruction he once gave to Silsbee — by which he meant that there should be no spires, no stained-glass windows, no trace of ritualistic tradition. The new building must express, even more than the old, the down-to-earth directness of his gospel which he liked to compare with the unvarnished humanitarianism of Lincoln.

Among the more liberal metropolitan Christian groups, such a church has become routine; many of the type have been built in the twentieth century in cities like Chicago and New York. But in 1897, the idea was startlingly original. The Rev. Mr. Lloyd-Jones, a canny man, realized that he could not have found an architect more sympathetic to the idea than his by-now successful nephew, who was as great a rebel as he; as it turned out, however, uncle and nephew were too closely bound, not only by common patterns of thought but also by their common inheritance of Welsh temperament. The whole Lincoln Center project was marked by one clash after another.

In the course of five years of negotiation,

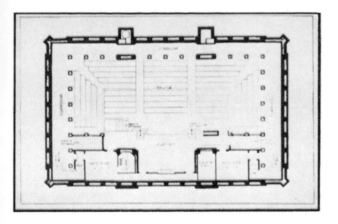

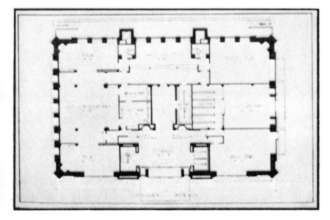

Fig. 103. Above: Plans for auditorium floor (top) and ground floor (bottom) of the Abraham Lincoln Center, Chicago. Above right: Preliminary drawing published in Spencer's article of 1900. Below: the plaster model shown in the Chicago Architectural Club's show of 1902.

Wright produced at least two and possibly more designs, varying in height but based upon an identical *parti*. The plaster model exhibited in the controversial display at the Chicago Architectural Club's annual show in 1902 is of a building of no more than five floors, while the perspective drawing published in the Spencer article of 1900 is considerably taller. Both designs (Fig. 103) are essentially a simple rectangular block enclosing somewhere within it an auditorium; in the taller scheme it is wholly unrevealed — in the lower, it is expressed by breaking and manipulating the fenestration, and incorporating a sculptured running frieze. It is unlike Wright to conceal function even as much as he did in the lower scheme, and we can only assume that some preconceptions of his uncle, obscurely arrived at as they may have been, carried the day. The taller design suggests an office

157

building rather than — let alone a church — a place of assembly. It is, furthermore, a Sullivan-esque office building, looking very much like Sullivan's famous Wainwright Building in St. Louis, of 1891. Only the two strong cornices serve to break the verticality of the design and bring it partially into harmony with Wright's instinctive cultivation of the level line.

The many plans and the model for Lincoln Center seem to have taken up an almost compulsive amount of Wright's energies, and in the end they came to nothing. They did not conform to the Rev. Mr. Lloyd-Jones's dream of a "four-square building for a four-square gospel," whatever this may imply; it was perhaps asking too much of any architect, no matter how sympathetic, to embody it in physical materials. When at length relations between uncle and nephew had reached the point of exhaustion, it was decided to call in another architect as consultant. It was in this capacity that Dwight Heald Perkins entered the affair, and formed a sort of *pro tem.* quasi-partnership with Wright. It was Perkins's intention to act only as the mediator who would set the negotiations back into operation, but he found himself alone when Wright defected in 1902. Perkins tried to execute the plans as they then stood; blueprints were made and construction begun. But the client continued to find fault with the "elaborateness" of the design and took pencil in hand to bring the building into line with his concept of Lincolnesque ruggedness. Confusion reigned, until one day Perkins walked out, too, writing in red crayon across the face of one of the blueprints "bldg. completed over protest of architect." As a matter of record, a Lincoln Center of sorts was finally ready for dedication in 1905, but it bears only a ghostly resemblance to the building that Wright designed, and cannot be included in the list of his executed work.

The second ecclesiastical commission, the designing of Unity Church in Oak Park, is a very different story; but we cannot escape the conclusion that something of the experience which Wright had with "four-square" ideas carried over from one to the other. There is a grandly spartan quality in Unity Church.

In the first week of June, 1904, the old frame church of the Unitarian congregation in Oak Park burned to the ground. In "An Autobiography," Wright tells of the visit paid him by Dr. Johonnot, Universalist[2] pastor of the congregation which the Rev. Miss Chapin had once led, to place the commission for the new church in his hands. Although the Wrights had been members of the congregation for many years, it was an unexpected move. Dr. Johonnot was not progressive in his tastes; strangely enough, he apparently had in mind a vision of a white New England meeting-house with a spire. He was, as Wright puts it, "out of luck." The gentle pastor was persuaded to "yield himself up 'in the cause of architecture,' " and what he got was an epochal, radical structure of concrete, cantilevers, flat planes and straight lines that the Rev. Mr. Lloyd-Jones might have had if he had been willing to leave well enough alone.

During the summer of 1904, Wright began work on the design of Unity Church. As in the case of the Larkin Building, which was still in progress, the broad concept of the design came to him at once, but the decision to build it of cast concrete, a newly-revived means of construction which was just entering its experimental phase both in Europe and the United States, was not immediate. In September, 1905, an announcement was made[3] that Wright was at work on the commission and had drawn plans, but it was said that the building would be constructed of "brick and stone." What led Wright to the decision to substitute concrete is not known; but it is significant that he was currently building the "E-Z" factory for the Martin brothers[4] of rough cast-concrete structural elements with brick in-filling. He was seeing, and reacting to, the wonderful design possibilities inherent in the nature of the new material. Also, the decision may have been dictated in part by need: the site for the new Unity Church, a corner property in Lake Street, was ample, but the funds for the building were severely limited — fine masonry was out of the question.

Note 2
The Unitarian congregation of Oak Park had by this time received many Universalist members and assumed a Universalist cast.
Note 3
Construction News (Chicago), Vol. 20, Sept. 23, 1905, p. 235.
Note 4
See the following chapter, p. 163, for an account of the "E-Z" factory.

Fig. 104 A. Unity Church, Oak Park.

Once made, the decision to build Unity Church of concrete had many results, both practical and aesthetic. In the first place, it caused serious delays in construction. It was, after all, one of the pioneer American monuments in this material. Wright called for bids in March, 1906,[5] and the building was still incomplete in April, 1907, at which time an article appeared in an Oak Park weekly[6] saying that the new church was "delayed several months beyond expectations." (It was dedicated, however, shortly afterward.) In the second place, the decision to use concrete had a

profound effect upon the design. Wright was determined that Unity Church, again like the Larkin Building, was to be an experimentation in mass and volume, but the elasticity of reinforced concrete invited the use of cantilevered slabs and resulted in a more tightly-organized and more aggressively cubical structure.

In hard reality, Wright's problem was this: for thirty-five thousand dollars,[7] he had to build a church consisting of an auditorium and parish-house for a congregation of four hundred people. And out of the same sum must come the inevi-

Note 5
Construction News (Chicago), Vol. 21, Mar. 3, 1906, p. 167.
Note 6
Oak Leaves (Oak Park), Vol. 26, April 27, 1907, pp. 101-102.

Note 7
There is a discrepancy in this sum: in "An Autobiography," Wright mentions the figure $45,000, but the announcement referred to in Note 3 (p. 158) gives the estimate as $35,000.

Fig. 104 B. The Unity Church exterior (above) and plan (facing page).

table price of attempting the unfamiliar, and of eliciting from workmen cooperation in experiments they could not approve or understand. These considerations, together with memories of Lincoln Center and the really simple nature of the Unitarian faith, focused Wright's thinking upon the church as a *room*, complete in itself, symbolizing the unity of man and God. This was a conception that was both in keeping with Unitarianism and strangely classic in essence. For an architect so often described as "romantic," Wright had certainly conjured up the complete antithesis of romantic architecture for his church. The room, furthermore, was to be scaled in proportion to man instead of an immense abstraction.

The whole process of thinking his problem through is winningly described in Wright's autobiography, and it needs no rephrasing here. The design, as it finally emerged (Fig. 104), is direct and powerful. Disposition of interior space is brilliantly revealed on the exterior, yet, much as volumes are stressed, we are never unaware of the dense, monolithic mass of the concrete or its rough pebbly surfaces, left entirely as they came from the wooden moulds in which they dried. In the course of time, these surfaces have weathered to a honey-golden hue which is the chromatic keynote of the building, and vines and creeper have grown over the walls to soften them. When seen from an angle, so that both the Lake and Kenilworth Street elevations are

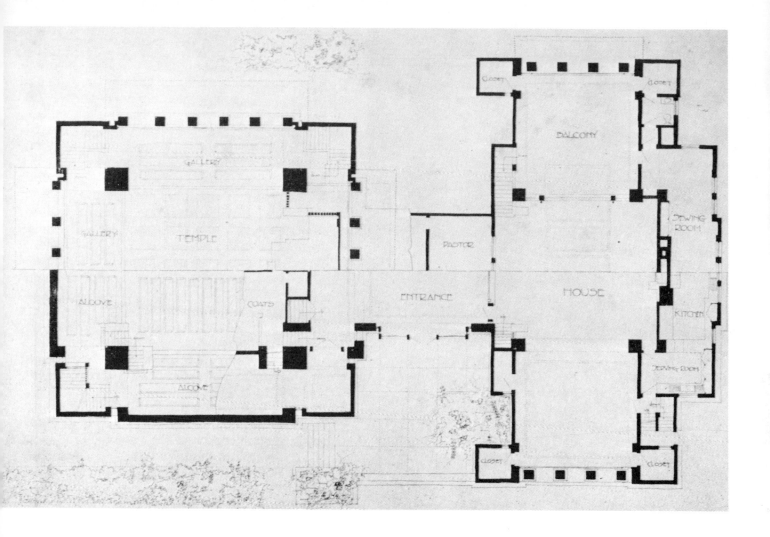

in view, the *parti* is clear: the auditorium itself is the major cube, at the front; to the rear of it, along Kenilworth Street, is a lower, smaller block which is the parish house; the two are connected by a joint, still lower, in which is a common entrance and vestibule, its portals screened by a parapet terminating in a geometrical urn. We are conscious of high blank walls breaking into openness and Wrightian detail at their upper stages — and the massive shadows of the roof-slabs in whose depth there is the gleam of glass. The overriding impression is that we are looking at an arrangement of Froebelian "gifts," building-blocks large and small piled upon each other, but by an immensely subtle mind and calculating hand. Last, perhaps the most startling realiza-

tion is that, for all its monumentality, this is a small building, with which we can feel at ease.

Of course, its simplicity is deceptive. The plan of the cube containing the auditorium — the *room* — takes a good deal of knowing before it is fully understood. It is a Greek cross inscribed in a square, and filled with many levels of seating and circulation. The center of the cross rises to the highest ceiling, almost entirely skylight; the four short arms rise to a somewhat lower ceiling and have banks of casements at their upper extremities; the four minor squares that fill in between the arms of the cross are stair-towers, and their summits are lower still. Access to the auditorium is by ramps under the speaker's rostrum, and then by passage around

Fig. 105. A skylit corner of the auditorium.

Fig. 106. The exterior expression of the stair-towers of Unity Church.

the four sides of the square and up the stairs to, first, the main floor of seats, which is at mezzanine, and finally to the balcony level slightly above, and sloping. The spatial effect of this manipulation of levels is surprisingly close and intimate: no member of the congregation feels himself to be either much lower or higher than the speaker. This close relationship, plus the great simplicity of decoration in the room and its astonishing brightness (Fig. 105), conspire to give a grand sense of the meaning of Unitarianism and its total lack of pomp and circumstance. There is nothing to overawe us, and our attention is quietly concentrated on the words of the service. There is nowhere any vista comparable to the protracted axes of Wright's larger Prairie Houses. The democratic tenets of the faith are superbly accommodated in this classic, self-contained cube.

The exterior expression of the cube is picked up, elaborated, and emphasized by many devices, such as the loose, slotted association of the rectangular prisms of the stair-towers to the outer faces of the cross (Fig. 106), further strengthening our impression of the mass as a piling-up of blocks whose lateral surfaces do not quite touch. We almost feel that we have the power to disassemble the building and re-erect it at will. There is something of this quality in the cubism of the Larkin Building, but bricks do not lend themselves so readily to this effect as does poured concrete.

Unity Church not only makes a sharp break with the age-old traditions of ecclesiastical architecture (and perhaps the first), but it shares with a handful of buildings in the world the distinction of being a beacon in the development of reinforced concrete construction. Only Perret and Garnier in France anticipated Wright[8] in the revolutionary concept of adapting reinforced concrete to the demands of sophisticated architecture, and by no more than four years at that.

Note 8
Perret's celebrated concrete apartment house, No. 25 bis, Rue Franklin, Paris, was constructed in 1903. Garnier's project in concrete, "La Cité Industrielle," was exhibited in 1904, but is thought to have been conceived in 1901.

4. Variations on a Theme

In mid-decade, The Studio entered two unusually busy years; in 1905 and 1906 twenty Prairie Houses came off the drafting-tables, as well as five or six non-domestic designs, some of them of first importance. The lull which had been caused in 1904 by Wright's almost continual absence in Buffalo was at an end. He now began to broaden the front of his activities and to turn his attention to such new fields as the factory, the retail shop, and interior design for commercial purposes. His staff at Oak Park had increased to impressive proportions and talent, including such names as Marion Mahony, William Drummond, Francis (Barry) Byrne, Isabel Roberts (secretary and bookkeeper), George Willis, Walter Burley Griffin, and Andrew Willatsen.[1]

The factory which Wright built in 1905 for the Martin brothers, the "E-Z" Polish plant on Chicago's West Side (Fig. 107), is an interesting anomaly in many respects: it is his first, it (like the Roloson houses) was lost to memory

Note 1
See Appendix, p. 217, for a complete list and a discussion of the apprentices of the Oak Park period.

Fig. 107. The E-Z Polish plant, Chicago, Wright's first use of reinforced concrete.

until 1939,[2] and it is the earliest experiment that he made in the use of reinforced concrete. It has been pointed out that this experiment was a sort of proving-ground for methods employed in Unity Church; and all of it constitutes what can be called the archaic period of the history of concrete in architecture of the twentieth century. By 1905, little had been attempted in the United States with the new material, and that little had failed to realize that concrete, if allowed to suggest its own forms, opened a whole new avenue for architectural design. Wright had first evinced interest in concrete in the "Village Bank" for Brickbuilder in 1900, but this was designed without steel reinforcement. Such use of concrete had been known and employed sporadically in this country for a quarter-century, as in the Ward house of 1873 at Port Chester, New York,[3] but "poured stone," as it was called, had been looked upon only as a cheap substitute for the genuine article, to be forced into an imitation of all the bastard shapes of the Revival Styles. That Wright had eschewed such a misconception of the nature of his material in the "Village Bank" was only to be expected from a designer of his sensitivity and genius, but the idea of the elastic strength of concrete was yet to come. When engineers like Ernest Ransome[4] began propounding the principles of concrete reinforced with embedded tensile members of steel, it was immediately seen that the new material could be turned to account as the gridwork of multi-story buildings, but still the tendency was to disguise it, in this case under a covering of applied traditional forms. Only if the building were to be strictly utilitarian, and, as such, not properly

"architecture," did designers consent to expose the material in its true forms. In 1903, Ransome erected a machine-shop at Greenburg, Pennsylvania, which, in its unself-conscious simplicity, had implications for a new architecture of concrete, but such a building had no influence except in the world of contractors. No real prominence had been accorded to reinforced concrete in the United States until 1904, when the Architectural Record published[5] the sixteen-story Ingalls Building at Cincinnati, by Elzner and Anderson. This skyscraper was loaded with Beaux Arts facades and crowned with a gigantic Renaissance cornice in order that no hint of its unconventional structure should escape to the man-in-the-street; but the accompanying article described in detail the technical processes involved in reinforced concrete, and there were many illustrations of the building in course of construction without its fancy-dress.

Whether or not Wright was influenced by the Ingalls Building to try his hand at reinforced concrete construction, it was certainly left to him to envision the way in which the course of architectural design might be seriously affected by it. He was, in every conceivable sense, both eligible and ready to take the part of the explorer, with a personal style that could have been, at almost any phase of its development, translated into concrete. It requires no effort, for instance, to think of the Larkin Building in such terms. The design of the "E-Z" factory does in fact resemble the long flank of the Larkin Building. Both are expressions of a rectangular grid of voids and solids contained between the vertical pylons of stair-towers; only the "E-Z" design is less dramatic, and makes no play with space-blocks. Its two-plane facade of piers and spandrels in an unrelieved pattern frankly reveals the structural uniformity of the building, and, since it is a street-facade wedged within a long line of adjoining factories, its stair-towers cannot protrude. It is faced with buff brick, and in this respect as well as others it cannot compare with the bold, granular effect of Unity Church, but its significance lies in the fact that all its forms are reduced to a simplicity compatible

Note 2
The "E-Z" factory is located on the Galena Division of the Chicago & Northwestern Railway, and was noticed by the author from the window of a train en route *to Geneva, Illinois.*
Note 3
See American Architect & Building News, Vol. 1, April 1, 1876, p. 112.
Note 4
Ransome's theories were eventually published, viz.: Ernest L. Ransome and Alexis Saubrey: "Reinforced Concrete Buildings," McGraw-Hill, New York, 1912.

Note 5
A. O. Elzner: "The First Concrete Skyscraper," Architectural Record, Vol. 15, June 1904, pp. 531-544.

Fig. 108. The remodeled shop for Pebbles and Balch, Oak Park.

with and dictated by the nature of a reinforced concrete framework. It was a signpost for much American architecture to come, both from Wright's hand and that of countless others.

There were also to be house designs in reinforced concrete before 1910, of which the most outstanding was the Lake Forest residence for Harold McCormick. This, which would have been his largest undertaking in domestic architecture, was unexecuted; it is discussed in the following chapter of this book.

The foregoing passages are a digression; but they complete the subject raised by the structural innovations of Unity Church, and they serve as a transition to the next. There is a fascination in the process, to which Wright now addressed himself, of recasting the ideas that resulted in the distinguished style of the Prairie House into a working formula appropriate to another area of design: shops and commercial interiors. His first commission of this kind was for the remodeling in 1906 of a little frame building in Lake Street, Oak Park, which was the business premises of a firm of interior deco-

rators, Pebbles and Balch (Fig. 108). Letting a new, low show-window, greatly reduced in height, into the commonplace little facade, running across its top a continuous, projecting sill surmounted by a ribbon of casements, the horizontal line is at once established as the dominant note. Then, purely decorative horizontals at a smaller scale are introduced in the muntins of the casements and the panes of glass at either side of the show-window. Over the whole motif, there is a segment of pitched roof. The effect is decidedly Japanese in spirit. It should be recalled that, only a few months before, Wright had made that absorbing journey to Japan to which reference was made in an earlier chapter and had fortified his impression of Japanese architectural traditions gained from the Ho-o-den, prints and books, with actual knowledge of the street architecture of Tokyo and Kyoto and the villages of central Japan. It was presumably this which made him suddenly seek opportunities, like shops, to put his new and more intimate knowledge to work in variations on the Prairie House theme.

Fig. 109 (above). The interior of the Pebbles and Balch shop.

The interior of the Pebbles and Balch shop (Fig. 109) was fresh and charming with plain surfaces and geometric forms in natural wood graced with cultivated Japanese overtones: rough pottery bowls with impressionistic glazes, and the substitution of oiled paper for glass in the cabinet doors. Other decorative elements remain unaffectedly Wrightian, such as the lighting-fixtures composed, like those of the Oak Park playroom of 1895, of cubes and spheres.

It was only natural that, upon his return from Japan, his new knowledge of actual Japanese customs, added to his already-established connoisseurship of Japanese prints and objects of art, should put him into relationship with dealers and other collectors as a consultant in interior design. Three or four commissions for pri-

vate and public galleries came his way. In these, Wright quite freely gave rein to his Japanophilia in terms of oiled paper, natural wood, and grass-cloth; yet it is really enchanting to see how at home in such a setting are all the other, more instinctive emanations of his art. His geometric chairs and tables, his cubes and spheres, his copper pots of dried oak leaves, his teazles settle down comfortably among the Japanese things, secure in their affinity.

He gloried, in these shop and gallery commissions, in the chance to design ingenious storage-places and exhibition-racks. Nothing that Wright ever did was more advanced for its time than his fittings for these premises — chests-of-drawers and case-pieces, their flush planes broken only by severe, unobtrusive pulls and knobs, wonderful devices of simple joinery to act as the servants and background for prints and porcelain. Such was the private gallery which he designed for the residence in Boston of W. S. Spaulding, the owner of a noted collection of Japanese prints which Wright helped to assemble — but this is well beyond 1910. For less exalted use were those shops in Chicago, Browne's Bookstore and Thurber's Art Gallery, which do lie within the scope of the period under discussion. Into the design of the Bookstore (1908) (Fig. 110) Wright contrived, despite its public nature, to inject the atmosphere of a private library, not only by the quiet mono-

chrome of browns in which it is worked out, but even more by the limitation of bookcases to shoulder-height, making every book within easy reach. The long, narrow room is broken up into alcoves, each large enough to hold a Wrightian table and four chairs; a second room containing rare editions has an informal arrangement of furniture around a Wrightian fireplace. The vestibule, with cashier's desk, is strongly reminiscent of the lobby of The Studio. Great, geometric lanterns of copper-bound glass, huge vases of leaves, casts from the Antique (including, of course, the Victory of Samothrace), and mottoes lettered in gold-leaf upon the walls provide the unmistakable Wrightian touch. Thurber's Art Gallery (Fig. 111) (1909) was similarly subdivided and given spatial variety. The chief adornment was the skylight, two long parallel panels of intricately-leaded glass very similar to those designed for The Studio. These glazed panels concealed batteries of electric lamps to be used on dark days — an archaic example of indirect lighting. The walls were finished in gilded cork and rough plaster. A contemporary critic, reviewing the Thurber shop in print,[6] came to the conclusion that its design was "a

Note 6
"Art Gallery Designed by Frank Lloyd Wright, Architect," International Studio, Vol. 39, Feb. 1910, pp. xcv-xcvi.

Fig. 110. Browne's Bookstore, Chicago (far left, near left, and below). The Winged Victory of Samothrace in one of her many appearances as a decorative adjunct in Wright's early work.

Fig. 111. Thurber's Art Gallery, Chicago.

Fig. 112. Wright's remodeling of the lobby of The Rookery, a famous old Chicago office building intimately associated with Wright's early career.

close study of Japanese refinement and elimination, with a slight touch of the modern German and Viennese Secessionist," an implausible mixture. What seemed so often to puzzled critics, in those days, to be Secessionist, or Arts and Crafts, or Art Nouveau in Wright's style was in reality the still unfamiliar essence of the "new architecture": its crisp geometry.

Wright also remodeled at this time (1905) the lobby of The Rookery, an old and popular La Salle Street office building which had been designed in the 1880's by the firm of Burnham and Root, pioneers in the aesthetics of the tall building who, for a brief moment, rivaled Sullivan. The original lobby was a very progressive affair of structural cast-iron, with an enormous skylight; but the effect was dated. Here, it was neither appropriate nor possible to recreate a Japanese atmosphere (Fig. 112); Wright accomplished the desired transformation with suitably strong, rigorous means. His first act was to clean away the iron ornament which writhed in every corner; he then substituted the crispness of simple, geometric planes and rectangular urns of creamy marble. From the trusses of the skylight he suspended several lighting-fixtures composed of a rectangular bronze plate punctured with hemispheres of milky glass containing the light-bulbs. The smaller, connecting lobby on the Adams Street side of the building he likewise encased in white marble, and a secondary staircase terminating here has flattened urns like those of the main lobby. His final touch, inexplicably enough, was to deface every surface with elaborate incised and gilded arabesques more suitable to a Turkish bath than a public lobby. Their embroidery-like patterns of curling lines are as unlike Wright as possible; they are also unlike the individualistic arabesques of Louis Sullivan. Was this, nevertheless, some final, belated flare-up of Sullivanesque influence?

The Rookery was associated with Wright in many ways. His "front office" was briefly there in 1898-99. The building was long under the management of his patron, Edward Waller, and it housed the headquarters of William Winslow and the American Luxfer Prism Company.

The curious structure erected in Wilson Avenue, Chicago, for P. C. Stohr was one of the last designs which Wright finished in 1909 before his flight to Europe. It is an agglomeration of shops and offices of the sort loosely referred to in the United States as an "arcade" (Fig. 113). No piece of property could have presented greater difficulties to an architect than the one which Stohr entrusted to Wright for improvement; it was triangular in shape, and directly under the overhead right-of-way of the Chicago "El." The building placed upon it had also to incorporate somehow sets of public stairs to the Wilson Avenue Station of the "El." Wright's horizontal style, somewhat mannered by now in its application to non-domestic architecture, was well-suited to cope with the exigencies of the situation under the "El." As erected, the Stohr Building was a continuous row of shops at street level, above which there was a mezzanine whose projecting sills and ribbon windows formed the dominant horizontal line of the composition. At the south end, where the building partially broke free from the overhead "El" structure, a third

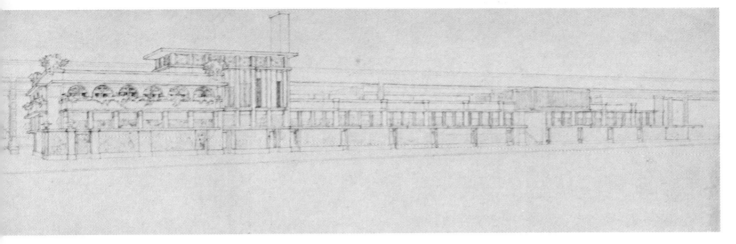

Fig. 113. A difficult site under the Chicago "El": The Stohr Arcade.

level with arcaded fenestration reminiscent of an earlier period of Wright's career was added. Just alongside it rose a stairwell lighted by very tall casements. This southern block of the building, also incorporating a heating-stack, makes the high point of the composition, balanced by the greater extension of the long northern section. Near the north end a public stair to the railway above is provided, its ticket-booths screened behind a typically Wrightian device of decorative planes and straight lines. There are also such other indispensables of Wright's style of the Oak Park period as the flat, geometrical flower-urns, continuous window-boxes for plants, cube-and-sphere lighting-fixtures, and decorative, mannered articulation of wall-surfaces. The Stohr Building was long ago demolished, and there is only one extant photograph, showing the building in construction. It is hard to judge, therefore, but it appears to have been a particularly fortunate combination of trying circumstances and the only contemporary architectural style which could have done them justice.

The largest non-domestic commission which Wright undertook between the completion of Unity Church and the commencement of Midway Gardens in 1913 was the City National Bank and Hotel at Mason City, Iowa (Fig. 114). This de-

Fig. 114 A. The City National Bank and Hotel, Mason City, Iowa. This view shows the bank and office block fronting on the main street with the hotel block to the rear.

Fig. 114 B. The Mason City building seen from another angle, showing only the block containing shops and the hotel known as the "Park Inn" — the first hotel in Wright's practice.

sign was begun in 1909; it was announced in The Mason City Times-Herald for March 6th of that year, and the working drawings were finished in December by those who remained on duty at The Studio after Wright's departure. The project was sponsored by the Mason City law firm of Blythe, Markley, Rule and Smith; Mr. Markley's daughters attended the Hillside Home School at Spring Green, and an accidental meeting of Markley and Wright at the Lloyd-Jones farm resulted in the commission. The project was a complicated one due to the desire of the firm that the building should be a sort of mercantile civic center fulfilling the functions of banking, hotel accommodations, and retail merchandising. The site was choice: a deep corner lot, fronting on the main street and having a small, leafy park on its flank. Wright's *parti* was to place the bank premises on the corner, with business offices over it, and shops and the hotel, which was to be known as the "Park Inn," along the quieter street overlooking the park and away from noisy traffic. Disclaiming any onus to "unify" this rather complex structure by obvious tricks of academic design, Wright let the various functions dictate the plan. The result is an asymmetrical, informal composition stretched out along the park side, the long axis of the property. What is lost in unity by this measure, is gained in legibility. A deep areaway

Fig. 114 C. Interior of the banking room.

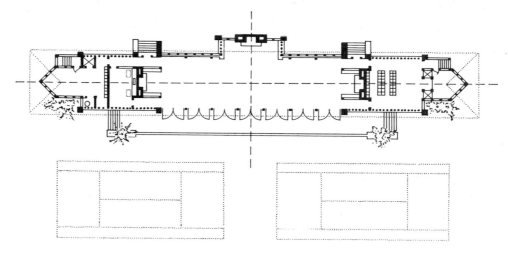

Fig. 115. The River Forest Tennis Club.

between the two main parts of the ensemble, the bank-office building and the hotel-shopping building, divorces them, and only the line of the heavily-projecting roof-slab carries through from one to the other; they are otherwise quite different in treatment.

The banking room, lighted by a clerestory, is expressed on the exterior by high blank walls of buff brick, the floor of offices above by rows of identical windows, the shops by huge, un-broken panes of plate glass, and the hotel over them by a very Wrightian balcony with urns and all the customary repertory of Wright's domestic style. The design is symmetrical on the main street front, featuring a monumental rectangular opening into the banking room, its starkness relieved by a pair of cubistic lamp-standards and some equally cubistic metal trim around the doors. The division of the main block into two horizontal elements of different char-acter but equal strength is bold, but there is an ambiguity in including the clerestory windows of the banking room in the upper one, as it gives

the impression of two floors of offices unless the floor-heights are closely studied. Another fault is that the twin entrances to the hotel are some-what lost among the show-windows and other doors at ground level in the rear block of the structure. The building was long in construction, and it was 1911 before the finishing touches were applied.

Among Wright's commissions for 1906-1907 were two clubhouses, of which one was executed in the style suggested by the Prairie House; the other, due to circumstances, is a decided curi-osity. The River Forest Tennis Club of 1906 (Fig. 115) is a strongly dynamic design dis-posed along an attenuated axis, with no vertical accents other than three squat chimneys, and terminating at the ends in diamond-shaped bays which put no real stop to its flowing lines of base, fenestration and eaves. It anticipates the ship-like quality of the Robie house. The Fox River Country Club, which stood in the river valley midway between Batavia and Geneva, Illinois, was one of the whims of the eccentric million-

Fig. 116. The Fox River Country Club, an alteration for Col. Fabyan of an existing building on his estate.

aire, Colonel Fabyan, who met Wright while he was supervising the construction of two Prairie Houses in the district.[7] Colonel Fabyan's large valley estate was already equipped, in 1906, with a variety of houses and outbuildings, including a real Dutch windmill which had been imported and re-erected on the estate, and which was for decades a prominent landmark. Colonel Fabyan's ideas were grandiose, and Wright became involved in them for some time. Among the many projects which were discussed, the only one that came to fruition was the remodeling by Wright,

Note 7
In 1906, Wright erected the Hoyt house in Geneva, Illinois; this led to the commission for the Gridley house in Batavia, Illinois, and it was through the Gridleys that he met Col. Fabyan. The whole series of events took place within a period of twelve months.

in 1907, of a large old building on the estate to serve as a private recreational center for a selected list of families in the valley. The resultant building (Fig. 116), whose design was partly dictated by the vagaries of the existing structure, reverts in feeling to an earlier phase of Wright's career when he at times entered a *cul-de-sac* in his search for the principles of the Prairie House. The Fox River Country Club has such anomalous features as a series of widely-spaced French doors and paneled, tapering chimneys which give it an unaccustomed verticality that low hip roofs and wide eaves cannot dispel. The building was destroyed by fire a few years after its rehabilitation. Wright also made a brief start on remodeling the house which Col. Fabyan used as his own residence, but his association with the project was brought to a close by mutual agreement before anything significant had been accomplished.

5. The Heyday of the Prairie House

The latter half of the period described in this book as "The First Golden Age" was the heyday of the Prairie House. Nearly two-thirds of all that were designed fall within the years 1905 to 1910 — some forty-odd houses — and, while the search for ways in which to vary and enrich the formula continues to result in invention, certain patterns of approach to the problem begin to repeat themselves and to suggest categories. There is, for example, the type of Prairie House which is scaled to a very limited budget, necessitating some mass-production techniques and a simplification of Wright's decorative vocabulary. Such are the Sutton, Mary Adams, Hunt, Fuller, Hoyt, Nicholas, Stockman and Waller Subdivision houses, to mention a few. The exigencies of the limited-budget house were met with a ruthless pruning of fine details of planning and craftsmanship, leaving only the basic principles of the Prairie House unmistakably but broadly expressed.

The Hoyt and Hunt houses (Fig. 117) are inexpensive buildings whose *parti* is the simple cube, the cheapest to erect and maintain. It was an inevitable scheme if the Prairie House was to be reduced to the economic level of popular housing, yet the square plan was to remain an exception in Wright's work until later years, never used if the budget permitted something more deployed in mass and flowing in space. To give plastic character to the elevations of these frame-and-stucco cubes without going to the expense of actually articulating the walls, the otherwise blank planes left by the concentration of windows elsewhere are paneled with applied wooden mouldings; occasionally, as in the Hoyt house, the panel bends around the corners of the house. The casements of these small houses were sometimes leaded in simple geometrical patterns, but were more often subdivided by wooden muntins into the conventional squares and diamonds. The tripartite window of the Walser house design was a variant in fenestration frequently incorporated, producing a marked decorative feature by inexpensive, sturdy means. The trim was wood stained dark brown, contrasting strongly with the light, sand-plastered walls, and approximating by linealism the structural horizontals of the larger Prairie Houses. The same sand-plaster and dark trim were used inside, in accordance with Wright's firm belief that as little distinction as possible should be made between the exterior and interior treatment of a house. When the budget permitted,

Fig. 117. Above: The Hoyt house, Geneva, Illinois. Below: The Hunt house, La Grange, Illinois. Both are examples of the "economical" Prairie House.

Fig. 118. Spaces and surfaces interestingly broken by inexpensive means — the interior of a budgeted Prairie House.

Wright indulged in the one luxury of "Tiffany bricks"[1] for the facing of the chimneypiece; but in any case, the wide mass of this dramatized element of plan was the principal adornment, as well as partition, of the living spaces of the house (Fig. 118). He also incorporated a wide, running rail, upon which pots and interesting arrangements of leaves could be placed, across the opening from living space to dining space, reducing the height of the opening to bare headroom; it not only introduced a strong horizontal to give style, but it helped to create spatial richness in an otherwise unbroken interior. Lighting-fixtures were simple geometrical abstractions in stained wood and clear glass.

Thus, everything about these modest Prairie Houses was simplified and minimized in conformance with the low price for which they were built, and calculated for the quick, broad effect. The resultant coarsening of Wright's domestic idiom detracts, in one sense, from its appeal. Wright is not only an architect, but he is a craftsman, for whom there is great fascination in the well-made thing, whether an arch of moulded bricks or a bronze vase. We can almost feel the reluctance with which he gives up, in closely budgeted designs, the terra-cotta pantiles, the raked brickwork, the leadings, the

Note 1
This was a term commonly used between 1890 and 1910 to designate Roman bricks of tan hue with small, dark vitreous spots and cavities where silicon had fused during firing. Presumably, it gave an "antique" appearance recalling that of Tiffany glass.

natural oak joinery, and all the panoply of fine craftsmanship with which he knew so well how to ennoble a domestic design. In comparison with the Dana house or the Darwin Martin house, the budgeted Prairie Houses seem impoverished, and they are; but the best of them still manage to achieve, despite drastic economy of means, something of that electrifying reorientation of the concept of the American dwelling that lies at the root of Wright's domestic architecture.

Wright is often criticized for "putting up a front" when he can't have his way in the matter of cost. Undoubtedly, it is a shock to see one of the cheaply-built Prairie Houses today, with its stucco loose, its overstrained wooden cantilevers sagging, its lath-and-plaster urns and outriders tilting on inadequate foundations; the effect is as depressing as that of an exhibition pavilion which has escaped demolition. But we must bear in mind that these occasional old ruins do not represent the norm of Wright's work in the Oak Park period. He knew perfectly well how to build solidly in durable materials, and, since so many of his structural innovations in house-design, such as the cantilever, depend upon tough materials for their success, it is safe to assume that he would have done so had the money always been available. He had too much to say, and its need to be said was too urgent, to wait for the perfect means and occasion to express it. When both these factors were present, as they fortunately were many times, Wright surpassed himself; when they weren't, he tried to show that his houses were in everyone's reach, and sometimes succeeded.

The next category, the medium-priced Prairie

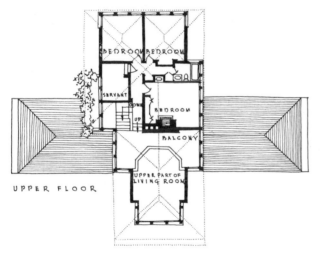

UPPER FLOOR

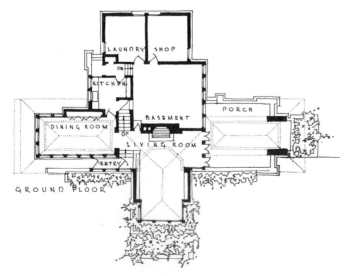

GROUND FLOOR

Fig. 119. The Isabel Roberts house, River Forest, Illinois. The interior views (facing page) show the complex spatial interrelationships of the two-story living room and the bed-room level above.

House, attests to a further review and reorganization, after 1904, of Wright's concept of the new house. A departure in plan makes its appearance, for example, in the much-admired Isabel Roberts house, in River Forest, of 1908, followed by the Baker, Davidson, Steffens, Guthrie and other designs. Its salient characteristic is the deceptive handling of levels, resulting in a two-story house which, on the outside, gives the effect of one. It is the acme of horizontality. The plan of the Roberts house (Fig. 119) is a cross, with the center of mass and the pylon of the single chimney roughly corresponding. The arm of the cross projecting toward the street is devoted to a two-story living room lighted by a casemented bay rising to the full height of the building, and by clerestories along the two sides, just under the jutting eaves. The second floor, for bedrooms, is mainly contained within the rearward arm of the cross, but it flows into the upper reaches of the living room by means of a balcony which crosses the chimney-breast, creating an ingle-nook beneath, and continues halfway down its sides. The soffit of this balcony and the undersides of the roof-parts above are

incorporated into the whole spatial scheme of the interior. The lateral arms of the cross are of one story only, containing on one side a dining room and the other a verandah. The weaving-together of these various levels and the centrifugal nature of the plan make for a strong, subtle, and immensely memorable effect which is the very quintessence of Wright's domestic style of the later Oak Park years. The Roberts house scheme, like so many of Wright's best ones, was capable of enlargement, as is seen in the un-executed Guthrie house and the Baker house in

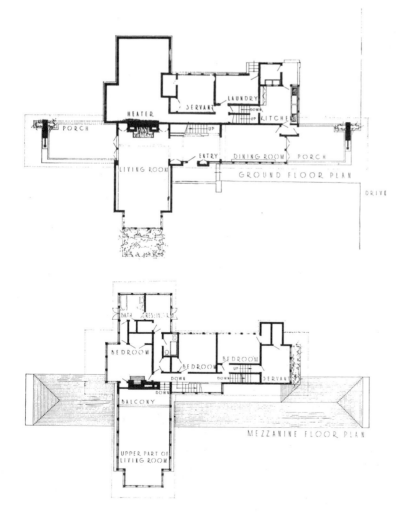

GROUND FLOOR PLAN

MEZZANINE FLOOR PLAN

Fig. 120. The Frank Baker house, Wilmette, Illinois. The "Baker bungalow" (as it is locally called) is an extreme example of reduction of vertical elements in a Prairie House.

Wilmette, identical twins[2] and offspring of the Roberts design. Like the Roberts house, the Frank Baker house (Fig. 120) impresses observers to such an extent with its low center of mass and its striking horizontality that it was popularly referred to by the citizens of Wilmette as the "Baker bungalow." The fascinating articulation of its surfaces, the sense it gives of a natural organism that has grown like a creeping plant, is so compelling that its obvious mannerisms are forgiven.

There were, as might be expected, actual "bungalows," or one-story houses, among the designs of this period. Discounting little vaca-

Note 2
When the Guthrie project (for a house in Sewanee, Tennessee) collapsed, the design was immediately submitted to the next client, Frank Baker, who accepted it in toto.

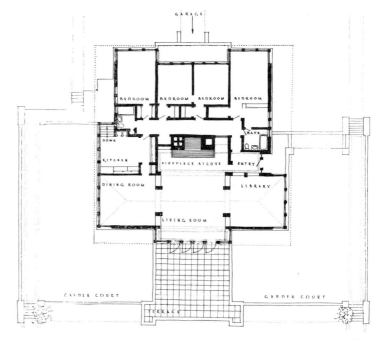

Fig. 121. The Edwin Cheney house, Oak Park, Illinois. A bungalow in fact, with all rooms on one level, and, biographically, a prelude to upheaval.

tion cottages for seasonal occupancy (of which there are several in the Indiana dunes and Michigan woods), Wright first seriously applied the principles of the Prairie House to the problem of the bungalow in the design of the Edwin Cheney house[3] in Oak Park in 1904 (Fig. 121). It is a design contemporary with and closely related to the Heurtley house in its compact plan and its restraint in handling the elements of the style; what it lacks in the elegance provided by the raised basement of the Heurtley design it makes up for in the handsome and extravagant paved and walled platform upon which it stands. The W. A. Glasner house, erected the following

Note 3
The Cheney house will be mentioned again in the last chapter, p. 211. Wright's connection with the Cheney family was to develop into a serious personal situation.

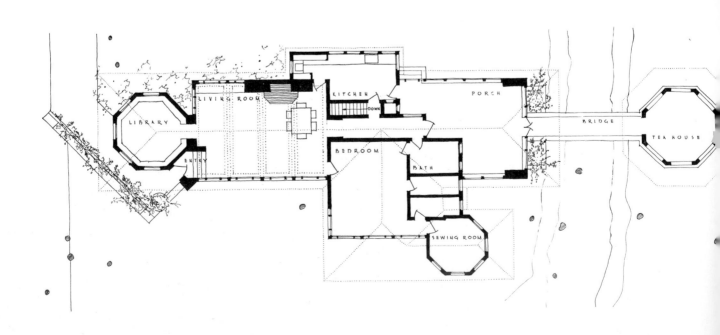

year in Glencoe, Illinois (Fig. 122), is more characteristic of Wright's mature manner in its prolonged axial plan and dramatic lines. Its design was conditioned by two special circumstances: the site was at the edge of one of those deep ravines which fall toward the beaches of Lake Michigan to the north of Chicago; and the Glasners were a childless couple who wanted a house that could be easily managed without a resident servant. The first condition suggested a house set very low to the ground on the south side so that its mass should not be overpowering on the north, or ravine, side. The second condition suggested the elimination of a service-block and, in line with the first, a one-story *parti*. Surprisingly, the plan called for three octagonal elements — a library, a sewing room, and a detached porch or tea-house — except for the tea-house, these were carried out, strange throwbacks to an earlier, picturesque solution to the problem of achieving centrifugality of plan. The unexecuted Elizabeth Stone and Adams houses, both to have occupied sloping sites at the edge of Lake Michigan, were likewise bungalows, larger but less complicated than the Glasner house, and

of the same year. All three designs had modest siding of brown clapboards to harmonize with their unspoiled wooded settings.

To continue the discussion of radical alterations of *parti* for Prairie Houses conforming with special circumstances, there are designs whose changes are those of technology rather than plan. Wright carried over into the realm of domestic architecture those experiments with the use of cast concrete which had been begun in the "Village Bank" and Unity Church. In 1906 and 1907, respectively, he designed a house for Richard Bock, the sculptor, and the third model house for the Curtis Publishing Company, both of which were to be of concrete construction. Neither was built, but their publication was important in staking a claim to Wright's title as innovator in this field.

The first two model houses for the Curtis Publishing Company had appeared, it will be recalled in the Ladies' Home Journal in 1901, and had raised the curtain on the era of the Prairie House. The third model house was published in the same periodical in April, 1907, under the title, "A Fireproof House for $5000,"

Fig. 122. The W. A. Glasner house, Glencoe, Illinois. The perspective on the facing page and the photograph below show the north side of the house, where a deep ravine leads down to the shore of Lake Michigan.

Fig. 123. "A Fireproof House for $5000," the third model house designed for the Ladies' Home Journal.

and it offers the greatest contrast with its predecessors (Fig. 123). The chief departures of the 1907 design arise directly from its different material. To facilitate and reduce the number of forms for casting the concrete, the house is essentially a cube covered with a simple flat slab; in this respect, it draws its inspiration from Unity Church. To avoid the starkness which would be unsuitable to domestic architecture, the cube is modeled by extruded fenestration, and its volume is extended at one side by a small wing, a long, trelissed terrace, and low parapets. But there is a marked absence of applied detail; everything is held to a minimum and calculated for the broad effect. The result is a building of greater force but less domestic appeal than the first model houses. A growing interest in the possibilities of new building materials, a concern with the problems of housing for people of limited means, actual experience with the impersonal, cold forms of monumental architecture — these combined to bring about the change. Although there had been a certain undeniable fussiness in Wright's earlier Prairie Houses, an over-exuberant fusion of architecture and the decorative arts to produce a total style, we cannot help feeling some regret when, due to Wright's concentration upon an architecture of more universal and democratic significance, all those wonderful, inventive emanations of Wright's talent for applied design are forced into temporary retirement. Wright himself must

have realized this, for, in the perspective drawing for the third model house, heavy reliance is placed upon non-architectural means — cascading vines and flourishing window-boxes — to mitigate the harshness of surface and profile.

The cast-concrete Bock project (Fig. 124), first published in The Architectural Record of March, 1908, was to have been the sculptor's combined Oak Park residence and atelier. Like the third model house, it has flat-slab roofs, a form which Wright might have adopted about this time quite independently of the techniques of concrete construction, since he used it in frame houses as well prior to 1910. Also like the third model house, the concrete surfaces of the Bock design demanded minimized and coarsened detail, and an appropriately monolithic effect. However, there is a burst of richness around the principal window, the focus of the composition: a striking arrangement of ornamental piers and a glazed grid of thick mullions which forecasts the massive decorative vocabulary of the much later concrete block houses in and around Los Angeles. The volumes of the Bock house are severely expressed. The reduced second floor added to the mass as a sort of glazed loggia is an element in Wright's domestic design which first appeared in the Heller house of 1898 and which comes back to play a part in this and other Prairie Houses of the later Oak Park period. Now, of course, it is low and subservient to the dominant horizontals; but it still has

Fig. 124. The unexecuted design for Richard Bock's house and studio. Similar in many ways to the third Ladies' Home Journal house, the Bock house also was to be built of cast concrete.

Fig. 125 A. The Robert W. Evans house, Chicago — a late Prairie House with an almost classic repose.

Fig. 125 B. The E. A. Gilmore house, Madison, Wisconsin, known locally as the "Airplane House." Unlike the Evans house, it has very dynamic lines.

Fig. 125 C. The Gridley house, Batavia, Illinois, shows the Prairie House dangerously approaching a condition of formula at one moment in the Oak Park Period.

Fig. 125 D. The Westcott house, Springfield, Ohio, is a house-and-garden with the garden strongly emphasized by architectural devices.

something of the quality of afterthought. It is repeated in the Tomek house in River Forest the following year.

Of the remaining Prairie Houses in the median range — medium-sized and average-priced — there are certain designs which stand alone and others which, because of common traits, can be grouped; but, again, only a sampling will be taken. The Evans house, like its prototype, the Willits house, is widespread and symmetrical; the Westcott and Gridley houses are irregular in plan and feature strong, balanced garden-façades with stressed second-story casements; the Beachey house is the last Prairie House with gabled roofs; the Hardy and Gilmore houses are dramatically related to site; and the Boynton

and Ingalls houses exemplify the Prairie House in a state of beautiful normality, so that they can be taken as paradigms. That they all display the extraordinary fertility of Wright's mind in applying the elements of his mature style to the evolution of a new answer to the central problem of American domestic architecture, the dwelling-house for the average family, is readily appreciated by leafing through their photographs (Fig. 125). To the mid-twentieth-century observer, they are dated in several ways, mostly, perhaps, by their dark accents, heavy massing, outmoded verandahs and decorative adjuncts; but their superb individuality and freedom from cant are as exciting as they ever were.

Finally, there are three Prairie Houses whose

Fig. 125 E. The Boynton house, Rochester, New York. A good Prairie House can perform the miracle of overcoming the banality of the standard city lot.

Fig. 125 F (above). The Hardy house, Racine, Wisconsin. Fig. 125 G (right). The Beachey house, Oak Park, Illinois. The "prairie" offers as wide a variety of settings as the Prairie House affords adaptations.

Fig. 125 H. The Ingalls house, River Forest, Illinois, a Prairie House without the prairie, shows a surprising degree of formality.

size or quality or circumstance place them in a class by themselves: the Coonley house, the Robie house, and the McCormick house project. They are roughly contemporary, falling in the years 1907-1909. Two were executed, and have been previously mentioned in this book as the "terminal masterpieces" of the Oak Park period — although the Coonley and Robie houses are very different from each other, they are a summation of Wright's principles of domestic architecture to their date. The third, the McCormick project, tragically abandoned at the eleventh hour, had a decisive effect upon the course of Wright's career; had it been built, it would have outranked the Coonley mansion as the *palazzo* of Prairie Houses. Judging by frequency of publication, the Coonley and Robie houses are the general favorites among executed Prairie House designs; Wright's own avowed preference is for the Coonley house, about which he remarks, "[it is] the most successful of my houses from my standpoint."

The Coonley house (Fig. 126) is the product of that rare set of factors in architectural history, a liberal client, a great designer, and perfect trust between the two. There is evidence on all sides that Mr. and Mrs. Avery Coonley were a most unusual and enlightened couple, seeking all the best that advanced thought and accomplishment in the new century afforded. They approached the task of erecting a house reflectively and rationally, determined to find the most progressive architect in practice and, having made their requirements plain, to interfere thenceforth in no way whatever with the creative processes which they had set in motion. Of the first meeting of clients and architect which led up to the famous Coonley house, Wright says: "About this time Mr. and Mrs. Avery Coonley came to build a home at Riverside, Illinois. Unknown to me they had gone to see nearly everything they could learn I had done before coming. The day they finally came into the Oak Park workshop Mrs. Coonley said that they had come because, it seemed to them, they saw in my houses 'the countenances of principle.' This was to me a great and sincere compliment. So, I put the best in me into the Coonley

Fig. 126. The Avery Coonley house, Riverside, Illinois, with little Miss Coonley looking like Alice in Wonderland.

Fig. 127 A. Rear view and plan of the Coonley house, the palazzo *of Prairie Houses and the product of harmony and "principle."*

house. I feel now, looking back upon it, that building was the best I could do then in the way of a house."

The exact year in which this memorable meeting took place is difficult to determine. An announcement appeared in Construction News (Chicago) in June, 1906, that the Riverside property had been bought with the view to erecting a residence, but no architect was mentioned; but by 1907 Wright was associated with the project and had done enough work to include the Coonley designs in the Chicago Architectural Club Annual Exhibition for that year, and in

March, 1908, he publicly stated[4] that the house was in process of construction. It would seem both safe and reasonable, therefore, to assign the date 1907 as the year of inception of the design, although the preliminary discussions may have been held some months earlier. In the *parti* of the Coonley design, two of Wright's most convinced beliefs had their greatest oppor-

Note 4
Frank Lloyd Wright: "In the Cause of Architecture," first paper, Architectural Record Vol. 23, March 1908, pp. 155-221.

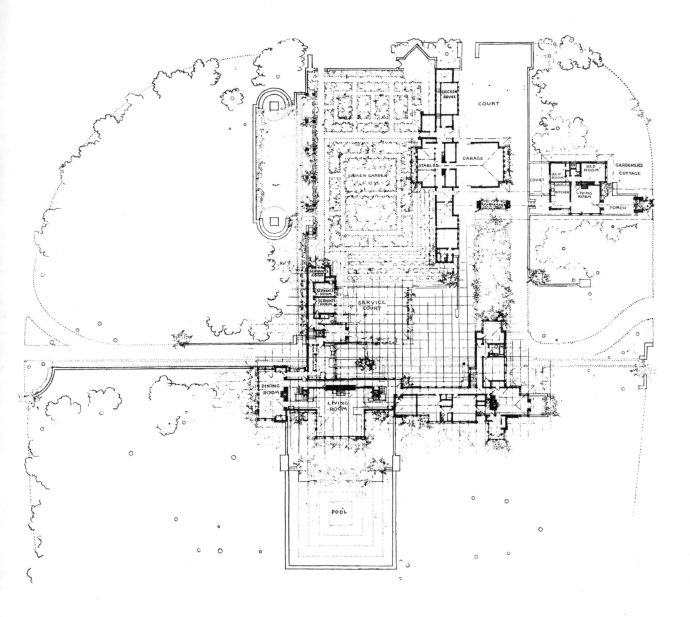

tunity for expression: the centrifugal plan and the raised basement. With the exception of a large, centrally located childrens' playroom, all principal rooms of the house are on the second level above grade; every room devoted to common enjoyment thus looks out over lawns and garden from a calculated height, although, by the magic of Wright's horizontal style, there is no sense of height on the exterior. The house fuses intimately with its setting (Fig. 127), and its great length, bent like the letter U and intricately jointed, is given variety by articulation of wall-surfaces and by the whole repertory of

Wrightian ornamentation. Oddly enough, it is frame construction, but there is no forced economy in the use of wood this time; everything is solidly and durably built. The treatment of exterior walls produces a banded effect: the lower registers are coated in fine sand-plaster of a creamy shade, the upper are faced with tilework in a simple geometric pattern whose subdued colors blend into a bronze tonality.

The view of the Coonley house most frequently published is the garden front, with its terraces, huge Wrightian urns, and reflecting pool. From this angle, the elements of the composition seem

Fig. 127 B. The Coonley house. Bedroom wing (above), living room terrace (left), and driveway penetrating the guest wing (facing page).

to reduce themselves to the plane of the water, the geometric solids of the ground story, the endless ribbons of casements in their deep band of shadow at the second level, the hovering, protecting roofs, and the low mass of the central chimney. The overriding impressions are those of a building with minimal head-heights and so perforated with openings everywhere beneath the eaves that it does not enclose space at all. It is only when we begin to move around the perimeter of the great house that we realize that it has many strongly defined space-blocks and that its plan is not symmetrical — that it is far more complex than it first seemed. The house is zoned within the confines of its U-shaped form. The living room, dining room and service quarters occupy the western half of the U; the bedrooms occupy the eastern. But, so that not only the communal rooms, but the master bedrooms as well, shall enjoy the south, or garden, exposure, the central bar of the U is again divided

in its function between living and sleeping accommodations; this accounts for the off-center placement of the main, or reflecting pool, elevation which, at first glance, seemed to be the exact center of the composition. The three blocks of the U are long, narrow and loosely connected; the length of the central block is projected at each end by pavilions, the western one containing the dining room, the eastern one containing the principal bedroom suite. The service wing and the guest-bedroom wing, the secondary blocks of the plan, are pierced at grade level by a driveway; the resultant isolation of the northern ground-floor spaces of these wings confirms the relative unimportance of the part which they play in the functioning of the house. In fact, almost the entire ground floor of the house is an extravagant substructure for what is essentially a one-level dwelling. Wright takes every aesthetic advantage, however, of this luxury. It is a fascinating experience (Fig. 128) to walk

Fig. 128. Above: West stairwell. Facing page: Corner of living room looking toward west stairwell and dining room in the Coonley house.

up one of the twin staircases from the entrance lobby into the great living space with its spatial surprises and its fantasy of moving, sloping ceilings emphasizing the fact that we are now under the great hovering roof itself. Here and there are leaded skylights set in separate peaked ceilings where the roofs have broken their flow to adjust themselves to the narrowed spots in plan caused by the joining of one element to another. In all this geometry of space and form, nature is constantly glimpsed through batteries of open casements in the distance, and is introduced into the room by jars of bittersweet and living plants. Across the long north wall, interrupted only by the raked brickwork of the enormous fireplace, there is a dim, painted frieze of

a birch forest.[5] These main spaces of the Coonley house combine to make what one is tempted to call a "noble apartment," for they have an undeniable grandeur, with their long vistas and

Note 5
There is some evidence that this mural was designed and executed by Marion Mahony.

their air of moneyed ease. Yet, the term conjures up the vision of monumental height, and there is no height here; on the contrary, everything is consciously scaled down to man. Wright replaces a senseless lavishness of height with a complete freedom of lateral movement, a luxury that human beings can *use*.

The harmony of shape and texture in the

Fig. 129. Above: Living room. Facing page: Dining room of the Coonley house.

Coonley house is also due to the fact that all of the furniture and fittings were custom-made to Wright's designs (Fig. 129). The color scheme of the decorations is expectedly autumnal: natural oak, brown, tan and gold stuffs, accents of verdigris. On the exterior, the tonality is established by the creamy tan of the plaster, the bronze of the tilework, and the russet terra-cotta roofing, with brown-stained trim providing sharp lineal definitions of breaks-of-plane. Rich-

ness of interest is accomplished by the prismatic gleam of the leaded casements and the constant, casual interruption of the strong lines of the architecture by vines and flowering plants in earth-pockets.

The word "harmonious" constantly comes to mind in connection with the Coonley house. It emerges first in the harmonious relation of client and architect and culminates in the perfectly harmonious relation of house to site—

the poetic statement of innermost meaning of that entire segment of Wright's creativity for which the term Prairie House has come to stand. Perhaps it is this thought which causes him to single out the Coonley house as the best. But its harmony is more than a thing of spirit; it is the sum-total of its material parts. Beginning with the shapes of the plan itself, the very *poché* of the drawings, harmony spreads to every detail of the superstructure and to every material of which it is made. Study will reveal that shapes in lead, in glass, in wood, in copper, in terra-cotta, in concrete are mirror-images, large or small, of each other and of the whole. In this very real sense, the Coonley house is an organic growth in which all cells are determined by and obedient to the central, ruling idea. Of very little architecture today can such be said.

Fig. 130. Above: Garden facade as originally built. Facing page: Garden facade after the pergola and playroom doors were added.

Shortly after the house was completed, a major alteration was made (Fig. 130). It was discovered that the playroom, the space directly beneath the living room, was too difficult of direct access to the outdoors, having only two lateral entrances from the terrace. Hence, a row of French doors, giving directly onto the pool, was installed where originally there had been three low windows under a continuous lintel. At the same time, two additional trellises were incorporated into the garden facade, one free and running across the entire width of the terrace, the other at the second-story level, just under the eaves, acting as an additional protection for the living room casements. The altered garden facade is thus somewhat overburdened, and loses the clear definition of the original design; but, to compensate, the terrace is a true outdoor living area, and as arresting in its spatial varieties as the rooms above. The added features are full of Wrightian decorative touches, both applied and inherent. With what sophisticated effect the shadow-bands of the upper trellis fall across the mullions and casements beneath!

The setting of the Coonley house recalls that of the Winslow house, its ancestor. Riverside, which was laid out in 1869 by Frederick Law Olmsted at the instigation of the Chicago, Burlington and Quincy Railroad as a model suburb, is perfectly flat but was given interest by an irregular, winding street plan. The Coonley property is a roughly triangular area at one edge of Olmsted's plan, nearly surrounded by the meanders of the Desplaines River. The casual quality of the site is reflected in the flowing plan of the house, which presents no definite facades and which, with its garages and outbuildings, rambles as freely over the land as the little river around it. The choice prairie scenery, the ample sweep of grounds, the impressive size of the building, and its fascinating summation

of all that went into the evolution of the Prairie House, makes it the first object of pilgrimage for those who travel to the western suburbs of Chicago to study in actuality Wright's early domestic work.

Because of its size and furnishings, the Coonley house was long in construction, but it was practically completed before Wright left Oak Park in 1909. It was first published in an article in House and Garden the following year.[6] The celebrated series of photographs used in this and ensuing publications was made in 1909-12 by the Chicago photographer Henry Fuermann; they are given added interest by the presence in the views of Mr. and Mrs. Coonley and their small daughter, for whom, in 1911, Wright was

Note 6
Hugh M. G. Garden: "Country Homes of the Western Plains," House & Garden, Vol. 18, Oct. 1910, pp. 230-35.

to erect a little building on the grounds as a playhouse and gathering-place for the children of the neighborhood. We get the impression that the Coonley family had a sensitive pleasure in their Prairie House which went beyond the norm, and the spirit of their appreciation of all its features was ever strong. Actually, there are legends. The story is still repeated in and around Chicago that, to keep everything in harmony with the "countenances of principle," Mrs. Coonley asked Wright to supply her with dress patterns for herself and her daughter; entertaining as this tale is, it must be consigned to the realm of folklore, but it bears witness to the unity of clients, house and architect which had much to do with the success of the design and which makes itself felt upon every observer. The house eventually passed to other hands, but subsequent owners have dealt with it sympathetically in an effort to preserve its crisp serenity.

A terminal masterpiece of a different order

Fig. 131 A. The Frederick Robie house, Chicago. This is perhaps the most dramatic Prairie House of all and still a cause cèlébre in 1958.

is the Frederick Robie house (Fig. 131) in Woodlawn Avenue on Chicago's South Side. This is a city house, built upon an average-sized city lot, though it must be remembered that when the house was erected in 1908 this part of Chicago still had something of the leafy quality of the open prairie. The amazingly long, dynamic lines of the house did not have to struggle in those days against the huddle of anomalous buildings which now crowds it. The Robie house is the culmination of those directional qualities in Wright's design which had been growing ever since the 1890's. Unlike the Coonley house, it is a massive structure of brickmasonry and concrete whose volumes are disposed along a single axis, parallel with the long dimension of the corner lot; the garage is integral, perhaps for the first time in the history of American architecture. Advanced concepts of function, such as this, together with a precision of edges which we associate with the machine, give to the design a technological spirit as great as that of the public structures, the Larkin Building and Unity Church. Strong planes, reliance upon the cantilever, and an uncompromising treatment of fenestration dominate the design in a way never before equalled in Wright's domestic work. Granted the validity of the ideal of horizontal flow in a dwelling, the design achieves its purpose without deviation or vagary.

Again, the *parti* is based upon a masterly adaptation of the raised basement theme, but the insertion of a long, sunken areaway at the center of composition, above which the main mass of the house seems suspended, gives it a subtlety and drama which are unprecedented. By this device and by the great prolongations of exterior masses of brick at the ends of the composition, terraces and parapets, we are almost confused by the relationship of level to level and house to site. It is as if everything were held in place by levitation. The one vertical, and the one fixed point in the entire complex of horizontal planes, is the huge chimney, which achieves an occult balance with the rest of the mass somewhat in the manner of a ship's stack. In fact, an analogy can be drawn between the Robie house and marine architecture; we begin to think of its levels as decks and of its topmost room as a bridge and of its projecting terraces as prows. It is no wonder that the Robie house was nicknamed "the Battleship."

Fig. 131 B. Dining room interior and plans of the Robie house.

The floor plan of the main level is a miracle of fluid spaces. Those areas which, by their function, demand the privacy of compartmentation —guest bedroom, kitchen, servants' quarters — are relegated to a parallel block at the rear that has a sliding relationship to the main block. The living room, the central stairwell, and the dining room are a unit, separated but not divided by the pylon of the chimney, and defined by the long walls of the house. Within this area, there is not a single cross-partition, nor do the walls themselves return at their ends. The two chief spaces terminate in diamond-shaped bays which are independent of the walls, and around which the spaces flow outward to open porches. The south wall is not exactly a wall; it is a parapet upon which rest the series of brick mullions between casements, and this glazed plane makes no acknowledgment whatever of the change in function from living to dining spaces — its rhythm is unbroken. The master bedrooms are contained within the reduced area of the third level of the house, a sort of glazed loggia seemingly composed of a low, umbrella-like roof resting upon panels of glass. Every major space has its access to the out-of-doors; but, because there can be no sweep of lawn and garden around the house, out-of-doors is man-made: porches and balconies, their brick parapets strongly demarcated by uninterrupted limestone cappings.

It is an absorbing exercise in the progress of Wright's style over fifteen years to compare the Robie house with the Winslow house. There are manifold changes; but perhaps the chief difference is in the degree of penetration of mass with surrounding atmosphere. Wall is important in the Winslow design, and the vertical planes are clear and unambiguous. Wall, as a supporting element, is non-existent in the Robie design. The effect is as of a loosely associated pile of horizontal planes, through and around which air flows uninhibitedly. The west front of the Winslow house is unified, self-contained; the Robie house is a temporary halt in a continuum which has neither beginning nor ending. It is part of some larger scheme of mass-in-space.

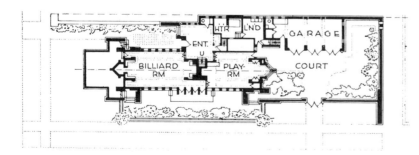

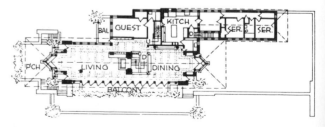

Fig. 132 A. Sketch for the Harold McCormick house, a spectacular project which died on the drafting-boards and may have carried with it to oblivion the whole future of the Chicago School.

The biggest private house that Wright has ever designed was intended as the Lake Forest residence of Harold McCormick, principal heir of the great reaper and farm-implement fortune which was an inheritance to be favorably compared with the Carnegie and Morgan holdings. That the project ended in failure was, as has already been indicated, a severe blow to Wright's early career and, indeed, the lowering of the curtain on the whole Chicago School. Mr. McCormick had apparently been interested in Wright for some time, and in 1907 proposed that he should present some ideas in sketch form for a new McCormick family seat in Lake Forest, some thirty miles north of Chicago. The site for this project was a large tract of land bordering the bluffs which rise there from the beaches of Lake Michigan. It was a dramatic setting similar to that of the Hardy house at Racine; in addition, there was a brook cascading to the Lake through a deep ravine at the southern edge of the property.

As the McCormick project gathered force in the favorable atmosphere of the client's approval, a *parti* for the huge complex of main house and ancillary buildings began to emerge (Fig. 132). Wright planned to reinforce and regularize the natural bluffs by means of a series of retaining walls, deeply articulated, which would also act as a great running base for the house proper. The levels of these walls were to be so varied that no one dominating horizontal would impose itself upon the natural landscape or make the scheme too rigid when seen from offshore; it would be a happy fusion of nature and Wright. Upon this partly synthetic platform, some fifty feet in height, the house would range itself in a long composition of freely associated pavilions and galleries. But the plan, of course, had an organization even though it was not obtrusive; a certain formality is necessary, even in a Prairie House, to a baronial way of life. The McCormick plan has its main axis along the bluff, jointed and staggered at places; extending westward and at right angles were two major wings and a minor one, forming landscaped courtyards open to the west. In its centrifugal, flowing quality, it resembles the plan of the smaller but equally luxurious Coonley house, with which it is contemporary. The *poché* of the plan indicates that the superstructure is carried on isolated masonry supports, with walls reduced to an absolute minimum. It is a complex of cantilevered hip roofs riding over vertical planes of glass. The long, free spans of covered verandahs, of which there are many, heighten the impression of a structure whose horizontal parts are rather mysteriously maintained in place. The extreme openness of plan is calculated to induce intimate living with nature — the Japanese ideal — and the extent to which client and designer were willing to go in approximating the quality of a gigantic gardenhouse is seen in the open gallery through which one must pass to reach the suite of master bedrooms. The owner's bedroom is somewhat recessed from the edge of the bluff for the sake of extra privacy, but it commands a wonderful view across the limitless expanse of the Lake and down into the wooded ravine. The great living and dining rooms are at the center of mass, projecting forward on bastions of masonry, and enjoying through their transparent outer skin a majestic seascape.

The McCormick design, had it been executed, would have placed Wright in the vanguard of successful American architects, and as the apostle of a new architecture to which the most serious attention must be given. It would have done even more: it would have placed the stamp of social approval on the whole progressive movement in Chicago and extended its scope immeasurably. It might have turned the tide of eclecticism. The rejection of the design marks a pivotal point in the history of a trend toward modern design in America which, as it was, went down in *débacle*, not to rise again until the late 1920's. The story of the rejection of the McCormick design has never been fully revealed. It has been suggested that it was Mrs. McCormick who refused it, saying that her mode of life simply could not be suited by a Prairie House. In any case it was she who suddenly went to New York in August, 1908, and placed the commission for the house which she eventually occupied in the hands of a master of traditional architecture, Charles Augustus Platt, who gave her a handsome Italian villa that is as knowing a piece of archaeology as can be seen in the Middle West. That it was erected upon the ruins of the Chicago School was, for him, unimportant.

Fig. 132 B. Aerial perspective of the proposed McCormick house, Lake Forest, Illinois.

6. Some Office Tragedies

Quite apart from the McCormick fiasco, The Studio had its share of "office tragedies" — unexecuted major designs. It is usually the nature of these ill-starred projects to drag on over a period of years, or to be undatable, in either case presenting problems to the student of the architect's work as well as to the architect himself. It will be recalled that there had been two of these projects in the transitional period of Wright's career, the Wolf Lake and Cheltenham Beach resorts. His office tragedies were mostly, like these, types of architecture which he did not ordinarily undertake. Then there had been that perennial frustration, commencing in 1898, of Lincoln Center. Of those which had their inception after 1900, the design of Lexington Terraces (Fig. 133) is the first, and a very characteristic example of its class. During almost ten years, this ambitious project for Edward Waller, Jr., was a recurrent drain upon the energies of everyone in The Studio; the drawings still on file at Taliesin range in date all the way from 1901 to 1909. At least two sites on the South Side of Chicago[1] were considered for Lexington Ter-

races, and there may have been others. It was a multiple-housing scheme: two identical units of small flats compressed into a square enclosing a landscaped court. Wright's solution of the problem is in many ways reminiscent of the smaller Francisco Terrace which he actually built for the senior Edward Waller in 1895. The three-story street fronts backed against the two-story courtyard fronts, the passageway through the body of the building as access to the courtyard, the idea of the courtyard itself, the communicating balcony at the second level, the corner stair-towers, and the severe, uniform horizontality of the design are all elements of the earlier structure. The chief difference is that Lexington Terraces is on a really large scale and is more intricate in its parts and surface enrichment. While there remain traces of Sullivanesque detail that suggest an early date for the *parti*, articulation of wall-surfaces is well advanced, and there is a brilliant example of geometrical intersections within the courtyard towers that is pure play, and that Nikolaus Pevsner[2] might call a "polyphony of abstract

Note 1
The sites of which there is record are: (1) the corner of Langley Avenue and 60th Street, and (2) the corner of Lexington and Spaulding Avenues.

Note 2
Nikolaus Pevsner: "Pioneers of Modern Design from William Morris to Walter Gropius," 2nd ed., Museum of Modern Art, New York, 1949, p. 102.

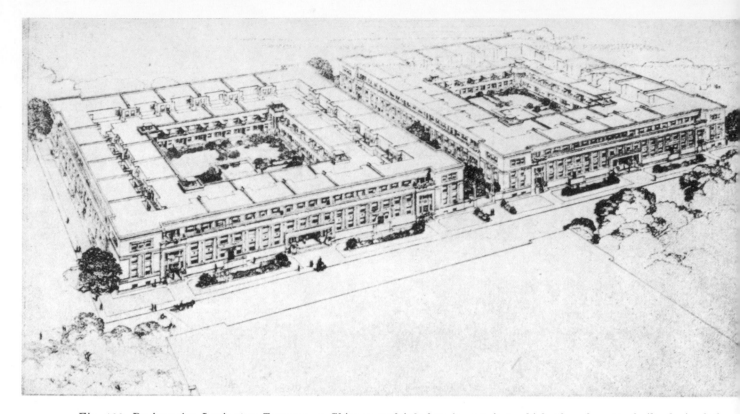

Fig. 133. Designs for Lexington Terraces, a Chicago multiple-housing project which, though never built, drained the energies of The Studio for almost ten years.

forms" had it been done by Glasgow's Charles Rennie Mackintosh. On the debit side, there are strange ineptitudes in Lexington Terraces, as in the repeated grouping together of a door, a bay, and a sash window; and the flower-boxes look rather small and incidental. As a piece of progressive city housing, too, the design has demerits; at any rate, modern practice would certainly condemn the narrow ribbon of light-wells that undulates between the outer and inner lines of flats.

The Wallers, father and son, were forever entertaining thoughts of further subdivision of their family property in River Forest, to the north of Auvergne Place. For these proposed "Waller Estates" Wright designed three houses with variants to be built speculatively. There are absurd discrepancies regarding the date of these designs. They were listed in the Museum of Modern Art (N.Y.) catalogue of 1932 as belonging to the year 1897; but the only extant drawings are those which were reproduced in the Wasmuth monograph of 1910, which are undated. In August, 1909, an announcement for the proposed "Waller Estates" was carried in Construction News (Chicago), saying that the designs for the houses were completed. While it is hard to believe that the designs could have been filed for twelve years, they are a sort of recapitulation of the whole process of development of the small Prairie House from about 1900 to 1910. They exhibit the three roof-forms which Wright favored: the early gable, the later deck, the perennial hip. They are cubical in *parti*, like that inexpensive house-type which Wright inaugurated in 1905 to democratize his architecture, but they retain the "outdoor living room," the long, roofed verandah which was characteristic of the more costly Prairie Houses all the way from the Bradley house of 1900 to the Robie house of 1908. Further, they illustrate the transformation of the flowing plan to a restricted rectangular unit-room and the coarsening of detail that was evolved for low-cost housing after 1905. There is one unaccountable feature: the continued use of the sash window; this kind of fenestration had become extinct in Wright's domestic work by 1909, the last example of its use having been the little clapboarded Charles Brown house in Evanston in 1905. The deck-roofed and gable-roofed designs for "Waller Estates" were destined, although neither Wright nor Waller built them, for a long life. They were often duplicated by the two members of Wright's Oak Park staff who, for a few years after the disbandment of the group, were his closest followers, Walter Griffin and John van Bergen.[3] Actually, in 1911, Wright himself played variations upon these Waller designs in five small houses which he built at Glencoe, Illinois, for Sherman Booth, his lawyer.

The project called "Como Orchards" became, in a sense, an office tragedy. It was surely the most unusual commission that came Wright's way before 1910 (Fig. 134). It was the scheme of some University of Chicago faculty members

Note 3
Cf. *van Bergen's Skillin house, 714 Ashland Ave., Wilmette, Ill., and the houses by Griffin at 10557 and 10561 So. Longwood Blvd., Chicago.*

Fig. 134. Como Orchards, the uncompleted Montana Utopia financed by University of Chicago professors.

Fig. 135. "Quadruple Block Plan," a recurring scheme never materialized but still hatching progeny at Taliesin.

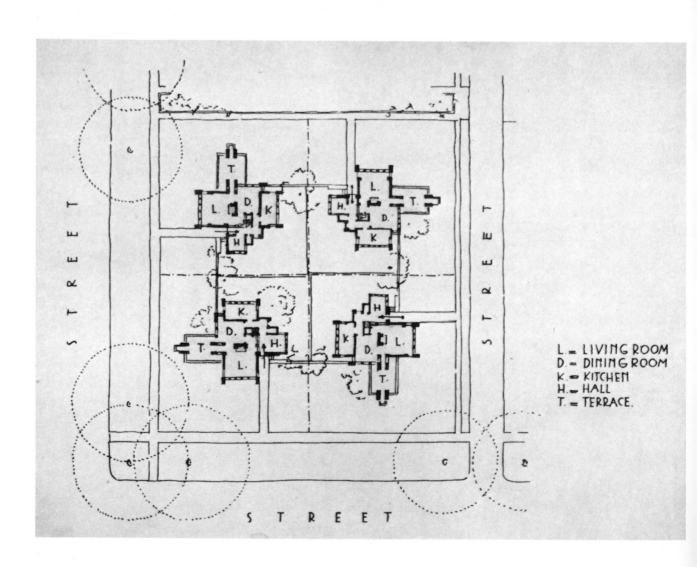

L. = LIVING ROOM
D. = DINING ROOM
K. = KITCHEN
H. = HALL
T. = TERRACE.

for a summer colony in the remote Bitter Root Mountains of western Montana that would combine the advantages of a holiday retreat for themselves and a financial investment which would bring some yearly profit. Like all Utopias, it failed to materialize as envisioned, and its failure damaged Wright as well as the professors, for he put some of his own scanty capital into it plus untold hours of time and thought. Eventually, a segment of the central building, the community lodge, was built under the supervision of Marion Mahony and William Drummond. The project, first broached in 1908, was most ambitious, including over fifty buildings. Wright's master plans, dated April, 1909, show several variants of the one-story Prairie House with hip roof and massive chimney arranged symmetrically around a long central axis of lodge, gardens, meadows and cascading pools. All the buildings were to have been of frame sheathed in brown lapped siding. Individually, the cottages are fine examples of Wright's Oak Park style, more compact and idealized than was normally possible because they had neither kitchens nor service quarters. Taken as a whole, the plan seems arbitrary and rigid for a wilderness site, there is no feeling for the roughness of terrain, and the cottages to the rear of the lodge are inexplicably close together, as if land were at a premium. Nevertheless, Como Orchards is really a very early landmark in the history of American town-planning, a development in which Wright, characteristically, took an immediate interest and expressed novel views.

The other project in town-planning was the "Quadruple Block Plan," which appears and re-appears throughout the Oak Park period, and even up to 1916,[4] like a will-o'-the-wisp (Fig. 135). The idea seems to have originated in the first year of the century as a housing project for Charles E. Roberts, to be erected on a tract of land in Oak Park south of Chicago Avenue and east of Fair Oaks; it was stopped by the citizens of that area of the town, who objected to it as too radical. The perspective drawings for the scheme then appeared as background for the Ladies' Home Journal model houses in 1901, and again, in the same periodical, for the concrete model house in 1907. Meanwhile, they had been included in the material exhibited at the Chicago Architectural Club Annual in 1902, and, eight years later, they were featured in the Wasmuth monograph. None of it was ever built. In essence, the "Quadruple Block Plan" was a scheme, with one variant, for placing a maximum number of individual dwellings on an average city block with maximum light and greenery. The houses were rather undistinguished two-story dwellings with hip roofs and stucco walls, but already completely recognizable as being within the Prairie House family. It is, perhaps, the greatest of the office tragedies that the scheme, in any of its guises, never got beyond the paper stage, for it might have stimulated Wright into more fruitful and significant efforts in the field of town-planning at the moment when its American phase was just beginning to assume importance.

Note 4
Frank Lloyd Wright: "A Non-Competitive Plan," in "City Residential Land Development," Alfred Yeomans (ed.), Univ. of Chicago Press, 1916, pp. 95-102.

FLIGHT

The End of an Era

Perhaps the chief clue to the fateful events of fall, 1909, is to be found in the following passage from "An Autobiography": "This absorbing, consuming phase of my experience as an architect ended about 1909. I had almost reached my fortieth year: weary, I was losing grip on my work and even interest in it." Behind this extraordinary statement — extraordinary because Wright might have seemed at this juncture to be in full career — lies an interlocking group of motives, professional and personal.

Professionally, there were ominous currents beneath the surface. Despite the triumphal progress of the Prairie House, the new architecture had suffered some serious blows which, in the mind of an ambitious and sensitive man, could add up to failure. It must be obvious to any reader of Wright's books and articles that there is a strong apostolic streak in his character. It was not enough that there stood in and around Chicago and Buffalo a few score of his buildings to prove that something fundamentally creative had been evolved; people were still mesmerized by the past, and too many of them still regarded the new architecture as a freak, and those who patronized it as unstable. It had come near, for a few months in 1908, to receiving the *cachet* of Society, only to be denied it at the last moment; whether it did or didn't, the very admission of the need was a galling thought. Wright undoubtedly evaluated the McCormick fiasco at its true significance: the requiem for a whole school of architecture which had had the will and the ability to make the United States the instigator of an architectural revolution that was long heralded and that could not, in any case, be in-definitely postponed. And, so far as the School was concerned, there was more than this public resistance that was wrong; the School could not fight resistance because it had no leader. Wright could have been that leader, but he had, through impatience and a certain arrogance, alienated his colleagues. Even those eager young people whom he had gathered around him at The Studio were, by 1909, disaffected. The tensions in "the house" were felt in the drafting room, and there were days on end when Wright was too distracted to work. The finances of the establishment had grown extremely precarious; there was lunch every day with the family, but less regularly a pay-check.

To these professional worries, whose power to sap the vitality of even a pioneer genius we can imagine, were added the very real troubles of pecuniary strain and family dissension. For the whole first half of his life, being short of cash was such a familiar demon that Wright may possibly have built up an immunity against it. He had, apparently, no patience with the grubby business of saving and budgeting. But the discordances of his private life, against which there was no magic charm, were playing havoc with him. By 1909, he and the first Mrs. Wright were totally estranged, and his six children had grown away from him. Wright frankly tells this in "An Autobiography," and it would be impertinent to attempt a further analysis of the difficulties here; but it should be pointed out that he had inherited from his father a stubborn ego coupled with an emotional instability that manifested itself when that ego was opposed. In the quarrels which broke out among Wright, his wife, and his eldest son, Lloyd, the issue at stake seems to have been the question of personal "freedom" against marital "slavery"; these words occur in the pertinent passage of "An Autobiography," and also the phrase "love is not property." Wright had fought for many years the mounting sense of outrage at being possessed, but when he suddenly released it, its pent-up pressure could not be controlled. The fact that he had found refuge in the sympathy of another woman only heightened the impasse.

Exactly repeating his father's behaviour of 1885, one day toward the end of October, 1909, Wright abruptly abandoned his family and his practice. It was an overnight decision. The following morning, he made frenzied rounds of his current clients in Chicago, collecting fees in advance and selling fistfuls of Japanese prints, but explaining his purpose to no one. That afternoon he took a train to New York, where he was joined by Mrs. Edwin Cheney (Mamah Borthwick).[1] A few hours later, they were on a ship bound for Europe. For nearly two weeks the scandal, while rumored, was kept from the public; but it broke into print on Sunday, November 7th, on the front pages of every Chicago newspaper.[2] There was general consternation and speculation, but Chicago heard nothing more from Wright for almost two years. All that was really known was that he and Mamah Cheney, after a sojourn in Berlin, were living quietly in a small villa above Florence, at Fiesole.

If the circumstances of this act can be con-

Note 1
It will be recalled that Wright built a small Prairie House in Oak Park in 1904 for Mr. and Mrs. Cheney; presumably, the intimacy between Wright and Mamah Cheney had been developing from that time until their elopement. The Cheneys had two children, aged seven and three in 1909.
Note 2
E. g., see the Chicago Tribune for Sunday, Nov. 7 and Monday and Tuesday, Nov. 8 and 9, 1909; apparently, discovery by some alert Chicago news correspondent in Berlin of a "Mr. and Mrs. Frank Lloyd Wright" in the registers of the Hotel Adlon gave the tip, and both Mrs. Wright and Mr. Cheney in Oak Park were immediately subjected to questioning.

doned, Wright's flight to Europe was as expected and "classic" a move as his running away to Chicago in 1887 to test himself against the background of a big city. For a great artist, his life to 1909 had remained strangely circumscribed; his one excursion to Japan must have left a hungry curiosity about the rest of the world. Furthermore, he had held long, stimulating conversations in 1908 with the German philosopher and critic Kuno Francke,[3] who had come to Chicago to have a look at a city whose accomplishments in architecture and social welfare had reached his receptive ears. Naturally, he found Wright. As a result of the contact, and of his enthusiastic reports, Ernst Wasmuth, the Berlin publisher, was at work on the now famous elephant-folio of Wright's architecture,[4] and it needed editing and comment by Wright himself. Wright's presence in Berlin had become a necessity. Thus, even under emotional duress, his flight to Europe was not wholly irresponsible; it was conditioned by the practical considerations of his career. We can conclude that, although his father's instable nature seemed at this moment dominant in Wright, the level-headed toughness of the Lloyd-Jones strain was by no means in abeyance.

As for The Studio, Wright paused long enough in that day of hasty preparation for departure to make a curious disposition of his practice: he simply turned it over, lock, stock, and barrel, to an architect named Herman von Holst. The link with von Holst was extremely tenuous — through Marion Mahony, who had worked in his office on occasion. There is no palpable reason for such a choice, and Wright has never offered an explanation. Perhaps that was not a day for rational decisions. Von Holst was born and

Note 3
Kuno Francke had come to the United States at the invitation of Harvard University in the capacity of Visiting Lecturer.
Note 4
Frank Lloyd Wright: "Ausgefuehrte Bauten und Entwuerfe," Wasmuth, Berlin, 1910 (previously cited); for any serious student of Wright's early career, this first great monograph is a key work; furthermore, its effect upon the dawning European school of modern architecture was incalculably important.

trained in Germany. His work in the Chicago area, where he had come to settle, had consisted of careful, utterly unimaginative designs, many of them ecclesiastic, and as far removed from Wright's style as it was possible to be. The two men had only recently been introduced and there had been no business connection of any kind. While there were a dozen architects immediately available both in The Studio and elsewhere in Chicago who had worked with Wright and who were familiar with his style and his clientele, it must have required painful adjustments for von Holst to attune himself, without warning, to the principles of the new architecture. Nevertheless, von Holst was chosen. He solved his dilemma in the only sensible way by placing Marion Mahony in charge of operations — the logical move, which Wright might have made directly. Walter Burley Griffin was also commandeered, and was given full responsibility for landscaping. These two people, then,[5] moved their desks to von Holst's office in town, there to complete and supervise, under von Holst's official banner, those commissions of Wright's which were still in the preliminary stages.[6]

It is ironical that Henry Ford made a tentative approach to Wright during this time of troubles. One story has it[7] that the approach was made upon Wright's return from Europe; the other, that it was made only a few days before his decampment. Ford was then thinking of his first enterprise in domestic architecture: the large family seat, eventually known as "Fair Lane," to be built on family land at Dearborn.

In any case, Wright was too emotionally disturbed to be able to make any adequate response, and turned Ford over to von Holst, who entirely failed to sustain Ford's interest. The contact was permanently lost; but it is fascinating to imagine what the consequences of an association of Henry Ford and Frank Lloyd Wright might have been.

On the day of Wright's flight, The Studio was busy with the normal volume of work-in-progress. Commissions which were nearly finished remained on the boards there and were carried to completion by William Drummond and John van Bergen. Obstacles were numerous and the work went forward slowly, but it was done. For one or two of the current designs which had really captured Wright's attention, he sent back from Europe, clandestinely, a few additional drawings. When these jobs were finished, Drummond and van Bergen closed and locked The Studio door, thereby ending an era in the chronicle of America's greatest living architect.

As everyone knows, and at this writing, almost a half-century of that chronicle lies beyond, filled with more experiment and more accomplishment. Only the future will reveal where the apex of so great a career actually falls; but it is self-evident, right now, that, had Wright's work been fated to terminate in 1910 instead of merely to pause, his place in the story of the emergence of modern architecture would still be first and no less secure. That part of his creative life which we can identify with Oak Park, was, indeed, a Golden Age.

Note 5
Marion Mahony (Mrs. Walter Burley Griffin; see Appendix F) is as interesting a personality in the world of architecture as her husband; she was one of the first women to graduate from the Massachusetts Institute of Technology and the first woman licensed to practice architecture in Illinois.
Note 6
The commisions which fell to von Holst's lot were: the Irving and Mueller houses in Decatur, Ill., and the Amberg house in Grand Rapids, Mich.; they were published under the attribution "H. V. von Holst & Marion Mahony, Associates." The furniture and fittings of these houses were made, as usual, by George Niedecken of Milwaukee.

Note 7
Keith Sward: "The Legend of Henry Ford," Rinehart, New York, 1948, p. 110; Sward attributes the impulse to visit Wright to Henry's son Edsel at the age of twenty, which would place the event in the year 1913—but he goes on to say that Wright was "vacationing in Europe" at the time, which is not the case; he was back in Wisconsin in 1911.
John van Bergen, who was one of those on duty at The Studio in the final weeks before the elopement, spoke to the author at length in February 1940; one of his strongest recollections about those weeks was the visit of Henry Ford and Wright's inability to maintain his customary, self-confident manner.

Appendix

APPENDIX A

The following program is transcribed from the Catalogue of the University of Wisconsin for the academic year 1885-1886. It was the standard curriculum for beginners in the Engineering School, and covers the entire period during which Wright was enrolled in the University as a "Special Student in Engineering."

Freshman Year:
  First Term
    German or French
    Algebra
    Drawing
    Shop Practice

  Second Term
    German or French
    Theory of Equations
    Rhetoric
    Drawing

  Third Term
    German or French
    Trigonometry
    Descriptive Geometry
    Drawing

Sophomore Year:
  First Term
    Analytical Geometry
    Chemistry
    Descriptive Geometry
    Drawing

  Second Term
    Calculus
    Chemistry
    Stereometry
    Physics
    Drawing

APPENDIX B

The following, transcribed from pertinent editions of The Lakeside City Directory of Chicago, shows the downtown offices which Wright occupied from the year in which his name first appeared until 1912:

1890 1600, Auditorium Bldg.
1892 1600, Auditorium Bldg.
[The above address is the office of Adler & Sullivan]
1893 1501, Schiller Bldg.
1894 1501, Schiller Bldg.
1895 1501, Schiller Bldg.
1896 1501, Schiller Bldg.
1897 1107, Steinway Hall
1898 1123, The Rookery
1899 1104, The Rookery
1900 (not listed)
1901 1106, Steinway Hall
1902 1106, Steinway Hall
1903 (not listed)
1904 1106, Steinway Hall
1905 1106, Steinway Hall
1906 1106, Steinway Hall
1907 1106, Steinway Hall
1908 1020, Fine Arts Bldg.
1909 (not listed)
1910 1020, Fine Arts Bldg.
1911 1020, Fine Arts Bldg.
1912 605, Orchestra Hall

APPENDIX C

The following is a list of those Japanese printmakers represented in Wright's collection at the time of forced sale at Anderson Galleries, New York, 1927:

Buncho   Kunimasa
Eishi   Masanobu
Eisho   Sharaku
Eirii   Shigemasa
Haronobu   Shunko
Hiroshige   Shunsho
Hokkei   Shunyei
Hokusai   Shunzan
Kiyomitsu   Toyokuni I
Kiyonaga   Toyonobu
Kiyonobu   Utamaro
Kiyotsune   Yeishi
Koriusai   Yeisho

APPENDIX D

The following list, compiled from the annual catalogues printed by the Club, itemizes all designs and objects exhibited by Wright in the Chicago Architectural Club Annual Exhibitions:

1894 Bagley house — a watercolor
        rendering by Ernest Albert
      "Residence"[1] — a watercolor
        rendering by Ernest Albert
      "Residence"[1] — a watercolor
        rendering by Ernest Albert
      "Residence"[1] — a watercolor
        rendering by Ernest Albert
      "The Hall"[1] — a watercolor
        rendering by Ernest Albert

Note 1
These designs cannot be identified.

Milwaukee Library and Museum[2]

1898 An example of electro-glazing for the American Luxfer Prism Co.

1899 Three examples of "Luxfer Electro-Glazed Art Glass"

1900 Devin house — plans, perspective drawing
Eckart house[3] — perspective drawing
Lincoln Center — plans, perspective drawing
McAfee house — plan, perspective drawing
Moore house — one photo of exterior
The Studio at Oak Park — plan, perspective drawing, one photo of exterior, two photos of interior
Waller house[4] — perspective drawing

1901 (No exhibitions, but the catalogue contained the full text of the Hull House lecture, "The Art and Craft of the Machine")

1902 All Souls' Church (Lincoln Center) — perspective drawing of the smaller scheme
Bradley house — two photos of exterior, three photos of interior
Henderson house — perspective drawing
Hickox house — one photo of exterior
Hillside Home School — plan, bird's-eye perspective drawing
Ladies' Home Journal Model Houses (and Quadruple Block Plan) for the Curtis Publishing Co. — plans, perspective drawings, sections
Lexington Terraces — two perspective drawings

Metzger house[5] — plan, perspective drawing
River Forest Golf Club — one photo of exterior
The Studio at Oak Park — drawings, details, photos of interior
Thomas house — perspective drawing
Village Bank for The Brickbuilder — perspective drawing
Winslow house — perspective drawing, details, photo of stables (furniture, objects, bric-a-brac)

1907 Adams, Mary, house
Beachey house
Cheney house
Clarke house[6]
Coonley house
Curtis Publishing Co. (model)
Dana house
Devin house, Eliot, Me.[7]
Gerts, Walter, house
Glasner house
Gridley house
Hardy house
Heath house
Henderson house
Hoyt house
Larkin Building
Larkin Co. (workmen's houses)
Ludington house[8]
Martin, Darwin, house
Metzger house
Millard house[9]

Note 5
This was an unexecuted design for Victor Metzger in 1902 for a rocky site near Sault Ste. Marie, Mich.

Note 6
This probably refers to the Little house in Peoria, Ill., first built in 1903 for Francis Little and later enlarged for its second owner, Robert Clarke.

Note 7
This was an unexecuted project for a summer house for the same Mrs. David (Aline) Devin for whom the projected design of circa 1895 was made.

Note 8
An unexecuted house design for R. S. Ludington at Dwight, Ill.

Note 9
This was the first house erected for Mrs. George Madison Millard — a typical Prairie House of 1906 at Highland Park, Ill. — who, in 1923, commissioned from Wright the celebrated "La Miniatura" at Pasadena, Calif.

Moore house
Pettit Mortuary Chapel[10]
de Rhodes house
River Forest Tennis Club
Shaw house[11]
Stone house
Sutton house
Thomas house
Tomek house
Unity Church
University of Wisconsin Boat Club[12]
Westcott house
Wolf Lake Resort

Note 10
A small family vault in Belvidere Cemetery, Ill.

Note 11
An unexecuted design, possibly of 1906, for a large granite Prairie House for Thaxter Shaw on the slope of the Mountain in Montreal, Canada; apparently part of the same commission was an alteration for Shaw's town-house in Peel St., Montreal.

Note 12
An unexecuted project of 1902 for the Yahara Boat Club at Madison, Wis.

APPENDIX E

Wright and Webster Tomlinson collaborated in the following commissions:

1. House for E. Arthur Davenport, River Forest, Ill., 1901
2. House for William G. Fricke, Oak Park, Ill., 1901[1]
3. House for F. B. Henderson, Elmhurst, Ill., 1901
4. House for Victor Metzger, Sault Ste. Marie, Mich., 1902 (unexecuted)
5. House for Frank Thomas, Oak Park, 1901[2]

Note 1
This house is sometimes referred to as the "Emma Martin" house; she was the second owner, and Wright carried out some additions and alterations under her name in 1907.

Note 2
This house is sometimes referred to as the "James Rogers" house; Rogers was Thomas's father-in-law, and actually gave the initial commission to Wright.

Note 2
This was a competition drawing of which nothing exists but one very poorly preserved sketch; it was in a Classic style, somewhat reminiscent of Perrault's east front of the Louvre.

Note 3
Robert Eckart was a Waller son-in-law; this was one of the unexecuted designs for "Waller Estates."

Note 4
Another executed design for "Waller Estates."

APPENDIX F

The active years of The Studio at Oak Park roughly corresponded with the first period of Wright's independent practice. It was built and equipped in 1895 and it was closed sometime in 1910. During these years, Wright employed many assistants at The Studio. An accurate and inclusive registry of these people, several of whom went on to independent careers of note, would be a valuable document, but it is unlikely that it will ever be compiled. Records were incomplete, and those that were saved from the debacle of 1909-1910 were destroyed in the Taliesin fire of 1914. Wright cannot remember all the facts. Certain former members of The Studio staff were interviewed by the author in 1939-1940; they cooperated as fully as they could, and much that had been mysterious was cleared up, but none of them had the whole story at his command. The chronicle of The Studio, although it was fresher in peoples' minds then, had already grown dim.

Fortunately, in 1908 Wright drew up a list of his assistants, as he could recall them, together with their terms of service at The Studio,[1] and this list is reproduced here:

Marion Mahony	11 years
William Drummond	7 years
Francis Byrne	5 years
Isabel Roberts	5 years
George Willis	4 years
Walter Griffin	4 years
Andrew Willatsen	3 years
Harry Robinson	2 years
Charles E. White, Jr.	1 year
Erwin Barglebaugh	1 year
Robert Hardin	1 year
Albert McArthur	new

This list is not exhaustive. We know, for example, of a woman named Anna Hicks who assisted Wright in the 1890's. Then, too, the list necessarily leaves unaccounted for the final eighteen months of operations. Sometime after 1908, we know, John van Bergen and Taylor Wooley joined the staff; and there may well have been others. The list, furthermore, is not entirely accurate in its figures if the recollections of certain staff-members themselves are to be given credence. Lastly, the list does not take any cognizance of those independent artists and craftsmen who collaborated in Wright's work. This is most unfortunate, as there is a good deal of significance for the whole story in these rather shadowy names. We know something of Richard Bock, the sculptor, and of George M. Niedecken, the decorator. It would be very valuable to have a complete dossier on Orlando Giannini, the glassmaker; the author has gleaned a little knowledge of him through correspondence with Alfonso Ianelli of Park Ridge, Illinois (who enters the story most prominently in 1913 as the potter and glassmaker of Midway Gardens and the post-Oak Park era). Another collaborator who appears fitfully in the story is Blanche Ostertag, the potter-muralist; it would be interesting to know precisely what her contribution was before she transferred her center of activities to New York in 1911 and painted, among other things, the "Sailing of the Claremont" in the foyer of the New Amsterdam Theater.

But to return to the regular staff at Oak Park, Marion Mahony is certainly the key figure. If The Studio had been organized along more conventional lines, she would have held the rank of "head designer." In conversations with the author in Chicago in 1940 (she was then the widow of Walter Burley Griffin), she stipulated that she came to The Studio in time to help with the drawings for the Francis Apartments, which was erected in 1895; by this reckoning, she would have been on duty at The Studio some thirteen years in 1908 instead of the eleven which Wright gives her. Although there were brief intervals when she worked elsewhere, it can be said that she remained to the end and saw her name joined with von Holst's in 1910-11 as "co-designer" of the Decatur and Grand Rapids houses. She was not only a skilled designer but a gifted draftswoman; many of the fine pen perspectives turned out by The Studio were hers, as well as most of the finished drawings for the Wasmuth monograph, and she may have designed some of the decorative murals of the Prairie Houses, such as that in the living room of the Coonley house.

There is good evidence that Walter Burley Griffin joined the staff of The Studio in 1901 rather than 1904. His special interest was landscape architecture, which he eventually broadened into town-planning. In 1914 he won the world-wide competition for the design of Canberra, the Australian Federal Capital; this took him and Mrs. Griffin to The Antipodes, where they remained until his death. William Drummond and John van Bergen were, for several years after The Studio closed, the chief imitators of the Wrightian style in domestic architecture; there are houses standing in the Chicago suburbs today which, although designed by them, are regularly taken by the uninitiated as Wright's. In later practice, each man developed an independent style. Barry Byrne (mentioned as "Francis" in Wright's list) entered after 1910 into partnership with an architect named Ryan and specialized in parochial buildings; his style was never pronouncedly Wrightian. Isabel Roberts, for whom one of the most celebrated Prairie Houses was built in River Forest in 1908, was not an architect; she was bookkeeper and general factotum at The Studio, but it is said that, caught up in the infectiously creative atmosphere of the place, she did occasionally try her hand at design and certainly worked on some of the detail-drawings of her own house. Albert McArthur was the son of that Warren McArthur for whom Wright built the most carefully detailed of the "bootlegged houses," and — many years later, — the Arizona Biltmore at Phoenix.

Note 1
Wright, Frank Lloyd: "In the Cause of Architecture," Architectural Record, Vol. 23, March 1908, pp. 155-221.

Bibliography

BOOKS

Andrews, Wayne. *Architecture, Ambition and Americans.* New York, Harper, 1955.

Architects' Year Book V. London, Elek, 1953.

Badovici, Jean (ed.). *Frank Lloyd Wright, Architecte Americain.* Paris, Morancé, 1932.

Behrendt, Walter C. *Modern Building; Its Nature, Problems and Forms.* New York, Harcourt, Brace, 1937.

Boston. Institute of Modern Art. *Frank Lloyd Wright; a Pictorial Record of Architectural Progress.* Boston, 1940.

Bragdon, Claude F. *More Lives Than One.* New York, Knopf, 1938.

Brownell, Baker. *Architecture and Modern Life.* 2d ed. New York, Harper, 1937.

Cheney, Sheldon. *The New World Architecture.* New York, Longmans, Green, 1930.

Chicago. Art Institute. Burnham Library of Architecture. *Buildings by Frank Lloyd Wright in Six Middle Western States.* Chicago, 1949.

Craven, Thomas. *Modern Art; the Men, the Movements, the Meaning.* New York, Simon and Schuster, 1934.

Edgell, George H. *The American Architecture of Today.* New York, Scribner, 1928.

Fitch, James M. *American Building; the Forces That Shape It.* Boston, Houghton Mifflin, 1948.

Fries, Heinrich de (ed.). *Frank Lloyd Wright; Aus dem Lebenswerke eines Architekten.* Berlin, Pollak, 1926.

Giedion, Sigfried. *Space, Time and Architecture.* 3rd ed. enlarged. Cambridge, Harvard University Press, 1954.

Hilbersheimer, Ludwig. *Groszstadt Architektur.* Stuttgart, Hoffmann, 1927.

Hitchcock, Henry R. *Frank Lloyd Wright.* Paris, Cahiers d'Art, 1928.

Hitchcock, Henry R. *In the Nature of Materials; 1887-1941; the Buildings of Frank Lloyd Wright.* New York, Duell, Sloan and Pearce, 1942.

Hitchcock, Henry R. *Modern Architecture; Romanticism and Reintegration.* New York, Payson and Clarke, 1929.

Kimball, Sidney Fiske. *American Architecture.* Indianapolis, Bobbs-Merrill, 1928.

McGrath, Raymond. *Twentieth-Century Houses.* London, Faber and Faber, 1934.

Morrison, Hugh. *Louis Sullivan, Prophet of Modern Architecture.* New York, Museum of Modern Art, Norton, 1935.

Mumford, Lewis. *The Culture of Cities.* New York, Harcourt, Brace, 1938.

Mumford, Lewis. *Roots of Contemporary American Architecture.* New York, Reinhold, 1952.

Neutra, Richard J. *Amerika; die Stilbildung des Neuen Baues in den Vereinigten Staaten.* Vienna, Schroll, 1930.

Neutra, Richard J. *Wie Baut Amerika?* Stuttgart, Hoffmann, 1927.

New York. Museum of Modern Art. *Modern Architects.* New York, Museum of Modern Art, Norton, 1932.

New York. Museum of Modern Art. *Modern Architecture; International Exhibition . . . Feb. 10 to March 23, 1932.* New York, 1932.

Oud, Jacobus J. P. *Holländische Architektur.* Munich, Langen, 1926.

Pevsner, Nikolaus. *Pioneers of Modern Design from William Morris to Walter Gropius.* 2d ed. New York, Museum of Modern Art, 1949.

Platz, Gustav A. *Die Baukunst der Neuesten Zeit.* 2d ed. Berlin, Propyläen-Verlag, 1930.

Price, Charles M. *The Practical Book of Architecture.* Philadelphia, Lippincott, 1916.

Richards, James M. *An Introduction to Modern Architecture.* Revised and reprinted. Harmondsworth, Middlesex, Penguin Books, 1956.

Robb, David M. *Art in the Western World.* 3rd ed. New York, Harper, 1953.

Sartoris, Alberto. *Encyclopédie de l'Architecture Nouvelle.* Vol. III. Milan, Hoepli, 1954.

Scully, Vincent J., Jr. *The Shingle Style; Architectural Theory and Design from Richardson to the Origins of Wright.* New Haven, Yale University Press, 1955.

Tallmadge, Thomas E. *The Story of Architecture in America.* Revised ed. New York, Norton, 1936.

Untermeyer, Louis. *Makers of the Modern World.* New York, Simon and Schuster, 1955.

Wijdeveld, Hendricus T. (ed.) *The Life Work of the American Architect, Frank Lloyd Wright.* Santpoort, Holland, C. A. Mees, 1925.

Wright, Frank Lloyd. *An American Architecture.* Edited by Edgar Kaufmann. New York, Horizon Press, 1955.

Wright, Frank Lloyd. *Ausgeführte Bauten und Entwürfe.* Berlin, Wasmuth, 1910.

Wright, Frank Lloyd. *An Autobiography.* New York, Longmans, Green, 1932.

Wright, Frank Lloyd. *An Autobiography.* New York, Duell, Sloan, and Pearce, 1943.

Wright, Frank Lloyd. *Frank Lloyd Wright; Ausgeführte Bauten.* Preface by Charles R. Ashbee. Berlin, Wasmuth, 1911.

Wright, Frank Lloyd. *Frank Lloyd Wright on Architecture; Selected Writings 1894-1940.* Edited, with an Introduction by Frederick Gutheim. New York, Duell, Sloan and Pearce, 1941.

Wright, Frank Lloyd. *The Future of Architecture.* New York, Horizon Press, 1953.

Wright, Frank Lloyd. *Genius and the Mobocracy.* New York, Duell, Sloan and Pearce, 1949.

Wright, Frank Lloyd. *The Japanese Print; an Interpretation.* Chicago, Ralph Fletcher Seymour, 1912.

Wright, Frank Lloyd. *Modern Architecture . . . Kahn Lectures for 1930.* Princeton, Princeton University Press, 1931.

Wright, Frank Lloyd. *Sechzig Jahre Lebendige Architektur. Sixty Years of Living Architecture.* Ein Bildbericht von Werner M. Moser. Winterthur, Verlag Buchdruckerei Winterthur, 1952.

Wright, Frank Lloyd. *A Testament.* New York, Horizon Press, 1957.

Wright, John L. *My Father Who Is on Earth.* New York, Putnam, 1946.

Yeomans, Alfred B. (ed.). *City Residential Land Development . . . Plans for Subdividing a Typical Quarter Section of Land in the Outskirts of Chicago.* Chicago, University of Chicago Press, 1916.

Zevi, Bruno. *Frank Lloyd Wright.* Milan, Il Balcone, 1947.

Zevi, Bruno. *Storia dell'Architettura Moderna.* 2d ed. revised. Turin, Einaudi, 1953.

Zevi, Bruno. *Storia dell'Architettura chitecture.* London, Faber and Faber, 1950.

PERIODICALS

Alford, John. "Modern Architecture and the Symbolism of Creative Process," *College Art Journal,* XIV (Winter, 1955), 102-23.

Andrews, Wayne. "The Great Uncompromiser," *Saturday Review,* XXXVI (November 14, 1953), 15-16.

"Architectural Philosophy of Frank Lloyd Wright," *Western Architect,* XX (June, 1914), 58.

Argan, Giulio C. "Introduzione a Wright," *Metron,* (No. 18, 1947), 9-24.

"Art Gallery Designed by Frank Lloyd Wright," *International Studio,* XXXIX (February, 1910), xcv-xcvi.

Banham, Reyer. "Review 'An American Architecture,' by Frank Lloyd Wright," *Architectural Review (London),* CXX (October, 1956), 264.

Bauer, Catherine K. "The 'Exuberant and Romantic' Genius of Frank Lloyd Wright," *New Republic,* LXVII (July 8, 1931), 214-15.

Berlage, Hendrik P. "Neuere Amerikanische Architektur," *Schweizerische Bauzeitung* (September 14-28, 1912).

Blake, Peter. "Our Elder Spaceman." *Saturday Review,* XXXIX (August 4, 1956), 22-23.

Boyd, John T. "A Prophet of the New Architecture; an Interview with Frank Lloyd Wright," *Arts and Decoration,* XXXIII (May, 1930), 57-59, 100, 102, 116.

Boyd, Robin. "Two Ways with Modern Monuments," *Architects' Journal,* CXXV (April, 1957), 523-24.

Campo, Santiago del. "Afternoon with Frank Lloyd Wright," *Américas,* VI (April, 1954), 9-12, 44-46.

Chenev, Sheldon. "A Prophetic Artist." *Saturday Review of Literature,* VIII (April 23, 1932), 677-78.

"Chicago," *American Architect and Building News,* LXXVI (April 26, 1902), 29.

"Chicagoans Rally to Save Wright's Robie House," *Architectural Forum,* CVI (March, 1957), 9.

Churchill, Henry S. "Notes on Frank Lloyd Wright." *Magazine of Art,* XLI (February, 1948), 62-66.

"Current Periodicals." *Architectural Review (Boston),* XV (April, 1908), 78.

"A Departure from Classic Tradition," *Architectural Record,* XXX (October, 1911), 327-38.

Dos Passos, John. "Grand Old Man," *New Republic,* XXCVII (June 3, 1936), 94-95.

Duffus, Robert L. "Frank Lloyd Wright's Way to a Better World," *New York Times Book Review,* (January 2, 1938), 2.

Fitzpatrick, F. W. "Chicago," *Inland Architect and News Record,* XLV (June, 1905), 46-48.

"Frank Lloyd Wright," *Architectural Forum,* LXVIII (January, 1938), 1-102.

"Frank Lloyd Wright," *Architecture Française,* XIII (No. 123-24, 1952).

"Frank Lloyd Wright," *Metron,* (No. 41-42, May-August, 1951), 19-87.

"Frank Lloyd Wright; His Contribution to the Beauty of American Life," *House Beautiful,* XCVII (November, 1955), 233-90, 292, 294, 299-300, 302, 304, 306-14, 317-32, 335-58, 361-80.

Garden, Hugh M. G. "Country Homes of the Western Plains," *House and Garden,* XVIII (October, 1910), 230-35.

Goodman, Paul. "Frank Lloyd Wright on Architecture," *Kenyon Review,* IV (Winter, 1942), 7-28.

Gross, Martin L. "Frank Lloyd Wright, Master of the Broken Rule," *True,* XXXVIII (May, 1957), 19-20, 22, 24, 26, 122-26.

Hamlin, Talbot F. "F. L. W.; an Analysis," *Pencil Points,* XIX (March, 1948), 137-44.

Hamlin, Talbot F. "The Future of Architecture, by Frank Lloyd Wright," *New York Times Book Review,* (November 1, 1953), 7.

Hamlin, Talbot F. "A Great American Architect Pays Tribute to His Teacher." *New York Times Book Review,* (July 10, 1949), 3.

Haskell, Douglas. "Frank Lloyd Wright and the Chicago Fair," *Nation,* CXXXI (December 3, 1930), 605.

Haskell, Douglas. "Organic Architecture. Frank Lloyd Wright," *Creative Art,* III (November, 1928), li-lvii.

Hitchcock, Henry R. "The Evolution of Wright, Mies and Le Corbusier," *Perspecta. The Yale Architectural Journal,* I (Summer, 1952), 8-15.

Hitchcock, Henry R. "Frank Lloyd Wright and the 'Academic Tradition' of the Early Eighteen-Nineties," *Journal of the Warburg Institute,* VII (January-June, 1944), 46-63.

Hitchcock, Henry R. "Notes on Wright Buildings in Buffalo," *Buffalo Gallery Notes,* XI (June, 1947), 18-21.

Hitchcock, Henry R. "Wright's Influence Abroad," *Parnassus*, XII (December, 1940), 11-15.

Howe, George. "Review 'An Autobiography,' by Frank Lloyd Wright," *Shelter*, II (April, 1932), 27.

Huxtable, Ada L. "Larkin Company Administration Building, 1904," *Progressive Architecture*, XXXVIII (March, 1957), 141-42.

Kienitz, John F. "Fifty-two Years of Frank Lloyd Wright's Progressivism, 1893-1945," *Wisconsin Magazine of History*, XXIX (Sept., 1945), 61-71.

Kimball, Sidney Fiske. "Builder and Poet: Frank Lloyd Wright," *Architectural Record*, LXXI (June, 1932), 379-80.

Kramer, Hilton. "Architecture and Rhetoric," *New Republic*, CXXXIII (December 26, 1955), 20.

Kuo, Yuan-Hsi. "My Opinion of 'Don Quixote Atilt at His World,'" *T-Square*, II (January, 1932), 30-31.

Manson, Grant C. "Frank Lloyd Wright and the Fair of '93," *Art Quarterly*, XVI (Summer, 1953), 114-23.

Manson, Grant C. "Sullivan and Wright; an Uneasy Union of Celts," *Architectural Review (London)*, CXVIII (November, 1955), 297-300.

Manson, Grant C. "Wright in the Nursery; the Influence of Froebel Education on His Work," *Architectural Review (London)*, CXIII (June, 1953), 349-51.

Maza, Aquiles. "Frank Lloyd Wright, 'Miguel Angel del Siglo XX,'" *Arquitectura (Colegio Nacional de Arquitectos, Havana)*, XVIII (April, 1950), 123-35.

Mies van der Rohe, Ludwig. "A Tribute to Wright," *College Art Journal*, VI (Autumn, 1946), 41-42.

Moser, Werner. "Frank Lloyd Wright und Amerikanische Architektur," *Werk*, V. (May, 1925).

Mumford, Lewis. "American Architecture Today. II," *Architecture*, LVII (June 1928), 301-08.

Mumford, Lewis. "A Phoenix Too Infrequent," *New Yorker*, XXIX (November 28, 1953), 133-39.

Mumford, Lewis. "A Phoenix Too Infrequent. II," *New Yorker*, XXIX (December 12, 1953), 116-20, 123-27.

Mumford, Lewis. "Two Chicago Fairs," *New Republic*, LXV (January 21, 1931), 271-72.

"One Hundred Years of Significant Building. 9: Houses Since 1907," *Architectural Record*, CXXI (February, 1957), 199-206.

Pellegrin, Luigi. "Alla Ricera del Primo Wright," *L'Architettura*, II (June, 1956), 126-31.

Pellegrin, Luigi. "La Decorazione Funzionale del Primo Wright," *L'Architettura*, II (July, 1956), 198-203.

Pellegrin, Luigi, "L'Ora 'Classica' di Wright," *L'Architettura*, II (February, 1957), 742-45.

Pellegrin, Luigi. "La Sintesi Culturale del Primo Wright," *L'Architettura*, II (January, 1957), 666-71.

Persitz, Alexandre, "Frank Lloyd Wright," *L'Architecture d'Aujourd'hui*, XXIV (December, 1953), 10-24.

Pevsner, Nikolaus. "Frank Lloyd Wright's Peaceful Penetration of Europe," *Architects' Journal*, LXXXIX (May 4, 1939), 731-34.

Pokorny, Elizabeth. "Use, Form and Art," *Nation*, CXXCII (January 14, 1956), 35-36.

"Publishers' Department," *Architectural Review (Boston)*, XV (April, 1908), v.

Read, Herbert E. "Against the Betrayal of Architecture," *New Republic*, CXXIX (November 2, 1953), 20-21.

Rebori, Andrew N. "Frank Lloyd Wright's Textile-Block Slab Construction," *Architectural Record*, LXII (December, 1927), 449-56.

Reed, Henry H. "Viollet-le-Duc and the USA; a Footnote to History," *Liturgical Arts*, XXIII (November, 1954), 26-28.

Saarinen, Aline B. Loucheim, "Frank Lloyd Wright Discusses 'An American Architecture,'" *Architectural Record*, CXIX (April, 1956), 62, 66, 446.

Saarinen, Aline B. Loucheim. "Frank Lloyd Wright Talks of His Art," *New York Times Magazine* (October 4, 1953), 26-27, 47.

Sargeant, Winthrop. "Frank Lloyd Wright," *Life*, XXI (August 12, 1946), 84-88, 90, 93-94, 96.

Schindler, Pauline. "Modern Architecture Acknowledges the Light Which Kindled It," *California Arts and Architecture*, XLVII (January, 1935), 17.

Schuyler, Montgomery. "An Architectural Pioneer; Review of the Portfolios Containing the Works of Wright," *Architectural Record*, XXXI (April, 1912), 427-35.

Scully, Vincent J., Jr. "Architecture and Ancestor Worship," *Art News*, LIV (February, 1956), 26, 56.

Seckel, Harry. "Frank Lloyd Wright," *North American Review*, CCXLVI (Autumn, 1938), 48-64.

Sell, Henry B. "Interpretation Not Imitation," *International Studio*, LV (May, 1915), lxxix.

Shand, Philip Morton. "Scenario for a Human Drama . . . the House of Character," *Architectural Review (London)*, LXXVII (February, 1935), 61-64.

Spencer, Robert C., Jr. "Brick Architecture in and about Chicago," *Brickbuilder*, XII (September, 1903), 178-87.

Spencer, Robert C., Jr. "The Work of Frank Lloyd Wright," *Architectural Review (Boston)*, VII (June, 1900), 61-72.

Sturgis, Russell. "The Larkin Building in Buffalo," *Architectural Record*, XXIII (April, 1908), 311-21.

Tallmadge, Thomas E. "The Chicago School," *Architectural Review (Boston)*, XV (April, 1908), 69-74.

Torcapel, John. "A Propos de Frank Ll. Wright," *Werk*, XXXIX (October, 1952), 330-32.

Tselos, Dimitri. "Exotic Influences in the Architecture of Frank Lloyd Wright," *Magazine of Art*, XLVI (April, 1953), 160-69, 184.

Udall, Mary C. "Wright, Great U.S. Architect," *Art News*, XXXVIII (February 24, 1940), 6, 16.

"Usonian Architect," *Time*, XXXI (January 17, 1938), 29-32.

"The Value of Used Architecture," *Architectural Forum*, CVI (April, 1957), 107-08.

"The Village Bank Series. V: Frank Lloyd Wright," *Brickbuilder*, X (August, 1901), 160-61.

Watts, Harvey M. "Don Quixote Atilt at His World," *T-Square Club Journal of Philadelphia*, I (November, 1931), 14, 34-35.

Wheelwright, John. "Truth Against the World," *New Republic*, LXXI (June 29, 1932), 186.

Whitcomb, Mildred. "Begin with a Hoe; an Interview with Frank Lloyd Wright," *Nation's Schools*, XLII (November, 1948), 20-24.

Wils, Jan. "Frank Lloyd Wright," *Elsevier's Geïllustreerd Maandschrift*, LXI (1921), 217-25.

"The Work of Frank Lloyd Wright; Its Influence," *Architectural Record*, XVIII (July, 1905), 60-65.

Wright, Frank Lloyd. "Apprenticeship-Training for the Architect," *Architectural Record*, LXXX (September, 1936), 207-10.

Wright, Frank Lloyd. "The Architect," *Brickbuilder*, IX (June, 1900), 124-28.

Wright, Frank Lloyd. "For All May Raise the Flowers Now For All Have Got the Seed," *T-Square*, II (February, 1932), 6-8.

Wright, Frank Lloyd. "A Home in a Prairie Town," *Ladies' Home Journal*, XVIII (February, 1901), 17.

Wright, Frank Lloyd. "In the Cause of Architecture," *Architectural Record*, XXIII (March, 1908), 155-221.

Wright, Frank Lloyd. "In the Cause of Architecture; Second Paper," *Architectural Record*, XXXV (May, 1914), 405-13.

Wright, Frank Lloyd. "In the Cause of Architecture. I: The Architect and the Machine," *Architectural Record*, LXI (May, 1927), 394-96.

Wright Frank Lloyd. "In the Cause of Architecture. II: Standardization, the Soul of the Machine," *Architectural Record*, LXI (June, 1927), 478-80.

Wright, Frank Lloyd. "In the Cause of Architecture. III: Steel," *Architectural Record*, LXII (August, 1927), 163-66.

Wright, Frank Lloyd. "In the Cause of Architecture. IV: Fabrication and Imagination," *Architectural Record*, LXII (October, 1927), 318-24.

Wright, Frank Lloyd. "In the Cause of Architecture. I: The Logic of the Plan," *Architectural Record*, LXIII (January, 1928), 49-57.

Wright, Frank Lloyd. "In the Cause of

Architecture. II: What 'Style' Means to the Architect," *Architectural Record*, LXIII (February, 1928), 145-51.

Wright, Frank Lloyd. "In the Cause of Architecture. III: The Meaning of Materials; Stone," *Architectural Record*, LXIII (April, 1928), 350-56.

Wright, Frank Lloyd. "In the Cause of Architecture. IV: The Meaning of Materials; Wood." *Architectural Record*, LXIII (May, 1928), 481-88.

Wright, Frank Lloyd. "In the Cause of Architectural. V: The Meaning of Materials; the Kiln," *Architectural Record*, LXIII (June, 1928), 555-61.

Wright, Frank Lloyd. "In the Cause of Architecture. VI: The Meaning of Materials; Glass," *Architectural Record*, LXIV (July, 1928), 10-16.

Wright, Frank Lloyd. "In the Cause of Architecture. VII: The Meaning of Materials; Concrete," *Architectural Record*, LXIV (August, 1928), 99-104.

Wright, Frank Lloyd. "In the Cause of Architecture. VIII: Sheet Metal and a Modern Instance," *Architectural Record*, LXIV (October, 1928), 334-42.

Wright, Frank Lloyd. "In the Cause of Architecture. IX: The Terms," *Architectural Record*, LXIV (December, 1928), 507-14.

Wright, Frank Lloyd. "A Letter to the Editor." *T-Square*, II (February, 1932), 32.

Wright, Frank Lloyd. "Louis Henry Sullivan, Beloved Master," *Western Architect*, XXXIII (June, 1924), 64-66.

Wright, Frank Lloyd. "Of Thee I Sing," *Shelter*, II (April, 1932), 10-12.

Wright, Frank Lloyd. "Organic Architecture Looks at Modern Architecture," *Architectural Record*, CXI (May, 1952), 148-54.

Wright, Frank Lloyd. "Recollections; United States, 1893-1920," *Architects' Journal*, LXXXIV (July 16-August 6, 1936).

Wright, Frank Lloyd. "A Small Home with 'Lots of Room in It,'" *Ladies' Home Journal*, XVIII (July, 1901), 15.

Wright, Frank Lloyd. "Sullivan Against the World," *Architectural Review (London)*, CV (June, 1949), 295-98.

Wright, Frank Lloyd. "To the Young Architect in America," *Architects' Journal*, LXXIV (July, 1931), 48-50.

Zevi, Bruno. "Frank Lloyd Wright and the Conquest of Space," *Magazine of Art*, XLIII (May, 1950), 186-91.

UNPUBLISHED MATERIAL

Cousens, Gertrude. "Frank Lloyd Wright; an Annotated Bibliography." Unpublished Master's thesis, Columbia University School of Library Service, 1938.

Manson, Grant C. "Frank Lloyd Wright's Work Before 1910." Unpublished Ph.D. dissertation, Harvard University, 1940.

Index

ILLUSTRATION CREDITS

Most of the illustrative material in this book, either from the files at Taliesin North or from the plates of the Wasmuth Monograph of 1910, were most generously loaned for the purpose by Mr. Wright. Another invaluable source of illustrations of erected buildings of the Oak Park Period are the remaining photographs of the set made around 1910 by Henry Fuermann of Chicago; these are in the possession of the Chicago Architectural Photographing Company, whose president kindly gave permission to include a selection of them in this book. Other illustrations came from Gilman Lane (Figs. 36, 49, 52 left, 125 D, 125 H), Myron H. Davis (Fig. 71), William G. Bland (Fig. 125 E), and Richard Nickel (Fig. 131 A lower).